Principles of Statutory Interpretation

Principles of Statutory Interpretation

RICHARD CALNAN
Partner, Norton Rose Fulbright LLP and Visiting Professor, University College London

OXFORD
UNIVERSITY PRESS

OXFORD
UNIVERSITY PRESS

Great Clarendon Street, Oxford, OX2 6DP,
United Kingdom

Oxford University Press is a department of the University of Oxford.
It furthers the University's objective of excellence in research, scholarship,
and education by publishing worldwide. Oxford is a registered trade mark of
Oxford University Press in the UK and in certain other countries

First Edition published in 2023

Impression: 1

Published in the United States of America by Oxford University Press
198 Madison Avenue, New York, NY 10016, United States of America

British Library Cataloguing in Publication Data

Data available

Library of Congress Control Number is on file at the Library of Congress

ISBN 978–0–19–286467–3

DOI: 10.1093/oso/9780192864673.001.0001

Printed and bound by
CPI Group (UK) Ltd, Croydon, CR0 4YY

For Scarlett and Fionn

Preface

Statutes now play a much greater part in the law than they have ever done. Gone are the days in which they impinged only marginally on the common law and were kept in their place by restrictive interpretation. Many areas of our law are firmly based on statute; and legislation affects most parts of the common law to some degree.

The length of statutes has also increased. I was brought up on the Companies Act 1948. One only has to compare that with the 2006 Act to see the difference. And even that is not a true comparison: the 1948 Act covered corporate insolvency, which is now the subject of a mass of statutes and regulations.

Much of our time as practitioners is therefore spent in trying to understand what is meant by the statutes, secondary legislation and regulations that govern our lives.

The problem with statutory interpretation is to get the balance right. Interpretation of any legal text is ultimately a question of judgement, but that judgement must be exercised in a way that is consistent with the rule of law. There are no such things as rules of interpretation, but there are principles that the courts have established over the last five centuries that guide the interpreter towards an understanding of how to exercise that judgement.

It is the purpose of this book to try to explain these principles and to illustrate their application in practice. I hope it will supplement the established practitioner texts. The principles are not self-contained precepts: they need to be understood as a whole. Which is why I have kept the book relatively brief.

This book is a companion to *Principles of Contractual Interpretation*, the second edition of which was published by Oxford University Press in 2017. The basic principles of interpretation are common to all legal texts, but the different nature of contracts and statutes means that their application can differ. As well as explaining how statutes are interpreted, I have discussed how the process differs from contractual interpretation.

The principles of statutory interpretation are largely derived from the common law but, in recent years, legislation has impinged in the form of section 3 of the Human Rights Act 1998. In June 2022, the Bill of Rights Bill was introduced to Parliament. If passed in its present form, it would repeal section 3. Chapter 7 contains a discussion of the way in which the courts have interpreted section 3. That will continue to be relevant unless and until section 3 is actually repealed.

Perhaps even more importantly, an understanding of the various ways in which section 3 was understood will continue to be of relevance in practice because it goes to the heart of the relationship between Parliament and the courts and the proper role of the courts when interpreting legislation.

I am very grateful to my colleagues at Norton Rose Fulbright and to my students at University College London for the discussions we have had over the years that have informed the content of the book. Particular thanks must go to my secretary, Jan Ball, who has—patiently and with great skill and good humour—coped with my constant rewriting of the text.

Richard Calnan
June 2022

Principles of Statutory Interpretation

Part I: The Guiding Principle

Principle 1: Objective Intention

1. The purpose of interpreting a statute is to establish what the legislature intended the statute to mean. This is done objectively: what would a reasonable person understand the legislature's intention to be from the words it has used in the statute?

Part II: Text and Context

Principle 2: The Text

2. The words of the statute are the source of the legislature's objective intention.

Principle 3: The Whole Text

3. The words of the statute are read in the context of the statute as a whole.

Principle 4: The Context

4.1. The words of the statute are read in the context of its relevant background.
4.2. The relevant background consists of publicly available information concerning the law as it was before the statute was passed and the problems that it caused.
4.3. The object of the relevant background is to provide the context in which the statutory words were used in order to help to establish their purpose.
4.4. The clearer the statutory words, the more unlikely it is that they can be influenced by the relevant background.
4.5. The relevant background cannot be used to alter or supplement the statutory words.

Part III: The Meaning of the Words

Principle 5: Natural Meaning

5. The words of the statute are nearly always given their ordinary meaning in context, taking account of the purpose of the statute.

Principle 6: Ambiguity

6. If the words of the statute are reasonably capable of more than one ordinary meaning, they are given the meaning the legislature is most likely objectively to have intended.

Principle 7: Unnatural Meaning

7.1. Very occasionally, it is clear that the legislature cannot objectively have intended the words it has used in the statute to have their ordinary meaning. If so, they are given the meaning that the legislature must objectively have intended.
7.2. The more unreasonable or unfair the result, the more unlikely it is that the legislature can have intended it.
7.3. Clear words are therefore needed to override a person's fundamental liberties.

Contents

Table of Cases

AUSTRALIA

NEW ZEALAND

SINGAPORE

UNITED KINGDOM

UNITED STATES

Table of Legislation

Secondary Legislation

Table of Treaties and International Instruments

Prologue

A. The Purpose of this Book

The purpose of this book is to explain the principles by which statutes are interpreted.[1] One might ask why this is necessary. Surely all that is required is to read the words? Do we really need to analyse the process any further? **Pr.1**

It is a fair question. Why is guidance needed on such an instinctive process? And therein lies the problem. The interpretation of any document—whether it is a statute, a contract or anything else—is ultimately a matter of judgement. The cases on the interpretation of documents show how difficult it is to be certain how a court will interpret words. The books are littered with cases in which the interpretation placed on the meaning of a provision of a document by one court is overruled on appeal; and it is not uncommon for that decision itself to be overruled on a further appeal. **Pr.2**

The process involved in interpreting a document is fundamentally different from that which applies to other legal questions. If two lawyers are asked a question concerning land law or the law of torts, they will be guided towards a similar conclusion by the case law and statute law that govern the issue in hand. That is not to say that they will necessarily reach the same conclusion, but simply that the underlying law will guide them to the correct answer. **Pr.3**

Interpretation is different. There are no rules. Words take their meaning from their context. A particular phrase may mean one thing in one document, and something quite different in another. Its meaning in context is a question of judgement, and reaching a decision on a question of judgement is not a matter of following rules. It is common for experienced and reasonable lawyers to reach different conclusions on questions of interpretation. **Pr.4**

Kirby J put it this way in *Malika Holdings v Stretton*:[2] **Pr.5**

> Differences of opinion often arise in giving meaning to statutory language. This is because different readers approach the task of construction differently. They may or may not be inclined to examine the contested words in a wider context, having regard to perceived considerations of policy.

Rules may not help, but principles can. The more open-textured nature of principles—their ability to be stated at a higher level of generality—means that they can guide the interpreter in the right direction whilst acknowledging the ultimately judgemental nature of the exercise. **Pr.6**

The purpose of this book is to explain what those principles are and to provide examples of their application in practice. It is important to see this process as a whole. The principles are not a series of self-contained precepts that can be applied independently of each other. They **Pr.7**

[1] This process is referred to either as 'interpretation' or as 'construction'. In this context they are synonyms. The former expression is normally used in this book, but both expressions are used in practice.
[2] (2001) 204 CLR 290 at [104].

Principles of Statutory Interpretation. Richard Calnan, Oxford University Press. © Richard Calnan 2023.
DOI: 10.1093/oso/9780192864673.003.0001

need to be understood as a whole. And that is why this book is relatively brief. It needs to be read as a whole.

Pr.8 The main practitioner text is *Bennion, Bailey and Norbury on Statutory Interpretation.*[3] Francis Bennion was a distinguished Parliamentary Counsel, perhaps best known for the clarity of his drafting of the Consumer Credit Act 1974. The book is now in its seventh edition and is edited by Diggory Bailey and Luke Norbury. It is a detailed text that contains a wealth of material and discussion.

Pr.9 The leading texts on statutory interpretation in other common law jurisdictions are also of value to the practitioner in the United Kingdom. Of particular importance are the texts used in Australia and New Zealand. The leading texts are Dennis Pearce's *Statutory Interpretation in Australia*, which is in its ninth edition[4] and Ross Carter's *Burrows and Carter Statute Law in New Zealand*, now in its sixth edition.[5] The similarity (and, just occasionally, the difference) between the law of statutory interpretation in the United Kingdom, Australia and New Zealand gives these texts a real relevance to the practitioner in the United Kingdom. Both texts contain a clear and detailed discussion of the law in their jurisdictions.

Pr.10 Statutory interpretation is important in practice. So much of our law is now contained in statutes and regulations. It is therefore important to understand how the courts interpret them.

Pr.11 There is a great deal of discussion in the cases of the nature of statutory interpretation. There is a distinction here with contractual interpretation. Until recently, there was little case law on the theory of contractual interpretation, but there has been an explosion of its discussion in the last thirty years. The case law on statutory interpretation has a longer history, and there is consequently a great deal of it. The discussion in this book therefore concentrates on the decisions of the higher courts—mainly the House of Lords and the Supreme Court—although the decisions of lower courts are occasionally used where they help to explain a principle or to illustrate it.

Pr.12 The word 'statute' is given a broad meaning in this book. It covers any written instrument promulgated by a state or a governing body, and therefore includes statutory instruments and regulations. Nor is it confined to legislation passed by the UK Parliament. The principles that have guided the courts when interpreting UK statutes are equally relevant to legislation passed by regional legislatures, and, indeed, by those in other common law countries.

Pr.13 This book is a companion to *Principles of Contractual Interpretation.*[6] Statutory interpretation shares many common elements with contractual interpretation, but there are also very important differences in approach. Both books have been structured in the same way, around a series of principles. The principles have much in common, but their application can differ depending on whether the writing being interpreted is a statute or a contract. Those distinctions are discussed throughout this book and they are summarised in Part II of the Epilogue.

Pr.14 Both books are concerned with interpretation. They assume that the document to be interpreted is valid and binding, and they proceed to discuss what it means. So this book is not concerned with the way in which statutes are created or with public law questions of whether secondary legislation is binding—for instance, on the basis that it is *ultra vires* the primary

[3] D. Bailey and L. Norbury, *Bennion, Bailey and Norbury on Statutory Interpretation* (LexisNexis, 8th edn, 2020).
[4] D. Pearce, *Statutory Interpretation in Australia* (Lexis Nexis Australia, 9th edn, 2019).
[5] R. Carter, *Burrows and Carter Statute Law in New Zealand* (Lexis Nexis New Zealand, 6th edn, 2021).
[6] R. Calnan, *Principles of Contractual Interpretation* (Oxford University Press, 2nd edn, 2017).

legislation under which it is made. Nor is it concerned with legal rules that limit powers under public law—for instance, limitations on the exercise of discretions. This book is only concerned with the interpretative process.

B. The Interpretative Process

It has already been suggested that the interpretation of documents is of a different order from most legal issues. That is because any question of interpretation is ultimately a matter of judgement. The approaches of lawyers to questions of interpretation tend to fall on a spectrum between the extremes of literal and purposive interpretation. Some lawyers see interpretation in more black-and-white terms than others: words do have a natural meaning and that should be given effect, however odd the result. Others are more concerned to find an interpretation that they consider to be more sensible, even if this involves doing some violence to the actual words used. Few lawyers sit at either extreme. Most fall on a spectrum between them. **Pr.15**

One common misconception is that there has been a trajectory in the interpretation of documents—from the murky lowlands of literal interpretation to the sunlit uplands of contextual and purposive interpretation. It is a common narrative, but it is wrong. Interpretation does not move in a straight line. Like the economy, it tends to move in cycles. A period of strict interpretation gives way to a more liberal approach and that, in turn, is superseded by a process that places more emphasis on the text than the context. **Pr.16**

This should come as no surprise. A freewheeling approach to contextual interpretation carries with it as many problems as a blinkered insistence on the grammatical meaning of the words on the page. **Pr.17**

The overriding question—which comes up time and again in practice—is where to draw the line. Few lawyers would now argue for an entirely literal approach. They recognise that words take their colour from their context, and that the context encompasses not only the rest of the statute, but also the relevant background. Few lawyers are prepared to countenance a wholesale rewriting of the words in order to achieve a sensible and fair outcome. But where is the line to be drawn? **Pr.18**

This question is relevant to all legal systems at all times. It has always been necessary—and it will always be necessary—to decide at what point along this spectrum the law will settle. Different legal systems lean one way or the other. And the pendulum swings within a legal system—as has been illustrated very clearly over the last thirty years in relation to contractual interpretation.[7] **Pr.19**

One of the key requirements of any book on statutory interpretation is to establish where that line is to be drawn. It will be suggested that the line is drawn in a different place in relation to statutory interpretation than it is in relation to contractual interpretation. But the same forces are at play in each case and the distinction should not be carried too far. It is only in a minority of cases that the result will be different. **Pr.20**

[7] One only has to compare *Investors Compensation Scheme v West Bromwich Building Society* [1998] 1 WLR 896 with *Arnold v Britton* [2015] AC 19 to understand that.

Pr.21 The words of any document take their colour from their context. This is primarily the rest of the document, but it can also include the background against which the document is set. The meaning of an expression in one document may not be the same in another document. It follows that although the decision of a court on the meaning of words in a particular document will (depending on the rules of precedent) bind a subsequent court when interpreting that document, it will not have the same effect in relation to other documents. This is as true of statutes as it is of other types of document.

Pr.22 This point has never been better expressed than by Lord Diplock in *Carter v Bradbeer*:[8]

> A question of statutory construction is one in which the strict doctrine of precedent can only be of narrow application. The ratio decidendi of a judgment as to the meaning of particular words or combinations of words used in a particular statutory provision can have no more than a persuasive influence upon a court which is called upon to interpret the same word or combination of words appearing in some other statutory provision. It is not determinative of the meaning of that other provision. This is because the inherent flexibility of the English language may make it necessary for the interpreter to have recourse to a variety of aids or canons of construction, which are not merely lexicographical, in order to select from what may be a number of different meanings which the words as a matter of language are capable of bearing, the precise meaning in which the legislature intended them to be understood.

Pr.23 Because statutes normally remain in force for a considerable time and are relevant to large numbers of transactions, the rules of precedent do have a larger part to play in statutory interpretation than they do in contractual interpretation. But it is still necessary to be wary about simply transposing the approach to the interpretation of particular words from one statute to another. The context will always be different.

Pr.24 The problem with this approach is that it sounds rather like palm tree justice. But it would be a mistake to see it in that light. Interpretation may be a matter of judgement, but that does not give the interpreter carte blanche. The judgement must be legally defensible. It must derive from the words used in the statute and be based on the principles of interpretation that have been developed by the courts in relation to the interpretation of statutes and of other relevant documents. The rule of law requires judgments to be made within bounds. Interpretation can never be a simple process of applying rules, but judgements must be consistent with the principles of statutory interpretation.

Pr.25 Lord Neuberger made this point in *Cusack v Harrow London Borough Council*:[9]

> Interpretation of any document ultimately involves identifying the intention of Parliament, the drafter, or the parties. That intention must be determined by reference to the precise words used, their particular documentary and factual context, and, where identifiable, their aim or purpose. To that extent, almost every issue of interpretation is unique in terms of the nature of the various factors involved. However, that does not mean that the court has a completely free hand when it comes to interpreting documents: that would be inconsistent with the rule of law, and with the need for as much certainty and predictability as can be attained, bearing in mind that each case must be resolved by reference to its particular factors.

[8] [1975] 1 WLR 1204 at 1206.
[9] [2013] 1 WLR 2022 at [58].

C. A Question of Judgement

Principles are therefore necessary, and they can take the interpreter a long way down the road; but the final decision is always a matter of judgement. This can be illustrated by three examples: **Pr.26**

- *R (Morgan Grenfell & Co) v Special Commissioner of Income Tax*;[10]
- *Shanks v Unilever (No 2)*;[11] and
- *Wills v Bowley*.[12]

The first example is *R (Morgan Grenfell & Co) v Special Commissioner of Income Tax*.[13] Section 20(1) of the Taxes Management Act 1970 allowed a tax inspector, by delivering a notice to a person, to require to be delivered to the inspector 'such documents as are in the person's possession or power'. The question was whether this overrode legal professional privilege. All the judges in the case adopted the same principles, but they reached very different conclusions as to the application of those principles to the facts of the case. **Pr.27**

All the judges in the case accepted that a fundamental legal right can only be overridden by express provision or by necessary implication. They all agreed that legal professional privilege is a fundamental legal right. The Divisional Court (two judges) and the Court of Appeal (three judges) decided that the structure of the Act was such that legal professional privilege had been overridden by necessary implication in the statute. The House of Lords (five judges) disagreed. So, in the outcome, all ten judges based their decisions on the same principles, but five judges went one way and five went the other. **Pr.28**

Both the Divisional Court and the Court of Appeal were driven to conclude that the provisions of the Act taken as a whole did demonstrate that legal professional privilege was excluded except where it was expressly preserved. The House of Lords reached the diametrically opposite conclusion—there was no necessary implication that legal professional privilege had been overridden. **Pr.29**

This case illustrates the judgemental nature of statutory interpretation. It is not simply a matter of applying a system of rules.[14] **Pr.30**

The second example is the decision of the Supreme Court in *Shanks v Unilever (No 2)*.[15] The question was whether an employee was entitled to compensation from his employer for an invention which had been patented by it. He would be entitled to compensation if, having regard among other things to 'the size and nature of the employer's undertaking', it was 'of outstanding benefit to the employer'. **Pr.31**

The claim was heard by a hearing officer at the Patent Office who found that the benefit provided by the patent fell short of being outstanding in the context of the size of the employer's business. That decision was upheld by Arnold J at first instance and by a strong Court of **Pr.32**

[10] [2003] 1 AC 563.
[11] [2019] 1 WLR 5997.
[12] [1982] AC 47.
[13] [2003] 1 AC 563.
[14] For another illustration, see *Pinner v Everett* [1969] 1 WLR 1266, where the House of Lords, by a majority of four to one, overruled a decision of three members of the Queen's Bench Divisional Court, so that again the judges were actually split equally.
[15] [2019] 1 WLR 5997.

Appeal, but it was reversed by the Supreme Court. In the result, although the employee won the case, there were again five judges who went one way and five the other.

Pr.33 There was again no real difference between the judges as to the principles to be adopted. The question at issue was what was meant by 'outstanding benefit'. There was no suggestion that those words should be given anything other than their natural meaning in context. The lower courts decided that the invention was not of outstanding benefit to the employer because it was not sufficiently significant in the light of the size of the employer's undertaking. The Supreme Court held that the expression 'outstanding benefit' was 'both a relative and qualitative term',[16] and decided that the invention could be of outstanding benefit to the employer even though it was of a relatively small value in comparison with the size of the employer's undertaking.

Pr.34 The third example is *Wills v Bowley*[17] which concerned the interpretation of section 28 of the Town Police Clauses Act 1847, which authorised a constable to take into custody anyone who, in a street, to the obstruction, annoyance or danger of the residents or passengers, commits certain offences. If the offence had not actually been committed but the constable had reasonable grounds to believe that it had, was the constable entitled to arrest the person concerned? On the face of it, the constable had no such power. His power of arrest only arose in the event that the offence had actually been committed. And that is what two members of the House of Lords (Lords Elwyn-Jones and Lowry) decided. But the majority (Lords Wilberforce, Russell and Bridge) took the contrary view. They decided that if the constable did have reasonable grounds to believe that the offence had been committed, then he was entitled to take the person concerned into custody even if the offence had not actually been committed.

Pr.35 These cases are simply illustrations of how difficult statutory interpretation can be in practice. How can a book help to resolve these difficulties? It cannot lay down rules—they would be too fine-grained to serve a useful purpose. But it can propose broad principles. They will not lead all lawyers to the same conclusion, but they should help the interpreter to weigh up the sometimes contrary indications and to enable them to reach a rational conclusion that can be justified legally.

D. The Layout of this Book

Pr.36 It has been suggested that the interpretation of documents can best be understood by reference to principles, rather than rules. This book is therefore constructed around a discussion of seven principles that, it is suggested, can guide the interpreter towards a rational exercise of judgement.

Pr.37 The principles fall into three broad categories.

Pr.38 **Principle 1** is the guiding principle. It describes the ultimate purpose of statutory interpretation—which is to establish what the legislature intended the statute to mean. But it then goes on to make it clear that this is an objective exercise. It does not matter what the

[16] ibid at [39].
[17] [1983] AC 57.

legislature really wanted. What matters is what it said in the statute. What would a reasonable person understand the legislature's intention to be from the words it has used in the statute?

Principles 2 to 4 establish which materials are available to the interpreter. The source of the legislature's objective intention is the words of the statute itself. But those words are read in the light of the statute as a whole and in the context of its relevant background. The key questions here are how much background is available to the interpreter and the purposes to which that background can be put. **Pr.39**

Principles 5 to 7 are concerned with how the interpreter establishes what the words of the statute mean. There will always be scope for ambiguity, and one of the principles is concerned with how ambiguities are to be resolved. Even more importantly, these principles deal with the perennial conflict in the interpretation of any document between literal and purposive interpretation. There is no simple answer to that problem, which is why it takes two principles to answer it. Neither approach holds complete sway. The important question is where the line is drawn between them. **Pr.40**

Interpretation will always be a matter of judgement for the interpreter concerned, but the principles can help to guide the interpreter to exercise that judgement in a manner which is not arbitrary, but which is consistent with the rule of law. **Pr.41**

Finally, the **Epilogue** draws together the main themes discussed in this book. It is divided into two parts. Part I is a case study that discusses how the principles of statutory interpretation work together to guide the interpreter in the right direction. Part II explains the main differences between the interpretation of statutes and of contracts. **Pr.42**

PART I
THE GUIDING PRINCIPLE

Principle 1: Objective Intention

1. The purpose of interpreting a statute is to establish what the legislature intended the statute to mean. This is done objectively: what would a reasonable person understand the legislature's intention to be from the words it has used in the statute?

1
Principle 1: Objective Intention

Principle 1: The purpose of interpreting a statute is to establish what the legislature intended the statute to mean. This is done objectively: what would a reasonable person understand the legislature's intention to be from the words it has used in the statute?

A. Objective Intention

Principle 1 embodies two ideas that conflict. The first is that what we are concerned with is the intention of the legislature. In the case of UK statutes, this is the intention of Parliament. The second is the requirement of objectivity. We are not really interested in what the legislature actually intended but with how a reasonable person would understand the words that the legislature has used in the statute. **1.1**

Why is Principle 1 written in this way? Is it necessary for the principle to be Janus-faced? Would it not be simpler to say that the purpose of statutory interpretation is to establish the meaning of the words used in the statute? **1.2**

This is an important question, and it is worth exploring now because it underlies many of the issues discussed in this book. **1.3**

B. Objectivity

There is no doubt that the main role of anyone interpreting a statute is to give effect to the words of the statute. What the legislature intended to do is irrelevant. All that matters is what it actually did in the statute. It is therefore important not to be led astray by references to the intention of the legislature. The test is objective, not subjective. How would a reasonable person understand the words used by the legislature in the statute? **1.4**

Lord Reid made this point in *Black-Clawson International v Papierwerke Waldhof-Aschaffenburg*:[1] **1.5**

> We often say that we are looking for the intention of Parliament, but that is not quite accurate. We are seeking the meaning of the words which Parliament used. We are seeking not what Parliament meant but the true meaning of what they said.

Lord Simon made the same point in *Farrell v Alexander*:[2] **1.6**

> [In] the construction of all written instruments including statutes, what the court is concerned to ascertain is, not what the promulgators of the instruments meant to say, but the

[1] [1975] AC 591 at 613. The same point was made by the High Court of Australia in *Saeed v Minster for Immigration and Citizenship* (2010) 241 CLR 252 at [31] (French CJ, Gummow, Hayne, Crennan and Kiefel JJ).
[2] [1977] AC 59 at 81.

Principles of Statutory Interpretation. Richard Calnan, Oxford University Press. © Richard Calnan 2023.
DOI: 10.1093/oso/9780192864673.003.0002

meaning of what they have said. It is in this sense that 'intention' is used as a term of art in the construction of documents.

1.7 This is such an important point that it is also worth quoting what Lord Watson had to say about it in *Salomon v A. Salomon and Co*:[3]

> 'Intention of the Legislature' is a common but very slippery phrase, which, popularly understood, may signify anything from intention embodied in positive enactment to speculative opinion as to what the Legislature probably would have meant, although there has been an omission to enact it. In a Court of Law or Equity, what the Legislature intended to be done or not to be done can only be legitimately ascertained from that which it has chosen to enact, either in express words or by reasonable and necessary implication.

1.8 Why is the law concerned with the objective manifestation of intention rather than with its subjective reality?

1.9 There are good practical reasons for doing so. If the interpreter only has to establish what the text of the statute means—without having to consider whether it properly reflects what the legislature really intended—the process of interpretation is accelerated and there is more certainty in the outcome. That is as true of statutory interpretation as it is of contractual interpretation.

1.10 In the case of statutes, however, there is another reason that is even more important. It is a constitutional reason, derived from the nature of statutes.

1.11 A statute lays down the law. It is a unilateral act of the legislature of a state, and it binds all of the citizens of that state. It is a formal document, promulgated in a particular way and then published. It would be constitutionally unacceptable for citizens to be bound by statutes unless they knew what they were and could therefore comply with them. It follows that the meaning of the statute must be gleaned from its words. What the legislature really intended (if that were ever capable of being established) is irrelevant.

1.12 Objectivity is therefore as important to statutory interpretation as it is to contractual interpretation. What the individual members of the legislature thought they were doing is irrelevant. The only thing that matters is what they did. A person reading the statute should be able to understand its effect from the words used.

1.13 This point was explained by Lord Diplock in *Fothergill v Monarch Airlines*:[4]

> Elementary justice or … the need for legal certainty demands that the rules by which the citizen is to be bound should be ascertainable by him (or, more realistically, by a competent lawyer advising him) by reference to identifiable sources that are publicly accessible. The source to which Parliament must have intended the citizen to refer is the language of the Act itself. These are the words which Parliament has itself approved as accurately expressing its intentions. If the meaning of those words is clear and unambiguous and does not lead to a result that is manifestly absurd or unreasonable, it would be a confidence trick by Parliament and destructive of all legal certainty if the private citizen could not rely upon that meaning but was required to search through all that had happened before and in the course of the legislative process in order to see whether there was anything to be found

[3] [1897] AC 22 at 38.
[4] [1981] AC 251 at 279–280.

> from which it could be inferred that Parliament's real intention had not been accurately expressed by the actual words that Parliament had adopted to communicate it to those affected by the legislation.

Lord Simon made a similar point in *Black-Clawson International v Papierwerke Waldhof-Aschaffenburg*:[5] **1.14**

> [As] in interpretation of all written material, what is to be ascertained is the meaning of what Parliament has said and not what Parliament meant to say. This is not a self-evident juristic truth.

Lord Simon went on to describe the reasons why the principle has been adopted. These include pragmatism—limiting the available material to speed up the process of interpretation—and also the reasonable expectations of those who are affected by the legislation. But it is suggested that the overwhelmingly important reason in the context of statutory interpretation is the constitutional principle that Lord Diplock describes in the *Monarch Airlines* case. **1.15**

C. Intention

If the actual intention of the legislature is irrelevant, is there any point in referring to its—inevitably artificial—objective intention? Would it not be better to reformulate Principle 1 on the following lines: **1.16**

> The purpose of statutory interpretation is to establish the meaning of the words used in the statue.

There is certainly some support for such an approach in the cases. In *R v Secretary of State for the Environment, Transport and the Regions, ex parte Spath Holme*,[6] Lord Nicholls said: **1.17**

> Statutory interpretation is an exercise which requires the court to identify the meaning borne by the words in question in the particular context.

No mention there of the intention of Parliament. But, interestingly, Lord Nicholls then went on to say:[7] **1.18**

> The task of the court is often said to be to ascertain the intention of Parliament expressed in the language under consideration. This is correct and may be helpful, so long as it is remembered that the 'intention of Parliament' is an objective concept, not subjective.

Concentration on the meaning of the words rather than the intention of the parties has been a feature of a number of recent statements of the purpose of contractual interpretation. Recent formulations of the basic principle of contractual interpretation often refer to the meaning of the words used in the contract without mentioning the intention of the parties.[8] **1.19**

[5] [1975] AC 591 at 645.
[6] [2001] 2 AC 349 at 396.
[7] ibid, 396.
[8] See eg Lord Hoffmann's first principle in *Investors Compensation Scheme v West Bromwich Building Society* [1998] 1 WLR 896 at 912 and Lord Hodge's comments in *Wood v Capita Insurance Services* [2017] AC 1173 at [10].

1.20 It could be said that intention has a greater part to play in the law of contract than it does in relation to statutes. The ultimate aim of the law of contract is to give effect to the objective common intention of the parties. This is a theme that applies across the whole of the law of contract, not just its interpretation. It might therefore be thought that there is more justification for continuing to use intention in relation to contractual interpretation than to statutory interpretation.

1.21 But what this ignores is that there are occasions where the courts do give effect to what they think the legislature must really have meant rather than what it has actually said. This may—and should—happen infrequently, but it does still happen. And when it does happen, it does so because the courts consider that no reasonable and fair legislature could have intended to do what the ordinary meaning of the relevant words suggests. In addition, where there is an ambiguity, its resolution is made easier if it is appreciated that what the court is doing, in resolving the ambiguity, is to try to work out what the legislature must reasonably have intended.

1.22 The idea of the legislature in this context is an abstraction—an idealised conception. It is not the actual members of the legislature at the time the statute was passed who are in issue. What the courts have in mind when they refer to the intention of the legislature is an ideal legislature, which is passing laws for the good of the people in a way which is both reasonable and fair. That gives quite a lot of discretion to the court, which is why it needs to be used sparingly. But that is not to say that it is never used.

1.23 As will be seen from Principle 5, in most cases the courts give effect to the natural and ordinary meaning of the relevant words in context. There is a good reason for this. As Lord Lowry said in *Wills v Bowley*:[9]

> It is, in my opinion, not for the judges but for Parliament, which represents the subjects whose liberty has been accorded priority by the common law and by the rules of interpreting statutes, to say in a particular case whether [the consequences of giving effect to the natural meaning of the words] are not only inconvenient but insupportable. If they are indeed insupportable, Parliament can decide, after an informed debate, whether a statute should be amended and, if so, in what way.
>
> My Lords, it is not, in my respectful submission, our function to anticipate the will of Parliament and to forestall debate by deciding that it would produce a better result if we inserted into a statute at the expense of the liberty of innocent subjects words which are not there, and which are not needed in order to make the Act intelligible and workable. I stress the word 'needed' in contrast to a phrase like 'desirable, in the opinion of the court,' believing that the role of the judge is to construe and apply the legislation, and not to frame policy by rewriting it.

1.24 One concern with trying to establish the intention of Parliament—rather than the meaning of the words it has used—is that courts can be tempted to stray across a constitutional line. It is trite law that Parliament legislates and the courts interpret what Parliament has done, but it is nevertheless an important constitutional principle. It is not for unelected judges to legislate.

[9] [1983] AC 57 at 88–89.

A concern that too much stress on what Parliament intended can encourage the courts to legislate themselves can be seen in the judgment of Griffith CJ in the High Court of Australia in *Richardson v Austin*:[10] 1.25

> Then as to the argument from the assumed intention of the legislature, there is nothing more dangerous and fallacious in interpreting a Statute than first of all to assume that the legislature had a particular intention, and then, having made up one's mind what that intention was, to conclude that that intention must necessarily be expressed in the Statute, and then proceed to find it. [He then reviewed the objects of the Act]. But no one could predicate how the legislature would effect those objects. To do that you must look at what they have said.

The importance of drawing a clear line between the roles of the legislature and the judiciary was made very clearly by another Australian Chief Justice—Barwick CJ—in *Commissioner of Taxation v Westraders*,[11] In the context of whether or not a sophisticated tax avoidance scheme was effective, Barwick CJ said:[12] 1.26

> It is for the Parliament to specify, and to do so, in my opinion, as far as language will permit, with unambiguous clarity, the circumstances which will attract an obligation on the part of the citizen to pay tax. The function of the court is to interpret and apply the language in which the Parliament has specified those circumstances. The court is to do so by determining the meaning of the words employed by the Parliament according to the intention of the Parliament which is discoverable from the language used by the Parliament. It is not for the court to mould or to attempt to mould the language of the statute so as to produce some result which it might be thought the Parliament may have intended to achieve, though not expressed in the actual language employed. In this connection, I would indorse what was said by Deane J in his reasons for judgment in this case and which, in my opinion, are worthy of repetition. Speaking of the result of this case in upholding the taxpayer's claim to deduction, his Honour said:
>
>> That result may seem both contrary to the general policy of the Act (if it be possible to discern any general policy other than that people pay income tax) and unfair to the ordinary taxpayer who willingly or reluctantly contributes, without resort to tax avoidance, the share of his net income which the Parliament has determined is required by the nation for the common good. If there be, in truth, such contrariety or unfairness, the fault lies with the form of the legislation at the relevant time and not with the courts whose duty it is to apply the words which the Parliament has enacted. For a court to arrogate to itself, without legislative warrant, the function of overriding the plain words of an Act in any case where it considers that overall considerations of fairness or some general policy of the Act would be best served by a decision against the taxpayer would be to substitute arbitrary taxation for taxation under the rule law and, indeed, to subvert the rule of law itself...
>
> The principle to which his Honour calls attention is basic to the maintenance of a free society.

[10] (1911) 12 CLR 463 at 470.
[11] (1980) 144 CLR 55.
[12] ibid, 59–60.

1.27 The rule of law requires not only that the citizen should be able to understand what Parliament has said from the terms of the legislation itself, but also that the courts should not overstep their legitimate role.

1.28 But, as Principle 7 demonstrates, the courts do not always give effect to the natural meaning of words. It is important to understand why—and therefore when—the court will override the natural meaning in favour of an unnatural one. That can best be understood by realising that the court is giving effect to the meaning that it believes a reasonable and fair legislature would have intended.

1.29 It is common to refer to the 'objective intention' of a group of persons, such as the parties to a contract or the members of a legislative body. But it is important to appreciate that the requirement of objectivity applies as much to the identity of the members of the group as it does to their collective intention. There are two issues here.

1.30 First, an individual can have a subjective intention, and a court can establish what that intention is on the balance of probabilities. The members of a group of people can each have an individual subjective intention, but the group as a whole cannot. Their collective (or 'common') intention is necessarily objective. To establish common intention requires the court to understand what has passed between the members of the group. An intention can only be common to a group if the individual subjective intentions of its members have been communicated to the other members of the group and a consensus has been achieved. That consensus can never be subjective. It is the outcome of communications between the members of the group and it is therefore necessarily objective.

1.31 Secondly, and equally importantly, even if the common objective intention of the legislature can be established, it is of no relevance to statutory interpretation. The objective common intention of the parties to a contract can be relevant because there are few formalities for the creation of a contract under English law. In most cases, the aim of the law of contract is to give effect to what the parties objectively intended. But a statute is a formal document that has to be in writing and created in a particular, formal, way. The process of communication of intention is therefore more limited than in the case of a contract. The intention of a legislature can only be established from the words of the statute.

1.32 It follows that when a court interprets a statute it is required to establish what was meant by the legislature from the words it has used in the statute; and that not only are the subjective intentions of the members of the legislature irrelevant, but so also is their collective objective intention. What the members of the legislature thought subjectively—or appeared to think objectively—is irrelevant. With a formal legal act such as a statute, what matters is its words.

1.33 When courts use the expression 'the intention of the legislature' they are therefore referring to an abstraction—an idealised legislature which intends to act reasonably and fairly in the interests of its citizens.

1.34 It is possible to reformulate Principle 1 without referring to the intention of the legislature, but to do so would be to lose a piece of the jigsaw. It is only by appreciating the importance of the idealised conception of the legislature that we can understand why—and therefore when—the courts do move away from the natural meaning of the words in the statute in favour of a less natural interpretation.

PART II

TEXT AND CONTEXT

Principle 2: The Text

2. The words of the statute are the source of the legislature's objective intention.

Principle 3: The Whole Text

3. The words of the statute are read in the context of the statute as a whole.

Principle 4: The Context

4.1. The words of the statute are read in the context of its relevant background.
4.2. The relevant background consists of publicly available information concerning the law as it was before the statute was passed and the problems that it caused.
4.3. The object of the relevant background is to provide the context in which the statutory words were used in order to help to establish their purpose.
4.4. The clearer the statutory words, the more unlikely it is that they can be influenced by the relevant background.
4.5. The relevant background cannot be used to alter or supplement the statutory words.

2
Principle 2: The Text

Principle 2: The words of the statute are the source of the legislature's objective intention.

A. Text and Context

When interpreting any document, the interpreter is primarily concerned with the meaning of the words contained in the document itself. But that is subject to two qualifications. **2.1**

The first qualification is that the operative words of the transaction concerned can, in some cases, be found outside the document itself. There may be other words—written or oral—which form part of the transaction and therefore need to be interpreted along with the document. In addition, other provisions may be implied into the document. And it may be possible for the words of the document to be altered subsequently by a court in order to ensure that the document properly reflects the intended transaction that it documents. **2.2**

This first qualification is therefore concerned with the identification of the terms of the transaction concerned. Before its terms can be interpreted, they must first be identified. **2.3**

The second exception is quite different. It is not concerned with what the terms of the transaction are; it is concerned with how those terms are to be interpreted. Having identified the terms of the transaction, it is then necessary to establish what they mean, and that meaning is not necessarily only derived from the words used. Interpretation is a contextual exercise. The terms of the transaction need to be read in the light of the relevant background in the context in which they were used. **2.4**

There are therefore two enquiries that need to be made. The first is to establish the terms of the transaction. The second is to establish the context within which those terms are interpreted. The first issue is the subject of Principle 2. The second issue is the subject of Principles 3 and 4. **2.5**

B. The Text

A statute is a law promulgated by a legislature that lays down legal rules for its citizens—and sometimes others—to comply with. It is a unilateral act of the legislature that binds all those to whom it is addressed. It must be in writing, it must be made in the appropriate form and it must be approved in the proper way by the legislature concerned. **2.6**

Because a statute is a formal act of the legislature, it follows that the terms of the statute are found—and can only be found—in the formal document. **2.7**

Principles of Statutory Interpretation. Richard Calnan, Oxford University Press. © Richard Calnan 2023.
DOI: 10.1093/oso/9780192864673.003.0003

2.8 This is very different from a contract. A contract is very rarely a unilateral act. It only binds its parties. It has very few formalities. It rarely has to be made in writing. In most cases, all that is required is that the parties have in some way objectively manifested a common intention to be bound.

2.9 Even if the terms of a contract are written down in a formal document and signed by the parties, the document may not contain all of the terms of the contract. The terms of the contract are derived from the common intention of the parties, and it may be the objective common intention of the parties that other terms—whether written or oral—are to form part of the contract. That is not very likely if the parties have gone to the trouble of writing down the terms of the contract and signing them, but it is possible. And it is to guard against the concern that a court may have to look at a vast array of documentation in order to decide whether that was the parties' intention that it is common for commercial contracts to contain an entire agreement clause.

2.10 An entire agreement clause establishes that the written document (or a series of transaction documents) constitutes the entire agreement between the parties. The courts give effect to such provisions because they establish the objective common intention of the parties. If the parties have agreed that the contract is what is in the writing, and nothing else, then that is what the contract is.[1]

2.11 Statutes have a built-in entire agreement clause. Unlike contracts, a statute does have to be made in a particular—formal—way. Nothing outside the statute can form part of it. There is no need for an 'entire statute' clause because it is implicit in the statute itself.

2.12 The provisions of a statute are therefore found—and can only be found—in the words of the statute itself. It follows that, to the extent that an interpreter is trying to establish the intention of the legislature, that intention can only be found from the words of the statute when they are read in the relevant context.

2.13 As Lord Simon said in *Black-Clawson International v Papierwerke Waldhof-Aschaffenburg*:[2]

> Courts of construction interpret statutes with a view to ascertaining the intention of Parliament expressed therein. But, as in interpretation of all written material, what is to be ascertained is the meaning of what Parliament has said and not what Parliament meant to say. This is not a self-evident juristic truth.

2.14 In *Black-Clawson International v Papierwerke Waldhof-Aschaffenburg*,[3] Lord Diplock said:

> The acceptance of the rule of law as a constitutional principle requires that a citizen, before committing himself to any course of action, should be able to know in advance what are the legal consequences that will flow from it. Where those consequences are regulated by a statute the source of that knowledge is what the statute says. In construing it the court must give effect to what the words of the statute would be reasonably understood to mean by those whose conduct it regulates. That any or all of

[1] *Inntrepeneur Pub Co v East Crown* [2000] 2 Lloyd's Rep 611 at 614; *North Eastern Properties v Coleman* [2010] 2 EGLR 161 at [82].

[2] [1975] AC 591 at 645.

[3] ibid, 638. *R (O) v Secretary of State for the Home Department* [2022] 2 WLR 343 at [29] (Lord Hodge).

> the individual members of the two Houses of the Parliament that passed it may have thought the words bore a different meaning cannot affect the matter. Parliament, under our constitution, is sovereign only in respect of what it expresses by the words used in the legislation it has passed.

The importance of reading the words in the statute was emphasised by Lord Neuberger in *Williams v Central Bank of Nigeria*:[4] **2.15**

> Given the unambiguous way in which [the Limitation Acts] incorporate the definition in [the Trustee Act 1925], the definition of 'trustee' in the 1925 Act simply cannot have a different meaning in the later Acts from that which it has in the 1925 Act itself, simply because any wording is 'subject to the context', or because of 'the mischief being addressed' in the later Acts, or because of 'Parliament's evident intention when enacting' the later Acts. When interpreting a statute, the court's function is to determine the meaning of the words used in the statute. The fact that context and mischief are factors which must be taken into account does not mean that, when performing its interpretative rule, the court can take a free-wheeling view of the intention of Parliament looking at all admissible material, and treating the wording of the statute as merely one item. Context and mischief do not represent a licence to judges to ignore the plain meaning of the words that Parliament has used. As Lord Reid said [in the *Black-Clawson* case] 'We often say that we are looking for the intention of Parliament, but that is not quite accurate. We are seeking the meaning of the words which Parliament used'.

To emphasise the importance of reading the words in the text is not to deny the importance of reading those words in the relevant context. How this should be done in practice was explained by Edelman J in the Hugh Court of Australia in *SAS Trustee Corporation v Miles*.[5] He said: **2.16**

> The task of statutory construction involves the legal application of the meaning of statutory words, as interpreted, to the facts of a case ... [The] task of statutory construction must begin and end with the text of the statute. That statement does not mean that the text of a statute must be interpreted only according to the range of semantic meanings of the individual words. It means only that the interpretation of a statute, like any other legal instrument, is an interpretation of its words. Those words are interpreted in their context and in light of their purpose although legal rules can sometimes exclude or restrict the use of some context. In ascertaining the reasonably intended meaning of Parliament *con*text is, literally, those matters to be considered (simultaneously) together with the text. Context can give words an interpretation that is the opposite of their ordinary meaning and grammatical sense. Context can also permit a construction of words that excludes their application to matters that would have fallen within the application of their literal meaning. However, as with contractual interpretation, where 'the clearer the natural meaning the more difficult it is to justify departing from it', so too in statutory interpretation 'questions of degree arise' and it will be more difficult to displace an interpretation that 'has a powerful advantage in ordinary meaning and grammatical sense'.

[4] [2014] AC 1189 at [72].
[5] (2018) 265 CLR 137 at [64].

C. Changing the Text

2.17 One aspect of the sovereignty of Parliament is its ability to change its mind. There are no gradations of Acts of Parliament. They all carry the same weight, and they can all be changed by another Act of Parliament. It is commonplace for statutes to be amended or replaced.

2.18 This is also true of contracts. The parties are always free to change their minds and amend the terms of their contract. And, again, is commonplace to do so.

2.19 It follows that, in principle, there can be no such thing as an 'entrenched' statutory or contractual provision. Parliament may say that a particular provision is fundamental and cannot be changed, but it can always be amended by subsequent legislation. The parties may decide that the terms of their contract can only be amended in a particular way, but they are always free to change their minds. These are fundamental principles that should really go without saying, but they have been subject to attack in recent years in relation to both statutes and contracts.

2.20 In relation to the English law of contract, the attack has been successful. In *MWB Business Exchange Centres v Rock Advertising*,[6] the Supreme Court decided that a clause that limited the way in which the parties could amend the contract was effective. Party autonomy required the courts to give effect to such a clause.[7]

2.21 This approach sits very uneasily with the basic principle that the parties are free to change their collective mind and that, if they decide to amend the terms of a contract, and they intend that amendment to take effect immediately, then they must necessarily have overridden the terms of any clause in the contract that limited the power of variation.[8] Party autonomy requires the latest manifestation of their agreement to be given effect. The approach in *Rock Advertising* has been rejected in Singapore[9] but, in English law, a clause that limits the parties' power to vary an agreement is effective in accordance with its terms.

2.22 In New Zealand, an attempt had been made to do something similar in relation to statutes. In *R v Pora*,[10] the issue was whether a person who had been convicted of murder was liable to a minimum period of imprisonment. The New Zealand Supreme Court decided that he was not. The majority reached this conclusion on the basis of a detailed interpretation of the words of the relevant statute. But the minority would have reached the same conclusion for a broader and more general reason; and it is this broader issue that makes the case of such interest.

2.23 The problem was that two different statutes provided inconsistent ways of dealing with the same question. Section 4(2) of the Criminal Justice Act 1985 said:

> [Notwithstanding] any other enactment or rule of law to the contrary, no court shall have power, on the conviction of an offender of any offence, to impose any sentence or make any order in the nature of a penalty that it could not have imposed on or made against the offender at the time of the commission of the offence. . . .

6 [2019] AC 119.
7 ibid, [10] and [11].
8 See the illuminating judgment of Beatson LJ in *Globe Motors v GRW Lucas* [2016] 1 CLC 712.
9 *Charles Lim Teng Siang v Hong Choon Hau* [2021] SGCA 43.
10 [2001] 2 NZLR 37.

Section 80(2A)(a) of the same Act (which was a subsequent amendment in 1999) provided that: 'if a court is satisfied that the commission of an offence of murder involved home invasion', the court 'Must impose ... a minimum period of imprisonment of not less than 13 years'. Section 2(4) of Criminal Justice Amendment Act (No 2) 1999 then said: **2.24**

> Section 80 ... applies in respect of the making of any order under that section on or after the date of commencement of this section, even if the offence concerned was committed before that date.

The result was that section 4(2) of the 1985 Act prevented the court from imposing a sentence that it could not have imposed when the offence was committed; but section 2(4) of the 1999 Act required the court to impose a minimum sentence even if the offence was committed before it came into force. **2.25**

The defendant had committed an offence of murder involving home invasion. The offence was committed before section 80(2A)(a) came into force. Section 2(4) required the court to impose a minimum sentence of thirteen years. Section 4(2) prevented it from doing so. Which provision prevailed? **2.26**

The court decided that it could not impose the minimum sentence. The majority reached this conclusion as a result of a detailed reading of other relevant provisions of the legislation. Those other provisions meant that there was no inconsistency on the facts of the particular case. But the court also addressed the more general question of which provision should prevail if they were inconsistent. **2.27**

The result should have been straightforward. Parliament had second thoughts. The later provision was clearly intended to override the earlier provision. And that is what Gault, Keith and McGrath JJ decided. But Elias CJ and Tipping and Thomas JJ took a very different approach. Richardson P declined to comment on this more general point. So, in the result, three judges went one way and three went the other. **2.28**

The judgment of Gault, Keith and McGrath JJ was delivered by Keith J. Parliament had decided in 1985 that the sentencing power should not be retrospective, but it changed its mind in 1999, and that change was expressed clearly in the language of the amendment. What is interesting about this case is not that the majority took this view, but that three judges in the New Zealand Supreme Court took a different approach. **2.29**

The judgment of Elias CJ and Tipping J is particularly interesting because of the way in which they reached the opposite conclusion. The two relevant statutory provisions were inconsistent. Each was clear in itself. One must yield. Statutes apply to circumstances as they arise. Parliament had anticipated issues of incompatibility in section 4 itself and had provided that section 4(2) was to prevail in the case of incompatibility with other legislation. On that basis, section 2(4) did not apply because that was what the legislative will had determined. **2.30**

They appreciated that one objection to this approach was that section 2(4) was enacted later than section 4(2) and was therefore to be preferred as a statement of legislative will by reason of that temporal circumstance. They got round this (apparently insoluble) problem by deciding that, where there is an inconsistency within a statute, the court has to determine which has priority; and the mere fact that one appears later in the legislation is not a determining factor. They said:[11] **2.31**

[11] ibid, [38].

> We do not think that it matters greatly whether the (sequentially) later provision was enacted at the same time as the earlier one ... or later in time.... Preference for a later provision is equally a default one which presupposes a mechanical rather than a purposive approach to statutory interpretation. The later is not to be preferred if the earlier expressly provides that it is to prevail.

2.32 Elias CJ and Tipping J considered that this result did not affect the orthodoxy that Parliament cannot bind its successors.[12]

2.33 The problem with this approach is manifest. When reading a single piece of legislation, a provision that appears in section 5 cannot override a provision that appears in section 3 just because it appears later in the text. The text has to be read as a whole, and the interpreter must determine which provision was intended to prevail by reading the relevant words in context. It is one statutory provision, and inconsistencies must be resolved.

2.34 But the same is not true of two pieces of legislation passed at different times. If they say different things, the latter must prevail. There is no inconsistency to resolve. The legislature has changed its mind.

2.35 Nor is it relevant that the earlier provision anticipates conflicts with other legislation and specifically overrides inconsistent statutory provisions. That solves the problem of inconsistencies with existing legislation, but it cannot prevent the legislature from departing from its previous approach. If the legislature clearly requires something to be done, it must be done. The apparent inconsistency with earlier legislation is resolved because the later expression of the legislature's intention overrides any former expression to the contrary. Laws change.

2.36 Thomas J agreed with Elias CJ and Tipping J, regarding their judgment as 'a work of outstanding merit'.[13] Having considered the approaches of the majority and the minority, he preferred that of the minority. He said:[14]

> It will be apparent that the canons of construction constitute a premise which is entrenched in Keith J's approach to the resolution of the conflict between the two subsections. This premise is absent from the Chief Justice's thinking. She accepts, as I do, that there is a choice, and that in the modern era a rights-centred approached is required to resolve the conflict—and to resolve it in a manner which can be said to take rights seriously.

2.37 *R v Pora* is as clear an illustration as can be found of the problem of statutory interpretation. As Thomas J said:[15]

> The difference between the opposing points of view clearly emerges. In essence, the difference reflects a different judicial philosophy and approach resulting in a different perception of the Court's role.

2.38 *R v Pora* is an extreme example, but it does clearly illustrate the problem. Some judges are more inclined to twist the meaning of the words used in order to reflect what they think Parliament must have really intended. The problem with the approach of Elias CJ and Tipping and Thomas JJ is that it puts too much power into the hands of unelected judges. It was perfectly clear, reading the relevant sections, that Parliament had changed its mind, and

12 ibid, [52].
13 ibid, [118].
14 ibid, [128].
15 ibid, [124].

deliberately intended to override the earlier legislative provision. Whilst purporting to give effect to the intention of Parliament, the approach of the minority in this case was to override what Parliament had clearly determined.

In *R (O) v Secretary of State for the Home Department*,[16] Lord Hodge had to consider this issue. He confirmed that the central task of the court in such a case is to interpret the later statute and to establish whether, in using the words of the later statute, Parliament intended to override the earlier statute.[17] **2.39**

The interpretation of statutes is ultimately a matter of judgement. But that judgement must be exercised in accordance with the rule of law. *R v Pora* is a salutary warning for all the common law jurisdictions of the dangers of straying beyond the limits of the judicial role. **2.40**

D. Implication

The law of contract has a doctrine of implied terms that enables provisions to be implied into contracts in certain limited circumstances. No such doctrine is applicable to statutes. But even a brief review of the cases on statutory interpretation illustrates the fact that the courts do interpolate words into statutes. How is this done? **2.41**

This question is, in fact, as pertinent to the interpretation of contracts as it is to the interpretation of statutes; and the way it is resolved with contracts can help to explain how the courts deal with statutes. **2.42**

There are many examples of courts adding words to contracts as a matter of interpretation without any consideration of the doctrine of implied terms. Although this is commonplace in the case law, there is little explanation in the cases of how this is done. Why is it that, in some cases, the courts feel the necessity to leap the hurdles imposed by the doctrine of implied terms whilst, in other cases, they are perfectly prepared to add words to contracts as part of the interpretation exercise without any reference at all to the doctrine of implied terms? **2.43**

It is suggested that there is a logical distinction that can be drawn in order to explain the divergence of approach, and that it is as applicable to statutes as it is to contracts. **2.44**

The key question is to decide what it is that is being implied into the contract. Is the effect of the additional words to modify the terms of an existing promise in the contract, or is it to create a new promise? A new promise can only be added to a contract if the requirements of the implied terms doctrine are satisfied. An existing promise can be limited—or even occasionally extended—as part of the process of interpretation without the necessity to comply with the rules concerning implied terms. **2.45**

In some ways, this distinction is more important in relation to statutes than it is in relation to contracts. Statute law does not have a doctrine of implied terms. There is no basis on which new provisions can be added to a statute. It is only possible to modify an existing provision by interpretation. It is therefore even more important clearly to draw the line between the creation of a new provision and the modification of an existing provision. **2.46**

16 [2022] 2 WLR 343.
17 ibid, [42].

2.47 Paradoxically, it is in some ways easier to decide where the line should be drawn for contracts than it is for statutes. A contract consists of a series of promises made by the parties to each other. They are normally promises as to the future—to do, or not to do, certain things. Sometimes, they are promises of existing fact—that a certain state of affairs is true at a particular time. It is therefore possible to ask the question whether the addition of the words that are proposed to be added to the contract would result in:

- the creation of a new promise; or
- the modification of an existing promise.

If it is the former, it is necessary to satisfy the conditions of the implied terms doctrine. If it is the latter, it can be done as part of the process of interpretation without reference to the implied terms doctrine.

2.48 The distinction can be illustrated by two cases decided by the Supreme Court:

- *Marks and Spencer v BNP Paribas*;[18] and
- *Re Sigma Finance*.[19]

2.49 In *Marks and Spencer v BNP Paribas*,[20] the question was whether a provision could be implied into a lease that would require the landlord to apportion rent. The lease did not provide for apportionment. The Supreme Court decided that no such provision could be implied. They carefully considered the requirements for the implication of terms into contracts, and decided that the conditions had not been met. A new promise to apportion rent could only be inserted in the contract if it satisfied the requirements of the implied terms doctrine; and it did not.

2.50 In *Re Sigma Finance*,[21] the question concerned the extent of an obligation of a security trustee in a security trust deed to pay money to certain creditors. Giving the relevant clause its natural meaning in isolation, the trustee was under an obligation to pay the money. But the Supreme Court decided that, reading the contract as a whole, there was no such obligation where the company concerned was insolvent. The relevant clause was not expressly limited in that way, but that is what the Supreme Court decided that it meant. It reached that conclusion as a matter of interpretation, without any reference to the requirements for the implication of terms. It is suggested that this is because the additional words did not create a new promise; they simply limited the scope of an existing promise.

2.51 The *Marks and Spencer* case is therefore an illustration of the necessity to comply with the requirements of the implied terms doctrine where a new promise is to be incorporated into a contract; and *Sigma Finance* is an example of the ability of the courts to limit the scope of an existing promise by adding words to the contract in order to modify its scope.

2.52 It gets more difficult where the effect of the modification is to extend the scope of an existing promise. In practice, this is much less common than using words to limit the scope of an obligation, but it can happen and it is treated as a question of interpretation, not implication.[22]

[18] [2016] AC 742.
[19] [2010] 1 All ER 571.
[20] [2016] AC 742.
[21] [2010] 1 All ER 571.
[22] See eg *Charter Reinsurance Co v Fagan* [2009] AC 1101.

This distinction is equally applicable to statutes. Statutes are not normally drafted in the form of promises. But they do create obligations on citizens—whether to the state or to other citizens. A statutory obligation is the equivalent of the duty imposed on the promisor under a contract to perform their promise. **2.53**

It follows that, in the case of statutes, the court's power to interpolate words is limited to the modification of obligations imposed by the statute. What a court cannot do is to impose new obligations. That would not be interpretation, but legislation. **2.54**

In practice, it is not always apparent where the line between legislation and interpretation should be drawn. Two New Zealand cases illustrate the issues: **2.55**

- *Northland Milk Vendors Association v Northern Milk*;[23] and
- *Commerce Commission v Telecom Corporation of New Zealand*.[24]

In *Northland Milk Vendors Association v Northern Milk*,[25] an Act had been passed without properly thinking through all the consequences. In the result, the only way that the New Zealand Court of Appeal was able to make it work was to imply that Parliament had intended the existing statutory position to continue until arrangements had properly been made for the new Act to come into operation. This sounds like a very broad definition of interpretation, but the case was an extreme one. The new legislation had made sweeping changes and had not properly provided for how they were to be implemented. The court had to establish a practical interpretation that best accorded with the general intention of Parliament as embodied in the Act. **2.56**

The judgment of the court was given by Cooke P. He said:[26] **2.57**

> [The] Courts must try to make the Act work while taking care not themselves to usurp the policy-making function, which rightly belongs to Parliament. The Courts can in a sense fill gaps in an Act but only in order to make the Act work as Parliament must have intended.

Although this is a very broad statement, it needs to be read in context. The Act had to be made to work, but this could not be done without some degree of gerrymandering. The interpretation required in this case went far beyond what is normally required. **2.58**

That this is the case is illustrated by another decision of the New Zealand Court of Appeal a few years later—*Commerce Commission v Telecom Corporation of New Zealand*.[27] **2.59**

The question was whether the Commerce Commission had the power under the Commerce Act 1986 to conduct an enquiry into the development of competition in the telecommunications industry in New Zealand. The Commerce Act did not contain an express provision authorising the Commission to do this, but it argued that a power to do so should be implied as being implicit in the Act. **2.60**

Where powers are conferred on a body in a statute, it has long been the case that powers should be read in a way that would give the body the power to do 'whatever may fairly be regarded as incidental to, or consequential upon, what the legislature has authorised'.[28] The **2.61**

23 [1988] 1 NZLR 530.
24 [1994] 2 NZLR 421.
25 [1988] 1 NZLR 530.
26 ibid, 537–538.
27 [1994] 2 NZLR 421.
28 *Attorney-General v Great Eastern Railway Co* (1880) 5 App Cas 473 at 478.

New Zealand Court of Appeal adopted this approach but decided that, in the particular case concerned, 'the power of inquiry and public report claimed by the Commission go[es] beyond the incidental or the consequential'.[29]

2.62 In reaching this conclusion, the court considered the provisions of the Act as a whole, identified the functions of the Commission, accepted that the Commission had incidental express and implied powers to carry out investigations and inquiries, but decided that they did not extend to conduct an inquiry of the kind which was in issue.

2.63 The court must interpret the legislation, but cannot itself legislate. In the *Commerce Commission* case, the Court of Appeal decided that the Commerce Commission did not have the power that it claimed. To afford it that power would not be to extend by implication an existing statutory provision but to add a new provision. That would be legislation, not interpretation.

2.64 The distinction can be easier to state than to apply in practice, but it does provide a logical basis for deciding how far courts can go. Ultimately, it is a question of judgement which side of the line a particular case falls.

E. Rectification

2.65 If a written contract does not reflect what the parties had agreed at the time the contract was entered into, it can be rectified. The effect of the rectification is to alter the words of the written contract so that they do reflect what was agreed at the time. It is difficult to persuade a court that the contract as signed does not reflect the real agreement at the time, especially if one of the parties is arguing that it does. But it is possible, and it does happen.

2.66 Again, statutes are different. The court has no power to rectify a statute in order to bring it into line with what the legislature intended. If the words of the statute do not reflect the legislature's intention, then new legislation must be passed to rectify the problem. The remedy is in the hands of the legislature, not the courts.

2.67 That is not to deny that the courts do have the power to read the words of a statute in a unnatural way in order to give effect to what they consider to be the clear intention of the legislature, but that can only be done as a matter of interpretation.

2.68 If a party to a contract is unhappy with the ordinary meaning of words used in the contract, it has a choice. It can claim that, as a matter of interpretation, they do not mean what they appear to say. Or it can argue that the contract should be rectified in order to give effect to the parties' real common intention. Where there is a dispute of this kind, it is not uncommon for both interpretation and rectification to be pleaded, and the court can deal with both in the same hearing as it did, for instance, in *Chartbrook v Persimmon Homes*.[30]

2.69 This approach is not available in relation to statutory interpretation. If someone wants to challenge the ordinary meaning of the words of a statute, they can only do so as a matter of interpretation. That is the province of Principle 7.

[29] [1994] 2 NZLR 421 at 430.
[30] [2009] 1 AC 1101.

3
Principle 3: The Whole Text

Principle 3: The words of the statute are read in the context of the statute as a whole.

A. Reading the Statute as a Whole

The principle that it is necessary to read a document as a whole is universal. It is true of all documents. It seems to be true of all legal systems. But it is easier to state than to understand. What does it really mean? **3.1**

The basic point is that words take their colour from their context, and the most obvious context is the surrounding words and the other provisions of the document concerned. **3.2**

In *Customs and Excise Commissioners v Zielinski Baker and Partners*,[1] Lord Walker said: 'Undoubtedly, the relevant provisions of [an Act] must be construed as a whole . . .' **3.3**

In *Attorney-General v Prince Ernest Augustus of Hanover*,[2] Viscount Simonds explained why this is so: **3.4**

> [Words], and particularly general words, cannot be read in isolation: their colour and content are derived from their context. So it is that I conceive it to be my right and duty to examine every word of a statute in its context, and I use 'context' in its widest sense . . .

More recently, in *R (O) v Secretary of State for the Home Department*, Lord Hodge said:[3] **3.5**

> Words and passages in a statute derive their meaning from their context. A phrase or passage must be read in the context of the section as a whole and in the wider context of a relevant group of sections. Other provisions in a statute and the statute as a whole may provide the relevant context.

B. Resolving Ambiguity

If words are ambiguous, their true meaning can often be established from the rest of the statute. **3.6**

In *Re Agricultural Sector (Wales) Bill*,[4] the question at issue was whether the Welsh Assembly had the power to legislate for minimum terms and conditions of employment for agricultural workers. The Assembly was entitled to legislate for agriculture, but the problem was to decide what Parliament meant by agriculture in this context. **3.7**

1 [2004] 1 WLR 707 at [39].
2 [1957] AC 436 at 461.
3 [2022] 2 WLR 343 at [29].
4 [2014] 1 WLR 2622.

Principles of Statutory Interpretation. Richard Calnan, Oxford University Press. © Richard Calnan 2023.
DOI: 10.1093/oso/9780192864673.003.0004

3.8 The Supreme Court decided that a Bill that established a scheme for the regulation of agricultural wages could in principle be classified as relating either to agriculture or to employment. Which classification was the more apt depended on the purpose for which the classification was being carried out and the classificatory scheme that had been employed.

3.9 The court accepted that the words needed to be interpreted according to their ordinary meaning in the context of the legislation as a whole. And, in the context of legislation that devolved powers in relation to agriculture, the court decided that 'agriculture' could not be intended to refer solely to the cultivation of the soil or the rearing of livestock, but must be understood in a broader sense to mean the economic activity of agriculture in all its aspects. In the context of the legislation as a whole, the Supreme Court therefore decided that the power to legislate for agriculture included a power to legislate for minimum terms and conditions of employment for agricultural workers.

C. Altering Meaning

3.10 An analysis of the statute as a whole can therefore enable a court to choose between two meanings that are ambiguous. But even clear words that seem to mean one thing only in isolation can mean something different if they are read in the context of the statute as a whole. This can be illustrated by four examples:

- *Civil Aviation Authority of New Zealand v Witschke-Rudd*;[5]
- *West Coast ENT v Buller Coal*;[6]
- *Director of Public Prosecutions v Schildkamp*;[7] and
- *Inglis v Robertson and Baxter*.[8]

3.11 In some cases, all that is required is to read a particular word in the context of those that surround it. An example is *Civil Aviation Authority of New Zealand v Witschke-Rudd*.[9] This was a decision of the New Zealand Court of Appeal. A provision of the Civil Aviation Act 1990 provided that a person committed an offence if he or she made 'any fraudulent, misleading, or intentionally false statement for the purpose of obtaining a medical certificate'. The question was whether a person who had made an incorrect statement applying for a helicopter licence was guilty of this offence. The statement he had made was objectively misleading in the sense that the person reading it would be misled. But he had no intention to mislead.

3.12 The New Zealand Court of Appeal held that the word 'misleading' had to be read in the light of the surrounding words. Although, in isolation, it could be said not to require an intention to mislead, when it was viewed in the light of the surrounding words 'fraudulent' and 'intentionally false', it was reasonably clear that what was intended was an intentionally misleading statement. The word 'misleading' got its colour from the surrounding words.

3.13 Stevens J, giving the judgment of the Court of Appeal, said:[10]

5 [2015] NZLR 749.
6 [2014] NZLR 32.
7 [1971] AC 1.
8 [1898] AC 616.
9 [2015] 3 NZLR 749.
10 ibid, [32].

> It therefore falls to interpret the content (in terms of mens rea) of the word 'misleading' which is sandwiched between the words 'fraudulent' and 'intentionally false'. We think this provides a classic example of the 'linguistic canon of construction' whereby a statutory term is recognised by its associated words. This is sometimes referred to by the Latin maxim *noscitur a sociis*, translated as 'it is known by its associates'. In plain language it is a contextual principle whereby a word or phrase is not to be construed as if it stood alone but in the light of its surroundings. Each of the associated words imports intention as the mens rea. We consider that is what the drafters intended for the word 'misleading'.

The *Witschke-Rudd* case is an example of the courts reading a particular word in the context of the words that surround it. But, in many cases, the courts have to go further—to read a particular phrase in a statute in the light of the structure and purpose of the Act as a whole. An example is *West Coast ENT v Buller Coal*.[11] **3.14**

West Coast ENT v Buller Coal[12] was a decision of the Supreme Court of New Zealand. The question at issue was the meaning of the words 'actual or potential effects on the environment' in the Resource Management Act 1991. In their natural sense, those words encompassed a broad analysis of potential effects on the environment—including the impact on climate change of the discharge into the air of greenhouse gases that results indirectly from the activity concerned. But the majority of the court (McGrath, William Young and Glazebrook JJ) decided that those words had to be read in a more limited way in the light of the structure of the Act as a whole. They said:[13] **3.15**

> Such limitation seems to us to be justified as a matter of necessary implication, essentially on the basis that, when the amended [Act] is looked at as a whole, the limitation is so obvious that it goes without saying.

What is interesting about this decision is that the court used a concept familiar in the context of contractual implied terms—the idea that something is so obvious that it goes without saying—to justify a particular reading of a statutory provision. The court decided that it was implicit in the structure and purpose of the Act that the words 'actual or potential effects on the environment' must be given a narrower meaning than their natural meaning in isolation. **3.16**

In *Director of Public Prosecutions v Schildkamp*,[14] the House of Lords had to consider the effect of the fraudulent trading provisions of the Companies Act 1948. Section 332(1) made the directors personally responsible for the company's debts 'if in the course of winding-up of a company it appears that any business of the company has been carried on with intent to defraud creditors ...' This civil liability for fraudulent trading therefore only arose if the company was in liquidation. Section 332(3) then went on to create a criminal liability on the directors 'where any business of a company is carried on with such intent or for such purpose as is mentioned in subsection (1)'. **3.17**

The question was whether the criminal liability created by subsection (3) applied whenever there was fraudulent trading or whether it was limited to cases where the company concerned was in liquidation. **3.18**

11 [2014] 1 NZLR 32.
12 ibid.
13 ibid, [173].
14 [1971] AC 1.

3.19 On the face of it, subsection (3) created a criminal offence even if the company was not in liquidation. But, by a majority of three to two, the House of Lords decided that the words of subsection (3) must be read as being impliedly limited to a case where a company was in liquidation. In the result, a person could not be convicted under subsection (3) unless the company itself were in liquidation.

3.20 The reason for limiting the apparent breadth of subsection (3) was that it was part of a series of provisions of the Companies Act that dealt with the winding-up of companies. It could not, therefore, have been Parliament's intention that subsection (3) should stand alone and impose a liability outside of liquidation when the rest of that part of the Act was concerned only with liquidation.

3.21 The principal judgment was given by Lord Upjohn. He recognised that the natural meaning of the words of the subsection was that no liquidation was required, but he went on to say:[15]

> But, my Lords, this, in my opinion, is the wrong approach to the construction of an Act of Parliament. The task of the court is to ascertain the intention of Parliament; you cannot look at a section, still less a sub-section, in isolation, to ascertain that intention; you must look at all the admissible surrounding circumstances before starting to construe the Act.

3.22 The same approach was taken by Lords Reid[16] and Hodson,[17] but Lord Guest and Viscount Dilhorne dissented. Lord Guest[18] took the view that the natural meaning of the words was that an offence was committed whether or not the company was in liquidation, and that it was 'highly dangerous to speculate on what Parliament's intentions were from a consideration of the rest of the sections'. Parliament's intentions could only safely be gathered from the words of the statute according to their ordinary meaning.

3.23 This is an interesting case for two reasons. First, because it illustrates the importance of reading the statute as a whole. And, secondly, because it illustrates the judgemental nature of the exercise—three experienced judges being prepared to limit the apparent scope of a provision by reference to the rest of the legislation, the other two experienced judges giving effect to the natural and ordinary meaning of the words themselves.

3.24 The final example is *Inglis v Robertson and Baxter*.[19] Section 3 of the Factors Act 1889 provided that: 'A pledge of the documents of title to goods shall be deemed to be a pledge of the goods.' That is the case at common law in England, but this case concerned the law of Scotland. One of the questions was whether this provision had general application. It was expressed in general terms but was contained in a part of the Act dealing with 'Dispositions by Mercantile Agents'. Did this limit the apparent breadth of its operation?

3.25 The House of Lords decided that the effect of the section was limited by the part of the Act in which it appeared. It was therefore only applicable where there was a disposition by a mercantile agent. Although the provision was expressed in broad and general terms, it was one of a group of sections under the heading 'Dispositions by Mercantile Agents', and it had to be interpreted in the light of that.

15 ibid, 23.
16 ibid, 10.
17 ibid, 11.
18 ibid, 15.
19 [1898] AC 616.

These cases illustrate another point—that reading a provision in the light of the entirety of the document concerned will normally limit the effect of the words that have been used. Apparently broad words will be limited by the context in which they appear. That is as true of statutory interpretation as it is of contractual interpretation. **3.26**

D. Limits of the Principle

It has been seen from *DPP v Schildkamp* that decisions in this area involve the exercise of judgement and that judgements can vary. It is therefore necessary to be careful about the application of the principle. A court will often decide that the words of a particular provision are too clear to be cut down by the context. Four cases illustrate this point: **3.27**

- *Attorney-General v Prince Ernest Augustus of Hanover*;[20]
- *Attorney-General v Great Eastern Railway* Co;[21]
- *Ward v Holman*;[22] and
- *K & S Lake City Freighters v Gordon & Gotch*.[23]

Attorney-General v Prince Ernest Augustus of Hanover[24] concerned the interpretation of an Act of 1705 that provided that Princess Sophia (who was the daughter of Queen Anne) 'and the issue of her body, and all persons lineally descending from her, born or hereafter to be born, be and shall be ... deemed ... natural born subjects of this Kingdom'. In the 1950s, Prince Ernest Augustus of Hanover, who was a lineal descendent of Princess Sophia, claimed British citizenship under this Act. **3.28**

The Attorney-General argued that the Prince was not entitled to citizenship because the Act could not have been intended to apply to all Princess Sophia's lineal descendants for all time. The Preamble to the Act described the purpose of the Act to be that Princess Sophia 'and the issue of her body, and all persons lineally descending from her, may be encouraged to become acquainted with the laws and constitutions of this realm' and that 'it is just and highly reasonable, that they, in Your Majesty's Life Time ... should be naturalised'. The Attorney-General argued that these words limited the apparently open-ended words of the enacting clause. **3.29**

The House of Lords decided that the Prince was entitled to British citizenship because the general words of the relevant provision were not limited by the rest of the Act. Viscount Simonds recognised that it was no answer to the Attorney-General's submission that the enacting words were clear. The Act must be read as a whole[25] and the general words of the relevant provision could be restricted by their context:[26] **3.30**

> [It] must often be difficult to say that any terms are clear and unambiguous until they have been studied in their context.... [The] elementary rule must be observed that no one should profess to understand any part of a statute or of any other document before he had

[20] [1957] AC 436.
[21] (1880) 5 App Cas 473.
[22] [1964] 1 QB 580.
[23] (1985) 157 CLR 309.
[24] [1957] AC 436.
[25] ibid, 461.
[26] ibid, 463.

read the whole of it. Until he has done so he is not entitled to say that it or any part of it is clear and unambiguous.

3.31 It was therefore accepted that the Preamble could be used to create an ambiguity in the operative clause but, here, the Preamble itself was ambiguous. It might just mean that the Act needed to be passed in the lifetime of Queen Anne. In the result, it did not limit the operative words.

3.32 To similar effect is the decision of the House of Lords in *Attorney-General v Great Eastern Railway* Co.[27] In that case, it was argued that the powers of the company set out in a statute were limited by their context. The House of Lords recognised that this would be possible, but it considered that it would take a lot to persuade it that the natural meaning of the words should be restricted by the context. Not impossible, but difficult. On the facts, it was not appropriate to imply a limitation on the apparently clear words of the section concerned.

3.33 The third example is *Ward v Holman*.[28] A person was accused of using threatening words or behaviour with intent to provoke a breach of the peace under section 5 of the Public Order Act 1936. The issue arose in the context of a domestic dispute, and the question was whether he should properly have been charged under that section.

3.34 The Preamble to the Act referred to the wearing of uniforms in connection with political objects and the preservation of public order on the occasion of public processions and meetings. The Quarter Sessions were of the opinion that the Act was therefore limited to conduct at political meetings and the like and in the course of political and similar processions, and could not be extended to disputes between neighbours. They limited the apparently clear words of the section by reference to the Preamble.

3.35 The Queen's Bench Divisional Court overruled this decision, the principal judgment being given by Lord Parker CJ. He regarded section 5 as being unambiguous, and was therefore not prepared to limit its generality by reference to the Preamble. Although this reasoning is suspect (reading the Act as a whole can create an ambiguity, as can be seen from the *Prince Ernest Augustus* case), this case does illustrate that it is often quite difficult to persuade a court to limit the clear words of a particular section in an Act simply because it might be said to go against the spirit of the Act as a whole.

3.36 The final example is *K & S Lake City Freighters v Gordon & Gotch*.[29] A section of the Motor Vehicles Act 1959 of South Australia provided that a contractual provision was void if it purported to contract out of the right to claim damages for the negligence of any person driving a motor vehicle. On the face of it, therefore, it applied to any claim relating to negligent driving. But the section was contained in a part of the Act that was otherwise concerned with death or bodily injury. Although the words of the section themselves were clear, the question was therefore whether they were limited to claims for death or bodily injury by the part of the Act in which they appeared.

3.37 Mason J considered that those words did need to be limited by reference to their context. But the other four judges in the High Court of Australia disagreed. The principal judgment was

[27] (1880) 5 App Cas 473.
[28] [1964] 2 QB 580.
[29] (1985) 157 CLR 309.

given by Deane J. He accepted that the section must be read in the context of the other provisions of the part of the Act in which it appeared. But, having done that, he said:[30]

> It appears to me, however, that, even when they are so read, the plain words of the section cannot, by any legitimate process of statutory construction, be constricted or read back so as to exclude from the words 'any right to claim damages or any other remedy', any right to claim damages or any other remedy for anything other than death or bodily injury.

The majority accepted that the part of the Act in which the section appeared provided a somewhat inappropriate context for a section of its apparent purpose, but that was not a warrant for refusing to give effect to the words that the legislature had seen fit to use. **3.38**

The contrast with *DPP v Schildkamp* is instructive. In each case, the question was whether the apparently broad words of a provision should be restricted by the context of the part of the Act in which they appear. In *DPP v Schildkamp*, the House of Lords did accept that the meaning of the words should be limited. In the *K & S Lake City Freighters* case, the High Court of Australia took the opposite approach. In each case, there were dissentients. This does illustrate how difficult decisions of this kind can be, and how much ultimately depend on the exercise of judgement. The basic principle was accepted by all the judges, but its application to the facts of the case was not straightforward. **3.39**

E. What is the Whole Statute?

There have been questions in the past about what it is that constitutes the whole statute. Courts have sometimes limited the scope of the material that they are prepared to use, particularly where the operative provision itself is unambiguous on its face. So, for instance, in *R v Galvin*,[31] Lord Lane CJ was not prepared to use the long title of an Act in order to restrict the scope of the otherwise plain meaning of the enacting provisions. **3.40**

It is suggested that this is out of kilter with the modern approach to interpretation, which is to consider the entirety of the printed statute as being relevant and to require the statute to be read as a whole whether or not the enacting provisions are, on their face, unambiguous. **3.41**

An example of the modern approach is *R v Montila*.[32] In this case, the House of Lords decided that headings and side notes in Acts of Parliament could be used to interpret them in spite of previous authority to the contrary. Lord Hope said[33] that this limitation is 'out of keeping with the modern approach to the interpretation of statutes and statutory instruments'. That the law has moved in this direction should occasion no surprise. As Lord Steyn said 'the starting point is that language in all legal texts conveys meaning according to the circumstances in which it was used'.[34] **3.42**

There is also a lot of old case law about consolidation statutes that suggests that it is necessary to read the words in the consolidating statute as if they were in the original statute. But it is **3.43**

30 ibid, 322.
31 [1987] 1 QB 862 at 869.
32 [2004] 1 WLR 3141.
33 ibid, [33].
34 ibid, [36].

suggested that this is no longer the approach that the courts take. A person reading an Act will read its current version, and that is also what the courts do.

3.44 This point was made by Lord Bingham in *R v Secretary of State for the Environment, Transport and the Regions, ex parte Spath Holme*:[35]

> [It] is plain that courts should not routinely investigate the statutory predecessors of provisions in a consolidation statute, particularly where . . . the issue concerns the construction of a single word or expression. Such a practice would reduce the benefit to be derived from the process of consolidation.

3.45 But Lord Bingham recognised that there are circumstances in which it is necessary to have regard to the earlier iterations of a statute:[36]

> [The] overriding aim of the court must always be to give effect to the intention of Parliament as expressed in the words used. If, even in the absence of overt ambiguity, the court finds itself unable, in construing the later provision in isolation, to place itself in the draftsman's chair and interpret the provision in the social and factual context which originally led to its enactment, it seems to be legitimate for the court—even, as Lord Simon said, incumbent on it—to consider the earlier, consolidated, provision in its social and factual context for such help as it may give, the assumption, of course, being (in the absence of amendment) that no change in the law was intended.

3.46 Courts do sometimes need to read back through earlier versions of the legislation in order to establish the true meaning of the words in the latest Act, but that should only be where there is real ambiguity. The general principle is to give effect to the natural meaning of the words of the current statute in the context in which they appear in that statute. This point is discussed further in relation to Principle 4.

F. Reading All the Words

3.47 As part of the principle of reading a statute as a whole, the courts will also try to give effect to all the provisions of the legislation. As McHugh, Gummow, Kirby and Hayne JJ said in *Project Blue Sky v Australian Broadcasting Authority*:[37]

> [A] court construing a statutory provision must strive to give meaning to every word of the provision.

3.48 This is sometimes referred to as the doctrine of surplusage or the argument from redundancy. A court will try to read each provision of the statute so that it has meaning and, if the same matter appears to be dealt with twice, a court will try to find some way of giving effect to both provisions. But the courts do recognise that draftsmen of statutes (like draftsmen of contracts) are not afraid of spilling ink in order to make their point absolutely clear.[38] The courts recognise that this may result in the same thing being said twice.

[35] [2001] 2 AC 349 at 388.
[36] ibid, 388.
[37] (1998) 194 CLR 355 at [71].
[38] See the comments of Lord Simon in *Ealing Borough Council v Race Relations Board* [1972] AC 342 at 363.

This point was made by Nourse LJ in *Omar Parks v Elkington*,[39] when he said: **3.49**

> If a long experience of legislative drafting had brought with it a conviction that an Act of Parliament never included words of surplusage, that would no doubt have been a persuasive point. But that is not our experience and I for one do not complain of it. An emphasis of the obvious, unnecessary to a judge who has had the benefit of argument, may yet be welcome to a busy practitioner who has not.

In this case, it had been argued that particular words in a paragraph should not be given their natural meaning because, if they were, another provision would have been unnecessary. The Court of Appeal did not accept this interpretation, recognising that draftsmen often use more words than is necessary. This is as true of statutory interpretation as it is of contractual interpretation. **3.50**

In *Walker v Centaur Clothes Group*,[40] Lord Hoffmann said: **3.51**

> I seldom think that an argument from redundancy carries great weight . . . It is not unusual for Parliament to say expressly what the courts would have inferred anyway.

[39] [1992] 1 WLR 1270 at 1273.

[40] [2000] 1 WLR 799 at 805. Lord Hoffmann made the same point in relation to contractual interpretation in *Beaufont Development v Gilbert-Ash* [1999] 1 AC 225 at 274.

4
Principle 4: The Context

Principle 4:

4.1. The words of the statute are read in the context of its relevant background.
4.2. The relevant background consists of publicly available information concerning the law as it was before the statute was passed and the problems that it caused.
4.3. The object of the relevant background is to provide the context in which the statutory words were used in order to help to establish their purpose.
4.4. The clearer the statutory words, the more unlikely it is that they can be influenced by the relevant background.
4.5. The relevant background cannot be used to alter or supplement the statutory words.

A. The Structure of this Chapter

4.1 The purpose of this chapter is to discuss what materials are available to the interpreter in addition to the text of the statute. It has been seen that the role of the interpreter is to give effect to the words of the statute (Principle 2) and that this must be done in the context of the statute as a whole (Principle 3). But what other materials are available to the interpreter? That is the subject of this Chapter 4.

4.2 It is first necessary to make some general points about the types of material that are available, the circumstances in which they can be used and the purposes to which they can be put.

4.3 First, the interpreter of any text is always entitled to use his or her general knowledge and understanding as the context within which to place the words of the text. What the law regulates is not general knowledge and understanding but particular materials that would have to be put in evidence if the court were to take account of them. It is the identification of these external materials that is the main subject of this chapter.

4.4 Secondly, there is a distinction between statutory interpretation and contractual interpretation. The scope of background materials should be more limited in the case of statutory interpretation than contractual interpretation. The reasons for this difference of approach are discussed in Section B of this chapter.

4.5 Thirdly, there is a limit on the circumstances in which background materials can be used in the interpretation process. They can be used where the statutory words are ambiguous when read in the context of the statute as a whole; but, the clearer the statutory words, the more difficult it is for their meaning to be influenced by the context. That is the subject of Section C of this chapter.

Principles of Statutory Interpretation. Richard Calnan, Oxford University Press. © Richard Calnan 2023.
DOI: 10.1093/oso/9780192864673.003.0005

4.6 Fourthly, there is a limit on the use to which background materials can be put in the interpretation process. They provide background against which the statutory words are interpreted, but they cannot be used to replace the statutory words. That is the subject of Section D of this chapter.

4.7 Having considered those general limitations, the remaining sections of this chapter discuss the particular types of background material that have been used in the interpretation process. They are all publicly available and closely connected with the statute. They are not necessarily the only types of background material that can be used, but they represent the main types of material that are used in practice. They are described in Sections E to J of this chapter.

4.8 Finally, the particular rules applicable to the interpretation of treaties are discussed in Section K of this chapter.

B. Context: Comparing Statutes and Contracts

4.9 It is commonplace in the interpretation of any document that the words of that document need to be read in context. Words take their colour from their context, and that context is not limited to the document itself.

4.10 As Lord Diplock said in *Prestcold v Minister of Labour*:[1]

> In construing any document it is helpful to bear in mind the purpose for which it was prepared, the kind of person who drafted it and the kind of person by whom it was intended to be read and understood.

4.11 The necessity to read words in their context is the defining element of the changes that have overtaken the law of contractual interpretation over the last twenty-five years. The die was cast by Lord Hoffmann in *Investors Compensation Scheme v West Bromwich Building Society*[2] towards the end of the 1990s; and, although the approach to contractual interpretation has developed subsequently,[3] it is still generally accepted that the words of a written contract need to be understood not only in the light of the rest of the contract, but also in the context of the relevant background at the time the contract was entered into.[4]

4.12 It is generally recognised that statutes also need to be understood in the context in which they were passed. This point was clearly made by Brennan CJ and Dawson, Toohey and Gummow JJ in the High Court of Australia in *CIC Insurance v Bankstown Football Club*,[5] where they said:

> [The] modern approach to statutory interpretation (a) insists that the context be considered in the first instance, not merely at some later stage when ambiguity might be thought to arise, and (b) uses 'context' in its widest sense to include such things as the existing state of the law and the mischief which, by legitimate means such as those just mentioned, one may

1 [1969] 1 WLR 89 at 96.
2 [1998] 1 WLR 896.
3 Most notably in *Arnold v Britton* [2015] AC 1619.
4 *Chartbrook v Persimmon* [2009] 1 AC 1101.
5 (1997) 187 CLR 384 at 408.

> discern the statute was intended to remedy. Instances of general words in a statute being so constrained by their context are numerous. In particular, ... if the apparently plain words of a provision are read in the light of the mischief which the statute was designed to overcome and the objects of the legislation, they may wear a very different appearance.

It is nevertheless suggested that the extent of available context is more limited in relation to statutory interpretation than it is for contractual interpretation, and that there is a good reason why this should be so. The distinction derives from the different natures of statutes and contracts. A statute is a unilateral instrument that imposes rules on all those to whom it is addressed. A contract is voluntarily entered into between particular parties, and binds only those parties. **4.13**

For this purpose, there are four key differences between statutes and contracts: **4.14**

- First, a statute is a unilateral act. It is imposed by the legislature on all citizens. It is consensual only in the limited sense that, in a constitutional democracy, we may be taken to have consented to the legislature's power to do this. By contrast, a contract is a voluntary act.
- Secondly, a statute is a formal instrument. It must be in writing, it is written in a particular form and style and it must be enacted in a particular way. Something is only a statute if it complies with these formal requirements. This is in marked contrast to most contracts. They can be made informally—orally or even by conduct. Even if a contract is encapsulated in a document, it does not necessarily follow that all of the terms of the contract are contained in that document. And the drafting style can vary considerably, depending on the nature of the contract.
- Thirdly, statutes are always promulgated by the same body—the legislature of the state concerned. The identity of those who make up the legislature will change over time, but the nature of the body which promulgates the statute is always the same. This is quite different from a contract, which will be entered into by all sorts of different persons.
- Fourthly, the purpose of statutes is always the same. They create laws to bind citizens. The nature of the laws varies from statute to statute, but the basic purpose of statutes is broadly the same. Contracts, on the other hand, are infinitely varied. They are entered into for all sorts of reasons in a multitude of different circumstances and cover an infinite variety of subjects.

Why should these differences affect the scope of the context that is available to interpret the instrument concerned? There are two key reasons. One is practical; the other is constitutional. **4.15**

Taking the practical difference first, contracts are made in all sorts of different circumstances and between all sorts of different types of people in order to achieve all sorts of different purposes. Even in a formal written contract, the meaning of the words used must to some extent be coloured by the context. The identity of the parties, the market in which the parties are operating, the purpose of the contract—these are all relevant background facts that can influence the way in which the words in the contract will be interpreted. None of this is true in relation to a statute. It is a unilateral instrument, and it is always issued by the same body. It follows that words can be given a more conventional meaning without as much need to delve into the background. The reason for the background to influence the outcome is much more limited. **4.16**

4.17 The second reason for the distinction between statutes and contracts is even more important. We allow the legislature to pass laws that will govern our behaviour. The quid pro quo is that we must know what those laws are so that we can comply with them. We must be able to understand the laws that govern us. Any reasonable person should be able to understand what statutes mean.

4.18 This point cannot be carried too far. A lawyer may well be required in order to establish what the statute really means in practice. But this does not diminish the constitutional importance of our being able to understand what we have signed up to in our social contract.

4.19 Lord Nicholls put it this way in *R v Secretary of State for the Environment, Transport and the Regions, ex parte Spath Holme*:[6]

> Citizens, with the assistance of their advisers, are intended to be able to understand parliamentary enactments, so that they can regulate their conduct accordingly. They should be able to rely on what they read in an Act of Parliament.

4.20 The effect of all this on statutory interpretation is that there is:

- less need for background to influence the interpretation of the words of a statute; and
- a strong policy reason to require statutes to be read on their own terms.

4.21 A person interpreting a statute should therefore be cautious about allowing too much external context to influence the text of the statute.

C. The Need for Ambiguity

4.22 One of the most important general questions to be considered in relation to the interpretation of any document is whether relevant background materials can always be used to interpret the words of the document, or whether they can only be used where there is ambiguity on the face of the document.

4.23 In relation to contractual interpretation, it has become generally accepted over the last twenty-five years that in order to understand the words contained in a contract, they must be considered in the light of:

- the contract as a whole; and
- the relevant background facts that were available at the time the contract was entered into.

4.24 This is the subject of Lord Hoffmann's first two principles in *Investors Compensation Scheme v West Bromwich Building Society*:[7]

> (1) Interpretation is the ascertainment of the meaning which the document would convey to a reasonable person having all the background knowledge which would reasonably have been available to the parties in the situation in which they were at the time of the contract.

[6] [2001] 2 AC 349 at 397.
[7] [1998] 1 WLR 896 at 912–913.

> (2) The background … [subject to certain limitations] … includes absolutely anything which would have affected the way in which the language of the document would have been understood by a reasonable man.

In other words, interpretation of a contract requires the interpreter to establish what the parties meant by what they have said. In order to do this, it is necessary to read the words of the contract not only in the light of the rest of the contract but also in the context of the background against which the contract was made. **4.25**

In relation to contractual interpretation, it is also clear that this is the case whether or not the words are ambiguous on their face. Words must always be read in context, and the context may itself create, and then resolve, an ambiguity. **4.26**

Does the same principle apply to statutory interpretation? Lord Steyn certainly thought that it does so. In *R (Westminster City Council) v National Asylum Support Service*,[8] he said: **4.27**

> The starting point is that language in all legal texts conveys meaning according to the circumstances in which it was used. It follows that the context must always be identified and considered before the process of construction or during it. It is therefore wrong to say that the court may only resort to evidence of the contextual scene when an ambiguity has arisen.… The same applies to statutory construction.

Whilst understanding the conceptual reason for taking this approach, it is suggested that this is not always true in relation to statutory interpretation. There is no doubt that the words in the statute must be read in the context of the rest of the statute, whether or not those words are themselves ambiguous, but it is suggested that the same is not always true of external materials. There is a strong body of opinion in the case law that many types of external materials can only be used if the words are ambiguous on the face of the statute. **4.28**

In *R (D) v Secretary of State for Work and Pensions*,[9] Carnwath LJ referred to the analogy that Lord Steyn had drawn between contractual and statutory interpretation, and continued: **4.29**

> However, the analogy cannot be taken too far. The context of a particular contract may show that the parties used language in a particular way which departs from ordinary English usage; but the same inference cannot be readily be drawn in relation to the language of legislation directed to the public as a whole.

In that case, one of the questions at issue was whether explanatory notes could be used to help to interpret the words of a statute. Carnwath LJ described what he referred to as the orthodox position: '[An] explanatory note may be referred to as an aid to construction where the statutory instrument to which it is attached is ambiguous.'[10] **4.30**

The idea that extrinsic material can only be used in the interpretation of a statute if the words of the statute are themselves ambiguous has a long history. It is illustrated by the decision of a strong Court of Appeal in *Salomon v Commissioners of Customs and Excise*.[11] This case concerned the interpretation of legislation based on an international convention. The Court **4.31**

8 [2002] 1 WLR 2956 at [5].
9 [2010] 1 WLR 1782 at [45].
10 ibid, [48].
11 [1967] 2 QB 116.

of Appeal decided that the court could look at the convention in order to interpret the legislation if—but only if—the words of the statute itself were ambiguous.

4.32 The principal judgment on this point was given by Diplock LJ. He said, in relation to legislation that was introduced in order to give effect to treaty obligations:[12]

> If the terms of the legislation are clear and unambiguous, they must be given effect to, whether or not they carry out Her Majesty's treaty obligations, for the sovereign power of the Queen in Parliament extends to breaking treaties ..., and any remedy for such a breach of an international obligation lies in a forum other than Her Majesty's own courts. But if the terms of the legislation are not clear but are reasonably capable of more than one meaning, the treaty itself becomes relevant, for there is a prima facie presumption that Parliament does not intend to act in breach of international law, including therein specific treaty obligations; and if one of the meanings which can reasonably be ascribed to the legislation is consonant with the treaty obligations and another or others are not, the meaning which is consonant is to be preferred. Thus, in case of lack of clarity in the words used in the legislation, the terms of the treaty are relevant to enable the court to make its choice between the possible meanings of these words by applying this presumption.

4.33 Why is there a distinction between contractual and statutory interpretation? If words necessarily get their colour from their context, then surely the context should be available for the interpretation of all written documents?

4.34 In order to answer this question, it is important to see the issue in its historical context—by reference to the way in which it has evolved. In relation to contractual interpretation, there has always been a strong inclination by many commercial lawyers to give effect to the words of the contract itself in the context of the contract as a whole but without reference to extrinsic evidence. The reason for this approach is essentially pragmatic. The words can be interpreted more quickly, and with a greater degree of certainty, if one focuses on the words used in the contract. After all, that is one of the main reasons why parties write their contracts down.

4.35 In recent years, the courts have set their face against this sort of approach. This was evident in the 1970s in the judgments of Lord Wilberforce,[13] but it was most fully discussed by Lord Hoffmann in *Investors Compensation Scheme v West Bromwich Building Society*,[14] and it is this approach that has held sway in contractual interpretation ever since.

4.36 The reason for this approach is clear. Words have different shades of meaning, and the true meaning that the parties must have intended can only be established by reading the words in the context in which they appear. That does not just include the contract itself, but also the setting in which it is placed. It does not include pre-contractual negotiations or subsequent conduct, but it does include the background facts in existence at the time the contract was entered into.

4.37 So why is this not also true of statutory interpretation? There are essentially two reasons, which have been discussed in Section B of this chapter. The first is that a statute is a different type of document from a contract. A statute is a unilateral instrument that is always issued by

[12] ibid, 143.

[13] *Prenn v Simmonds* [1971] 1 WLR 1381 at 1383–1384; *Reardon Smith Line Ltd v Yngvar Hansen-Tangen* [1976] 1 WLR 989 at 995–996.

[14] [1998] 1 WLR 896 at 912–913.

the same body and that generally applies to the same group of people. There are not the variations of approach that apply in relation to contracts. Contracts—even written ones—are of all sorts of different types, cover a variety of different subject matter and are entered into in different forms by all sorts of different parties. These variations require the interpreter to consider the context in which the words in the contract were used when establishing what they mean. The same is simply not true of statutes. They are always issued by the same body to the same group of people in the same form.

The other reason—which is perhaps even more compelling—is a constitutional one. Citizens must be able to understand the laws that govern them from the text that the legislature issues. This constitutional imperative overrides the fact that all interpretation is contextual. The nature of the instrument limits the context. **4.38**

The distinction between contractual interpretation and statutory interpretation can be illustrated by two cases: **4.39**

- *Bank of Scotland v Dunedin Property Investment Co*;[15] and
- *R (D) v Secretary of State for Work and Pensions*.[16]

Bank of Scotland v Dunedin Property Investment Co[17] involved the interpretation of a loan stock deed. A company raised money by issuing fixed-rate loan stock to a bank. In order to protect itself against interest rate fluctuations, the bank entered into a swap contract with a third party. The loan stock deed enabled the company to redeem the stock early, subject to reimbursing the bank for all expenses incurred by it 'in connection with' the stock. The company gave notice to redeem the stock early. The bank therefore terminated the swap contract and then claimed the cost of doing so from the company on the basis that it was an expense incurred 'in connection with' the stock. **4.40**

The court decided that the expense was recoverable by the bank. In part, this was due to the natural—and broad—meaning of the expression 'in connection with'. But the court was reinforced in its conclusion by reference to evidence of the negotiations between the parties before the loan stock was issued. That evidence established that the company was aware that the bank would borrow money to subscribe for the loan stock and that the bank intended to hedge the transaction; and that, if the loan stock was redeemed early, there would be a cost of an uncertain amount associated with the hedge. **4.41**

There were two relevant pieces of information in this case—the words of the loan stock deed and the knowledge of the company that the bank intended to hedge its exposure. Both were relevant to the decision, whether or not the words of the particular contract were ambiguous. In contractual interpretation, the relevant context is always available to help to interpret the words of the contract. **4.42**

Statutory interpretation is different. A statute must always be read as a whole, but specific external context can often only be used if the words of the statute are ambiguous. **4.43**

In *R (D) v Secretary of State for Work and Pensions*,[18] one of the issues was the extent to which explanatory notes concerning legislation could be used in interpreting it. The Court **4.44**

[15] 1998 SC 657.
[16] [2010] 1 WLR 1782.
[17] 1998 SC 657.
[18] [2010] 1 WLR 1782.

of Appeal decided that they could only be used where the words of the legislation were ambiguous. The public (to whom the statute is addressed) are expected to read the statute themselves, but not necessarily any external materials.

4.45 The result is that the legislature is set a higher duty than the contracting parties. It must make the words it has used clear in the context of the legislation alone. And the reason for that is both pragmatic and constitutional.

D. The Purpose of Context

4.46 The purpose of the context is to set the scene against which the words of the statute are read. But what does that mean in practice?

4.47 The starting point is that the context cannot add new provisions to the statute. No rights, duties, powers or immunities can be created unless they emanate from the words of the statute. As has been seen in relation to Principle 2, there is no statutory equivalent of the implied terms doctrine for contracts.

4.48 Nor does the court have any power to alter the statutory words in order to make them comply with what it thinks Parliament intended. Again, as has been seen in relation to Principle 2, there is no statutory equivalent of the contractual doctrine of rectification. The expression 'rectification' is used in relation to statutes, but it has a different meaning than when it is used in connection with contracts. It is not concerned with changing the statutory words. It is a principle of interpretation, and it is discussed in Section E of Chapter 7.

4.49 In principle, therefore, the background can be used to set the scene within which the statutory words are used and to establish the mischief that the statute was intended to remedy and therefore the general purpose of the statute.[19] But it cannot create new provisions or substitute words for those that have been used in the statute.[20] As Lord Hodge has recently said in *R (O) v Secretary of State for the Home Department*,[21] statutory interpretation is concerned with the meaning of the words that Parliament has used in the statute. 'External aids to interpretation therefore must play a secondary role.'[22]

4.50 This is easy to say, but more difficult to apply in practice. The problem is illustrated by the decision of the House of Lords in *Pepper v Hart*.[23] In that case, the court had to decide the meaning of the following words in section 61 of the Finance Act 1976: 'the cost of a benefit is the amount of any expense incurred in or in connection with its provision'. Was the expense the marginal cost of providing the benefit for a particular transaction or a proportion of the total cost of providing the benefit? The House of Lords decided that the words were ambiguous and that they were entitled to look at the parliamentary speech of the minister who promoted the legislation, which was reported in Hansard, in order to establish which of the two possible meanings was intended. When doing so, did they use the minister's words to set

19 *Fothergill v Monarch Airlines* [1981] AC 251 at 281 (Lord Diplock).
20 *Assam Railways v Commissioners of Inland Revenue* [1935] AC 445 at 458–459 (Lord Wright).
21 [2022] 2 WLR 343 at [29]–[31].
22 ibid, [30].
23 [1993] AC 593.

the scene for the statutory words, or were they substituting the minister's words for the words of the statute?

The words of a ministerial statement in Parliament during the discussion of a Bill that are then reported in Hansard might be regarded as evidence of what the government wanted to do. It is not an infallible guide to the government's intention because intentions can—and often do—change. But the important point is that—whether or not those words establish what it was that the government wanted to achieve—it is irrelevant to the question of what the statute means. What matters is what Parliament actually said in the statute. There is no statutory doctrine of rectification. The minister's statement cannot be used as a substitute for the statutory words. **4.51**

The context can help to establish what was wrong with the existing law—the 'mischief' that the legislature was intending to rectify. It can therefore also help to establish the general aim of the legislation—its 'purpose'—because its purpose was to rectify the mischief. But that purpose could be achieved in a variety of ways, and to a greater or lesser extent. The actual way in which the legislature achieved the general purpose of avoiding the mischief can only be established by reading the statutory words; and what a minister says about what those words mean—or were intended to mean—is irrelevant. **4.52**

Pepper v Hart is a controversial case. This is partly because it extends the scope of the contextual material available when interpreting the words of a statute. There is a strong body of opinion that it is not appropriate to do this because it serves little useful purpose and simply increases the time it takes to resolve questions of interpretation. Indeed, this was why Lord Mackay dissented in the case itself. He pointed out the practical difficulties involved. Almost every question of statutory interpretation that comes to the courts will involve the types of issue that it was being suggested would enable Hansard to be used. It followed that the parties' legal advisers would need to study Hansard in practically every case. That would involve an immense increase in the cost of litigation.[24] These are all important points, and history suggests that Lord Mackay was right.[25] **4.53**

But there is an even stronger reason to doubt the approach in *Pepper v Hart*. This is because of the purpose for which the background material was used. It is legitimate for relevant background material to be used to establish the mischief that the legislation was intending to resolve. What is illegitimate is to use it to establish what the words of the statute mean. **4.54**

The problem can been seen in the judgment of Lord Browne-Wilkinson:[26] **4.55**

> In my judgment, subject to the questions of the privileges of the House of Commons, reference to Parliamentary material should be permitted as an aid to the construction of legislation which is ambiguous or obscure or the literal meaning of which leads to an absurdity. Even in such cases references in court to Parliamentary material should only be permitted where such material clearly discloses the mischief aimed at or the legislative intention lying behind the ambiguous or obscure words.

[24] ibid, 614–615.

[25] See the comments of Lord Hoffmann in *Robinson v Secretary of State for Northern Ireland* [2002] UKHL 32 at [39] and [40].

[26] [1993] AC 593 at 634.

4.56 In this context, the crucial sentence is the last one. The background material can be used not only to establish the mischief, but also the legislative intention. In principle, it is suggested, that is wrong. The former is legitimate; the latter is illegitimate.

4.57 Lord Steyn made this point in *R (Jackson) v Attorney General*:[27]

> I would be inclined to hold that the time has come to rule … that *Pepper v Hart* … should be confined to the situation which was before the House in *Pepper v Hart*. That would leave unaffected the use of Hansard material to identify the mischief at which legislation was directed and its objective setting. But trying to discover the intentions of the Government from ministerial statements in Parliament is constitutionally unacceptable.

4.58 Lord Hope took a similar approach in *R v Secretary of State for the Environment, Transport and the Regions, ex parte Spath Holme*:[28]

> In my opinion there are sound reasons of principle for rejecting the argument that statements made by ministers in Parliament may be used to identify the policy and objects of an enactment for the purpose of identifying the scope of a discretionary power which Parliament has conferred on the executive.… [The] policy and objects of the Act must be determined by construing the Act …
>
> The limited exception to the general rule that resort to Hansard is inadmissible which was recognised in *Pepper v Hart* …[29] is available to prevent the executive seeking to place a meaning on words used in legislation which is different from that which ministers attributed to those words when promoting the legislation in Parliament.

4.59 Ten years on from *Pepper v Hart*, Lord Hoffmann had to consider its effect in *Robinson v Secretary of State for Northern Ireland*.[30] He was concerned that the effect of *Pepper v Hart* had been to increase the amount of argument based around extrinsic material. He continued:

> I am not sure that it is sufficiently understood that it will be very rare indeed for an Act of Parliament to be construed by the courts as meaning something different from what it would be understood to mean by a member of the public who was aware of all of the material forming the background to its enactment but who was not privy to what had been said by individual members (including Ministers) during the debates in one or other House of Parliament.

4.60 Green J tried to reconcile *Pepper v Hart* with principle in *Solar Century Holdings v Secretary of State for Energy and Climate Change*:[31]

> Parliament is sovereign and its views are constitutionally discrete from those of the Executive. The gap can in some cases, however, be bridged.… [Where] there is a very clear pre-legislative statement which turns out to be inconsistent with the subsequent enactment the latter can be construed to mean the same as the former where this can properly be said to reflect the will of Parliament. In such a case the view of the Executive is not taking precedence over that of Parliament; it is simply that the earlier statement is said on analysis

27 [2006] 1 AC 262 at [97].
28 [2001] 2 AC 349 at 407–408.
29 [1993] AC 593.
30 [2002] UKHL 32 at [40].
31 [2014] EWHC 3677 (Admin) at [66].

> to be an accurate reflection of Parliament's will. At base this approach by the courts seeks to override infelicitous statutory language which the Court concludes is not a proper reflection of Parliament's actual will and it is aided in this endeavour by reference to admissible pre-legislative material.

It is suggested that *Pepper v Hart* cannot be reconciled with principle in this way. The effect of applying *Pepper v Hart* is to replace the words that the legislature has used with words that it might better have used, and that is an illegitimate role for a court.[32] As Lord Steyn said in *R (Westminster City Council) v National Asylum Support Service*:[33] **4.61**

> What is impermissible is to treat the wishes and desires of the Government about the scope of the statutory language as reflecting the will of Parliament. The aims of the Government in respect of the meaning of the clauses ... cannot be attributed to Parliament. The object is to see what is the intention expressed by the words enacted.

In *Wilson v First County Trust (No 2)*,[34] Lord Hobhouse put it this way: **4.62**

> Once one departs from the text of the statute construed as a whole and looks for expressions of intention to be found elsewhere, one is not looking for the intention of the legislature but that of some other source with no constitutional power to make law. The process of statutory construction/interpretation is objective not subjective ... The principles are also fully familiar (mutatis mutandis) to commercial lawyers in deciding what was the bargain struck between two commercial parties by a written agreement ...

As well as explaining the constitutional problem with *Pepper v Hart*, Lord Hobhouse also described the practical problems that it creates:[35] **4.63**

> Judicial experience has taught me, particularly since I was appointed a member of this House, that the attempt by advocates to use parliamentary material from Hansard as an aid to statutory construction has not proved helpful and the fears of those pessimists who saw it as simply a cause of additional expense in the conduct of litigation have been proved correct.

In summary, it is suggested that there is a distinction between the words of a statute and the context in which those words must be read. The context cannot be used to change or replace the statutory words. All the context can do is to establish the background against which the statutory words were used in order to assist the interpreter to understand what those statutory words mean. **4.64**

E. What Materials are Available?

Having discussed the general limitations on the use of background materials, it is now necessary to consider the types of material that can be used in the interpretation process. **4.65**

[32] To appropriate, in a different context, the words of Lord Mustill in *Charter Reinsurance Co v Fagan* [1997] AC 313 at 387–388.
[33] [2002] 1 WLR 2956 at [6].
[34] [2004] 1 AC 816 at [139]. *R (SC) v Secretary of State for Work and Pensions* [2022] AC 223 at [163]–[172].
[35] [2004] 1 AC 816 at [140].

4.66 Apart from the necessity that the materials must relate directly to the statute concerned, there is one general limitation on the type of material available.

4.67 Background material can only be used to interpret a statute if it was publicly available at the time the statute was passed. This is very similar to the position in relation to the interpretation of contracts, where the background information must have been reasonably available to the parties at the time the contract was made.[36]

4.68 The reason for this requirement is the same in each case. It is the principle of objectivity. What needs to be established is not what the legislature or the parties wanted to do. It is what a reasonable person would understand they meant from what they have actually done.

4.69 This principle is applied even more strictly to statutes than to contracts. This is because of the constitutional element involved in the interpretation of statutes. We are bound by the laws the legislature has passed—not by what it intended, but by what it did. So if a statute is to be read in the light of something else, it must be something that is reasonably available to the general public—to whom the statute is addressed.

4.70 This principle was explained by Sales J in *R (Public and Commercial Services Union) v Minister for the Civil Service*:[37]

> An Act of Parliament creates law applicable to all citizens. In my judgment, it is fundamental that all materials which are relevant to the proper interpretation of such an instrument should be available to any person who wishes to inform himself about the meaning of that law.

4.71 Lord Reid made the same point in *Black-Clawson International v Papierwerke Waldhof-Aschaffenburg*:[38]

> The general rule in construing any document is that one should put oneself 'in the shoes' of the maker or makers and take into account relevant facts known to them when the document was made. The same must apply to Acts of Parliament subject to one qualification. An Act is addressed to all the lieges and it would seem wrong to take into account anything that was not public knowledge at the time.

4.72 The importance of this point was illustrated in the decision of the Supreme Court in *Re Agricultural Sector (Wales) Bill*.[39] One of the questions in this case was whether correspondence between government departments that had never been made public could be used to assist in the interpretation of particular legislation. The Supreme Court made it clear that evidence outside the words of the statute itself can only be taken into account if it is in the public domain. It said:[40]

> In our view it would be wholly inconsistent with the transparent and open democratic process under which Parliament enacts legislation to take into account matters that have passed in private between two departments of the Executive or between the Executive of the UK and a devolved Executive.

[36] *Investors Compensation Scheme v West Bromwich Building Society* [1998] 1 WLR 896 at 912.
[37] [2011] 3 All ER 54 at [55].
[38] [1975] AC 591 at 613–614.
[39] [2014] 1 WLR 2622.
[40] ibid, [39].

There is no *numerus clausus* of the types of background materials that are available in the interpretation of statutes, but particular types of background materials have proved to be important in practice, and they are discussed in the following sections of this chapter: **4.73**

- judicial interpretation of the statute and its predecessors (Section F);
- legislative history (Section G);
- explanatory notes (Section H);
- public reports on which the statute is based (Section I); and
- ministerial statements in Parliament (Section J).

There are also particular rules for treaties that are briefly discussed in Section K. **4.74**

F. Judicial Interpretation of the Statute and its Predecessors

One of the issues that distinguishes statutes from contracts is that they apply to a wider body of persons and they tend to last longer. It is common for particular statutes to be interpreted in more than one case, and it is common for statutes to be amended and restated over time. **4.75**

In relation to contractual interpretation, the doctrine of precedent has a small role to play. When a court interprets the meaning of a particular expression, it is doing so in the context of the particular contract concerned. The approach of the court in an earlier case may be of relevance to a later court interpreting the same words in a different contract, but it cannot be binding. **4.76**

The same is not entirely true of statutes. Statutory provisions can remain in force for a long time. If a court has decided that a particular expression in a statute has a particular meaning, then that will be binding on subsequent courts in accordance with the normal rules of precedent. But what if the words used in one statute are used in a later statute in a similar context? **4.77**

In *Barras v Aberdeen Steam Trawling and Fishing Co*,[41] the question was what was meant by the words 'wreck or loss of a ship' in the Merchant Shipping (International Labour Conventions) Act 1925. The same expression had been used in the Merchant Shipping Act 1894, and had been interpreted by the Court of Appeal. The House of Lords decided that there was a presumption that Parliament, by using the same words in the same context, intended the words to have the meaning given by the decision of the Court of Appeal. But this was only a presumption. **4.78**

A number of the judges quoted the judgment of James LJ in *Ex parte Campbell*:[42] **4.79**

> Where once certain words in an Act of Parliament have received a judicial construction in one of the Superior Courts, and the Legislature has repeated them without alteration in a subsequent statute, I conceive that the Legislature must be taken to have used them according to the meaning which a Court of competent jurisdiction has given to them.

In the *Barras* case, Viscount Buckmaster expressed the position in these terms:[43] **4.80**

[41] [1933] AC 402.
[42] LR 5 Ch 703 at 706.
[43] [1933] AC 402 at 411.

> It has long been a well established principle to be applied in the consideration of Acts of Parliament that where a word of doubtful meaning has received a clear judicial interpretation, the subsequent statute which incorporates the same word or the same phrase in a similar context, must be construed so that the word or phrase is interpreted according to the meaning that has previously been assigned to it.

4.81 This is not a rule of law. It is a presumption—a starting point in the process of interpretation. This point was made by Lord Lloyd in *Lowsley v Forbes*:[44]

> It has long been a rule of construction that when Parliament uses a word or term, the meaning of which has been the subject of judicial ruling in the same or similar context, then it may be presumed that the word or term was intended to bear the same meaning ... The rule, like other rules of construction, is not in any way conclusive. It is an aid: no more.

4.82 There is always a danger in using presumptions in the interpretative process. Interpretation involves the exercise of judgement. It is not assisted by formalistic processes. They just detract from the real job in hand. This issue was discussed by Lords Simon and Wilberforce in *Farrell v Alexander*.[45]

4.83 Lord Simon said:[46]

> If therefore the object of statutory interpretation were to ascertain what Parliament meant to say, the *Barras* doctrine would indeed be potent and primary. But the object of statutory interpretation is rather to ascertain the meaning of what Parliament has said. On this approach the previous judicial interpretation is merely one of the facts within the knowledge of the draftsman in the light of which he will draft.

4.84 Lord Wilberforce commented:[47]

> My Lords, I have never been attracted by the doctrine of Parliamentary endorsement of decided cases: it seems to me to be based upon a theory of legislative formation which is possibly fictional. But if there are cases in which this doctrine may be applied, and I must respect the opinions of those judges who have so held, any case must be a clear one ... This case is certainly not such as case.

4.85 In reality, this is just one of the factors that a court will take into account when deciding the true meaning of the particular words in question.

G. Legislative History

4.86 Statutes very rarely stand still. They are frequently amended, and are often replaced or consolidated. If you are reading words in a statute that has a legislative history, to what extent should you look at the legislative history?

4.87 The starting point is that the interpreter should not generally look to the legislative history of the statute that is being interpreted. The interpreter should read the legislation

[44] [1999] 1 AC 329 at 340.
[45] [1977] AC 59.
[46] ibid, 90.
[47] ibid, 74.

in its current form. The reason for this approach was explained by Lord Diplock in *R v Cuthbertson*:[48]

> [Your] Lordships have been invited to trace the history of various kinds of forfeiture known to the law over the centuries, from the concept of Anglo-Saxon deodand ... That it should be necessary to have recourse to such erudite and intricate arguments in order to ascertain the meaning of a provision in a criminal statute which needs to be administered with reasonable consistency by hundreds of criminal courts throughout the land if justice is to be done, would be discreditable to the English legal system. I have not, however, been persuaded that it is necessary to do so in order to find out what [the relevant section] means. It is indeed more likely to distract attention from what is the real issue in the case. The words of the section, in my view, speak for themselves clearly, without resort to extraneous aids.

In *Farrell v Alexander*,[49] Lord Wilberforce made the same point: **4.88**

> [It] is quite wrong that, in every case where a consolidation Act is under consideration, one should automatically look back through the history of its various provisions, and the cases decided upon them, and minutely trace the language from Act to Act ... I think that this tendency should be firmly resisted; that self-contained statutes, whether consolidating previous law, or doing so with amendments, should be interpreted, if reasonably possible, without recourse to antecedents, and that the recourse should only be had when there is a real and substantial difficulty or ambiguity which classical methods of construction cannot resolve. This is particularly true of Acts ... which have to be applied by county courts, and which have to be understood or at least explained to great numbers of citizens."

The reasons for this approach are obvious. A person reading a statute should be able to understand it without having to work through its antecedents. A requirement to trawl through the undergrowth (to coin an expression used by Lightman J in relation to contracts) would not only increase the amount of time required in order to resolve the issue, but would also be constitutionally unacceptable. It should be possible for a citizen to be able to understand legislation in its own terms. **4.89**

That is not to say that the courts will never trawl through the legislative history. If the legislation is ambiguous, a court can look to the history of the legislation to see if it casts light on which of the alternative meanings was intended. This can be illustrated by two cases: **4.90**

- *Goodes v East Sussex County Council*;[50] and
- *Mitsui Sumitomo Insurance Co v Mayor's Office for Policing and Crime*.[51]

In *Goodes v East Sussex County Council*,[52] the plaintiffs sued the council for failure to salt or grit a road in freezing conditions. The claim was made under section 41(1) of the Highways Act 1980, which requires a highway authority 'to maintain the highway'. **4.91**

The House of Lords held that maintenance did not include a duty to salt and grit the roads. They accepted that the words were capable of more than one meaning. The words could include steps to keep the road safe for ordinary use by motor cars, but they held that in this **4.92**

48 [1981] AC 470 at 480.
49 [1977] AC 59 at 72–73.
50 [2000] 1 WLR 1356.
51 [2016] AC 1488.
52 [2000] 1 WLR 1356.

context they had the narrower meaning of keeping the fabric of the highway in such good repair as to render its physical condition safe for ordinary traffic to pass at all seasons of the year, and that did not include a duty to prevent the formation of ice or to remove the accumulation of snow on the road.

4.93 The reason the court reached this conclusion was that it read the legislation by reference to its historical antecedents. It read the words of the Act in the context of the earlier legislation. Lord Hoffmann, in particular, went into great detail through the earlier statutory duties of highway authorities going back over the centuries.

4.94 A similar approach was taken by the Supreme Court in *Mitsui Sumitomo Insurance Co v Mayor's Office for Policing and Crime*.[53] The case concerned the meaning of section 2(1) of the Riot (Damages) Act 1886 that provided for compensation from a public fund where damage to a building or the property in it has been sustained as a result of a riot. The question was whether the damage that could be recovered was limited to physical damage, or whether it also extended to consequential loss. The first instance judge held that it was limited to physical damage, the Court of Appeal that it was not and the Supreme Court that it was.

4.95 In the Supreme Court, the judgment of the court was given by Lord Hodge. He considered that the statute was ambiguous. The statutory words did not disclose whether the loss that was recoverable was limited to damage to the value of the property concerned, or whether it extended to consequential loss. Lord Hodge said:[54] 'In my view this is a case in which history rather than legal theory casts light, revealing the correct answer.'

4.96 Lord Hodge carried out a detailed review of the prior legislative history since 1714. He decided that the words of the legislation should be interpreted in the light of the prior legislation and that they supported the conclusion that the most recent Act, like its predecessors, contained a self-contained statutory scheme that did not mirror the common law of tort.

4.97 In summary, prior legislative history can be used to interpret words in a statute which are ambiguous. Otherwise, the court should generally read the words of the latest legislation without reference back to its antecedents.

H. Explanatory Notes

4.98 Statutes frequently contain explanatory notes that are expressed not to form part of the statute itself but that are intended to assist the reader to understand the statute. Explanatory notes are frequently printed as part of the document that contains the statute itself.

4.99 This raises the question whether recourse can only be had to the explanatory notes if the statute itself is ambiguous. It has been seen that the basic principle is that the statute itself must be read as a whole regardless of whether particular words are ambiguous, but that external background materials are generally only available if there is ambiguity. Where do explanatory notes fall?

[53] [2016] AC 1488.
[54] ibid, [13].

There are suggestions in some cases that ambiguity is not a requirement for the court to take explanatory notes into account. In *Flora v Wakom (Heathrow)*,[55] Brooke LJ said: 'The text of an Act does not have to be ambiguous before a court may be permitted to take into account explanatory notes in order to understand the contextual scene in which the Act is set.' **4.100**

But in *R (D) v Secretary of State for Work and Pensions*,[56] Carnwath LJ said: '[An] explanatory note may be referred to as an aid to construction where the statutory instrument to which it is attached is ambiguous.' **4.101**

Although the explanatory notes are contained in the same document as the statute, they are not part of the statute itself, and they serve a different purpose. It is therefore suggested that they should only be used to resolve an ambiguity. **4.102**

It is also important to appreciate the purpose for which the explanatory notes can be used. This was explained by Carnwath LJ in *R (D) v Secretary of State for Work and Pensions*:[57] **4.103**

> [They] remain only aids to construction and no more. The essential task is to construe the language of the legislation, not that of the explanatory material. Thus in the present case, the memoranda may help to explain the background and general purpose of the [relevant regulations]. They do nothing to explain why [words were used in a particular way]. For the answer for this question, in the default of other aids, one is driven back to analysis of the words of the legislation.

This is a point that is occasionally overlooked in the cases. An extreme example is *R (Confederation of Passenger Transport UK) v Humber Bridge Board*,[58] that concerned a statutory instrument under which tolls were levied for traffic crossing the Humber Bridge. The expression 'large bus' was defined in the Order, but there was no provision in the operative part that expressly levied a toll on large buses. The Court of Appeal nevertheless decided that the Order should be interpreted as including a provision for tolls to be levied on large buses. **4.104**

One of the reasons the Court of Appeal took this view was that the explanatory note said that the statutory instrument did impose a toll on large buses.[59] Clarke LJ gave the principal judgment. He said:[60] 'I see no reason why [the explanatory note] should not be used to help to resolve the question whether any words were omitted from the statutory instrument by mistake.' **4.105**

In the result, the court decided that the Order should be read as including a 'large bus' in the appropriate place—even though it was not actually there. **4.106**

It is suggested that this is an illegitimate use of explanatory notes. They can be used to place the words in the statute in context but, ultimately, the only words that create laws are the words in the statute themselves, and the statute did not levy a toll on large buses. **4.107**

55 [2007] 1 WLR 482 at [16].
56 [2010] 1 WLR 1782 at [48].
57 ibid, [51].
58 [2004] QB 310.
59 ibid, [19].
60 ibid, [49].

I. Public Reports on which the Statute is Based

4.108 Acts of Parliament are sometimes introduced in order to give effect to Law Commission reports, and are preceded by White Papers and similar public reports. The courts use these reports as background for the purpose of interpreting the words of a statute if those words are ambiguous.[61] But it is important to appreciate that they can only be used for the purpose of explaining the background against which the words of the legislation are to be interpreted. They cannot be used to replace those words.

J. Ministerial Statements in Parliament

4.109 Until *Pepper v Hart*[62] in the early 1990s, it was clear that a court should not have regard to parliamentary debates for the purpose of interpreting statutes. In Australia, the principle was reaffirmed in the late 1970s in *South Australian Commissioner for Prices and Consumer Affairs v Charles Moore*.[63] In that case, the High Court of Australia confirmed the importance of the principle and declined to alter it.[64] Gibbs J observed:[65]

> The need to have regard to the parliamentary debates for the purpose of construing a statute would render the law less certain, and the burden of having this additional material available for consideration, and examining it, in many cases for no worthwhile result, would tend to aggravate the delay and increase the cost of litigation.

4.110 In spite of these compelling reasons to preserve the principle, fifteen years later it was abrogated in the United Kingdom by the House of Lords in *Pepper v Hart*.[66]

4.111 *Pepper v Hart*[67] has been discussed in Section D of this chapter. In that case, the House of Lords decided that when interpreting ambiguous words in a statute, the courts were entitled to look at the speech of the minister who promoted the Act concerned, as it was reported in Hansard, if it is clear and it is directed to the point in issue.[68] The court recognised that materials of this kind had not previously been available in evidence.

4.112 The principal judgment was given by Lord Browne-Wilkinson. He expressed the position this way:[69]

> In my judgment, subject to the questions of the privileges of the House of Commons, reference to Parliamentary material should be permitted as an aid to the construction of legislation which is ambiguous or obscure or the literal meaning of which leads to an absurdity. Even in such cases references in court to Parliamentary material should only be permitted where such material clearly discloses the mischief aimed at or the legislative intention lying behind the ambiguous or obscure words.

[61] *R v G* [2014] 1 AC 1034.
[62] [1993] AC 593.
[63] (1977) 139 CLR 449.
[64] ibid, 457 (Barwick CJ), 461 (Gibbs J), 470 (Stephen J) and 476–478 (Mason J).
[65] ibid, 461.
[66] [1993] AC 593.
[67] ibid.
[68] *Melluish v BMI* [1996] 1 AC 454 at 481 (Lord Browne-Wilkinson).
[69] [1993] AC 593 at 634.

The House of Lords reached this conclusion by a majority of six to one. Lord Mackay dissented, but even those judges who decided in favour of using the material had their doubts. Lord Oliver described himself as a 'somewhat reluctant convert'.[70] Lord Bridge[71] considered that this material should only be used in those rare cases where the very issue of interpretation that arose in the case had been addressed in the parliamentary debate and where the promotor of the legislation had made a clear statement directed at that very issue. **4.113**

There are certainly occasions—albeit rare—where a court has found material from Hansard to be useful in the interpretation exercise. In *A. E. Beckett & Sons v Midland Electricity*,[72] there was a dispute about the meaning of the word 'supply' in section 21 of the Electricity Act 1989. There were two possible meanings of the word in this context, and the Court of Appeal 'found these rival contentions based on textual analysis of the statute to be nicely balanced and inconclusive'.[73] **4.114**

The court therefore asked counsel to find out whether any help could be obtained from Hansard, and the court continued:[74] **4.115**

> In accordance with *Pepper v Hart* ... counsel referred us to passages of parliamentary debate in relation to the clause in the Bill which was to become section 21. These immediately made clear what had previously been obscure.

The Court of Appeal concluded:[75] **4.116**

> We have concluded that this is a rare case where material admitted under *Pepper v Hart* has resolved an ambiguity in the statute being construed.

This is an interesting case for two reasons. First, it shows that *Pepper v Hart* can be of use where there a real ambiguity in the statute and that dispute can be resolved clearly by reference to Hansard. Secondly, it also demonstrates (as the court acknowledged) how limited the types of case are in which *Pepper v Hart* will assist. But, whether or not it can help in limited cases, there are formidable practical and constitutional problems with its use. **4.117**

In *Pepper v Hart*, Lord Browne-Wilkinson explained why the courts had not previously used material of this kind:[76] **4.118**

> [The] the reasons put forward for the present rule are first, that it preserves the constitutional proprieties leaving Parliament to legislate in words and the courts (not Parliamentary speakers), to construe the meaning of the words finally enacted; second, the practical difficulty of the expense of researching Parliamentary material which would arise if the material could be looked at; third, the need for the citizen to have access to a known defined text which regulates his legal rights; fourth the improbability of finding helpful guidance from Hansard.

There are two key issues here. One is practical, the other constitutional. **4.119**

[70] ibid, 619.
[71] ibid, 617.
[72] [2001] 1 WLR 281.
[73] ibid, [30].
[74] ibid, [34].
[75] ibid, [39].
[76] [1993] AC 593 at 633.

4.120 The practical issue is a concern that the use of parliamentary material of this kind will simply add to the amount of time required to consider cases of statutory interpretation. A great deal more information will be made available, and it will almost certainly be of no real value in practice. This was the principal reason for Lord Mackay's dissent. He considered that practically every question of statutory interpretation that comes before the courts will involve the types of issue that it was being suggested would enable Hansard to be used. It followed that the parties' legal advisers would need to study Hansard in practically every case, and that would involve an immense increase in the cost of litigation. Commenting on this point in *Robinson v Secretary of State for Northern Ireland*,[77] Lord Hoffmann regarded Lord Mackay as being the better prophet on this point.

4.121 There is a very strong echo here of the reasons why, in *Chartbrook v Persimmon Homes*,[78] the House of Lords decided that pre-contractual negotiations were not to be considered when interpreting a contract. As Lord Hoffmann said in that case:[79] 'There is certainly a view in the profession that the less one has to resort to any sort of background in aid of interpretation, the better.' That promotes certainty and reduces the amount of time and expense required to resolve disputes.

4.122 This is an important point. But even more important are the constitutional issues. As Lord Oliver said in *Pepper v Hart*:[80]

> A statute is, after all, the formal and complete intimation to the citizen of a particular rule of the law which he is enjoined, sometimes under penalty, to obey and by which he is both expected and entitled to regulate his conduct. We must, therefore, I believe, be very cautious in opening the door to the reception of material not readily or ordinarily accessible to the citizen whose rights and duties are to be affected by the words in which the legislature has elected to express its will.

4.123 Lord Oliver is here echoing Lords Reid and Wilberforce in the *Black-Clawson* case[81] and Lord Diplock in *Fothergill v Monarch Airlines*,[82] who said that the purpose of statutory interpretation is to establish what Parliament said, not what it meant, and that citizens should be able to rely on the words Parliament did use.

4.124 There are strong practical reasons for limiting the amount of background material available—both in order to establish more certainty and to limit the time and cost of disputes. But the most important point is that citizens are entitled to understand the laws that govern them from the words of the published statute.

4.125 The approach in *Pepper v Hart* has been criticised in other common law jurisdictions. There is a particularly useful discussion of the issues in the judgment of the Court of Appeal of New South Wales in *Harrison v Melhem*.[83] Mason P gave the principal judgment. He said:[84]

[77] [2002] UKHL 32 at [39] and [40].
[78] [2009] 1 AC 1101.
[79] ibid, [36].
[80] [1993] AC 593 at 619–620.
[81] [1975] AC 591.
[82] [1981] AC 251.
[83] (2008) 72 NSWLR 380.
[84] ibid, [159].

> There are many authoritative statements that legislation must be construed by reference to what Parliament has said through its enactment, as distinct from what others, including ministers, may wish or think Parliament intended …

Mason P then considered *Pepper v Hart*. He said:[85] **4.126**

> Statements in Parliament, even by ministers during the Second Reading debate, will however seldom be available to elucidate the meaning of the later-enacted text. Identification of mischief and purpose is one thing, statement of meaning is another. *Pepper* … was and, to my mind, remains a controversial decision. … I am unaware of any authoritative Australian decision that goes as far as *Pepper* or its English progeny.

Mason P was concerned not only with the practical, but also with the constitutional, problems inherent in *Pepper v Hart*. He considered that there were 'large issues about the correctness of *Pepper* to the extent that it goes beyond allowing resort to ministerial statements to discern the context of the Bill in question and the mischief to which it is addressed'.[86] He continued:[87] **4.127**

> In my view, the idea that a Minister can stamp his or her interpretation upon an Act of Parliament by no more than (and I emphasise 'no more than') stating a view as to its meaning is constitutionally unacceptable. Nor is it supported by legitimate canons of statutory construction.

Spigelman CJ threw his weight behind these observations. He said:[88] **4.128**

> Statements of intention as to the meaning of words by ministers in a Second Reading speech, let alone other statements in parliamentary speeches are virtually never useful … I only refrain from using the word 'never' to allow for a truly exceptional case, which I am not at present able to envisage.

Spigelman CJ accepted that ministerial statements can be of use in order to establish the mischief, and therefore the general purpose, of the legislation, but he continued:[89] **4.129**

> The task of the court is to interpret the words used by Parliament. It is not to define the intent of Parliament … The courts must determine what Parliament meant by the words it used. The courts do not determine what Parliament intended to say.

In *Pepper v Hart* itself, the statement by the promoting minister was used for the benefit of the taxpayer. It has subsequently been suggested that the actual decision in the case might be justified on the basis that the government is estopped from denying that the ambiguous words of the statute mean what the minister said. In *Wilson v First County Trust (No 2)*,[90] Lord Hope saw the justification for *Pepper v Hart* as being 'to prevent the executive seeking to place a meaning on words used in legislation which is different from that which ministers attributed to those words when promoting the legislation in Parliament'. Even this more limited approach has not met with universal approval. In *Harrison v Melhem*,[91] Mason P in the New South Wales Court of Appeal commented that 'the notion that the meaning of a **4.130**

[85] ibid, [162].
[86] ibid, [167].
[87] ibid, [182].
[88] ibid, [12].
[89] ibid, [16].
[90] [2004] 1 AC 816 at [113].
[91] (2008) 72 NSWLR 380 at [163].

statute might turn upon such private law notions strikes me, with respect, as constitutionally untenable'.

4.131 There are those who are in favour of the rule in *Pepper v Hart*. One is Lord Nicholls, who spoke in favour of it in *R (Jackson) v Attorney General*[92] and in *Wilson v First County Trust (No 2)*[93] but there have been powerful arguments against, on the grounds both of practicality and of constitutional propriety. This was the view of Lord Steyn in *R (Westminster City Council) v National Asylum Support Service*[94] and of Lord Hoffmann in *Robinson v Secretary of State for Northern Ireland*.[95]

4.132 *Pepper v Hart* offends against the fundamental principle of statutory interpretation that the law is what the legislature has written in the statute, not what the legislature intended, and that citizens must be able to understand the statutes that govern them from what they actually say. There has been sufficient doubt cast on the case to make it possible that the Supreme Court might one day return to principle.

K. Treaties

4.133 In *Revenue and Customs Commissioners v Anson*,[96] Lord Reed said:

> It is a matter of agreement that, as international treaties, [conventions] have to be interpreted in accordance with arts 31 and 32 of the Vienna Convention on the Law of Treaties . . .

4.134 Although the Vienna Convention on the Law of Treaties adopts an approach to interpretation that is more consistent with civil law jurisdictions than common law ones, it is generally accepted that the principles that it establishes are also relevant in common law jurisdictions. Common law courts accept that treaties have to be interpreted in accordance with the international rules of interpretation, and that they have been codified in the Vienna Convention on the Law of Treaties. An example of this approach is provided by the High Court of Australia in *Thiel v Commission of Taxation*.[97]

4.135 Article 31 provides:

> 1. A treaty shall be interpreted in good faith in accordance with the ordinary meaning to be given to the terms of the treaty in their context and in the light of its object and purpose.
> 2. The context for the purpose of the interpretation of a treaty shall comprise, in addition to the text, including its preamble and annexes:
>   (a) Any agreement relating to the treaty which was made between all the parties in connexion with the conclusion of the treaty;
>   (b) Any instrument which was made by one or more parties in connexion with the conclusion of the treaty and accepted by the other parties as an instrument related to the treaty.

92 [2006] 1 AC 262 at [65].
93 [2004] 1 AC 816 at [56]–[60].
94 [2002] 1 WLR 2956 at [6].
95 [2002] UKHL 32 at [39] and [40].
96 [2015] 4 All ER 288 at [54].
97 (1990) 171 CLR 338 (see the discussion by McHugh J at 356).

3. There shall be taken into account, together with the context:
   (a) Any subsequent agreement between the parties regarding the interpretation of the treaty or the application of its provisions;
   (b) Any subsequent practice in the application of the treaty which establishes the agreement of the parties regarding its interpretation;
   (c) Any relevant rules of international law applicable in the relations between the parties.
4. A special meaning shall be given to a term if it is established that the parties so intended.

Article 32 provides: **4.136**

> Recourse may be had to supplementary means of interpretation, including the preparatory work of the treaty and the circumstances of its conclusion, in order to confirm the meaning resulting from the application of article 31, or to determine the meaning when the interpretation according to article 31:
>
> (a) Leaves the meaning ambiguous or obscure; or
> (b) Leads to a result which is manifestly absurd or unreasonable.

Applying these principles, in *Fothergill v Monarch Airlines*[98] four members of the House of Lords considered that the *travaux préparatoires* can be used in the interpretation of international conventions. **4.137**

98 [1981] AC 251.

PART III
THE MEANING OF THE WORDS

Principle 5: Natural Meaning

5. The words of the statute are nearly always given their ordinary meaning in context, taking account of the purpose of the statute.

Principle 6: Ambiguity

6. If the words of the statute are reasonably capable of more than one ordinary meaning, they are given the meaning the legislature is most likely objectively to have intended.

Principle 7: Unnatural Meaning

7.1. Very occasionally, it is clear that the legislature cannot objectively have intended the words it has used in the statute to have their ordinary meaning. If so, they are given the meaning that the legislature must objectively have intended.
7.2. The more unreasonable or unfair the result, the more unlikely it is that the legislature can have intended it.
7.3. Clear words are therefore needed to override a person's fundamental liberties.

5
Principle 5: Natural Meaning

Principle 5: The words of the statute are nearly always given their ordinary meaning in context, taking account of the purpose of the statute.

A. Natural and Ordinary Meaning

The starting point when interpreting a statute is to give the words of the statute their natural and ordinary meaning.[1] **5.1**

This is also true of contractual interpretation: the starting point is the natural and ordinary meaning of the words of the contract. **5.2**

In *Selvey v Director of Public Prosecutions*,[2] Viscount Dilhorne said: 'The words of the statute must be given their ordinary natural meaning.' **5.3**

Lord Simon made the same point in *Black-Clawson International v Papierwerke Waldhof-Aschaffenburg*:[3] **5.4**

> After all, the first and most elementary (and, I would add, salutary) rule of construction is that the words of a statute must be read in the most natural sense which they bear in their context.

More recently, in *Re Agricultural Sector (Wales) Bill*,[4] the Supreme Court had to decide whether a particular proposed Bill was within the competence of the Welsh Assembly. It said: **5.5**

> [The] question whether a provision is outside the competence of the Assembly must be determined according to the particular rules that [the relevant sections] have laid down. These rules must be interpreted according to the ordinary meaning of the words used. In that way a coherent, stable and workable outcome can be achieved.

This statement is of interest because it not only states the principle but also explains its rationale. By interpreting words according to their normal meaning in context, a coherent, stable and workable outcome can be achieved. **5.6**

There is also a constitutional reason for giving effect to the natural and ordinary meaning of the words of the statute. This point was made by Lord Diplock in *Duport Steels v Sirs*:[5] **5.7**

> My Lords, at a time when more and more cases involve the application of legislation which gives effect to policies that are the subject of bitter public and parliamentary controversy, it

[1] The words 'natural' and 'ordinary' are used interchangeably in the cases. There is nothing wrong with that. They are synonyms in this context. They are also frequently used in conjunction. That approach is generally avoided in this book. It seems wasteful to use three words where one will do just as well.
[2] [1970] AC 304 at 339.
[3] [1975] AC 591 at 650.
[4] [2014] 1 WLR 2622 at [66].
[5] [1980] 1 WLR 142 at 157.

Principles of Statutory Interpretation. Richard Calnan, Oxford University Press. © Richard Calnan 2023.
DOI: 10.1093/oso/9780192864673.003.0006

> cannot be too strongly emphasised that the British constitution, though largely unwritten, is firmly based upon the separation of powers; Parliament makes the laws, the judiciary interpret them. When Parliament legislates to remedy what the majority of its members at the time perceive to be a defect or lacuna in the existing law …, the role of the judiciary is confined to ascertaining from the words that Parliament has approved as expressing its intention what that intention was, and to giving effect to it. Where the meaning of the statutory words is plain and unambiguous, it is not for the judges to invent fancied ambiguities as an excuse for failing to give effect to its plain meaning because they themselves consider that the consequences of doing so would be inexpedient, or even unjust or immoral. In controversial matters … there is room for differences of opinion as to what is expedient, what is just and what is morally justifiable. Under our constitution it is Parliament's opinion on these matters that is paramount.

5.8 Lord Diplock went on to say that if a statute turned out to have injurious results, then it is for Parliament not the judiciary to change it. He continued:[6]

> It endangers continued public confidence in the political impartiality of the judiciary, which is essential to the continuance of the rule of law, if judges, under the guise of interpretation, provide their own preferred amendments to statutes which experience of their operation has shown to have had consequences that members of the court before whom the matter comes consider to be injurious to the public interest.

5.9 As Holt CJ said in 1701:[7] 'An Act of Parliament can do no wrong, although it may do several things that look pretty odd.'

5.10 The way in which the principle is applied in practice can be illustrated by cases concerning criminal law, tax law and the law of contract:

- *R v Bentham*;[8]
- *R v Boyesen*;[9]
- *Police v Emirali*;[10]
- *Customs and Excise Commissioners v Mechanical Services (Trailer Engineers)*;[11]
- *Customs and Excise Commissioners v Zielinski Baker and Partners*;[12] and
- *Actionstrength v International Glass Engineering*.[13]

5.11 In *R v Bentham*,[14] the defendant put his hands inside his jacket and, forcing out the material to give the appearance of a gun, he pointed his fingers at the victim, demanding money. The defendant was charged under section 17(2) of the Firearms Act 1968 with having 'in his possession a firearm or imitation firearm'. The House of Lords decided that, since a person's hand or fingers were not a separate thing but were part of himself, he could not possess them and therefore that he could not have been in possession of an imitation firearm.

[6] ibid, 157.
[7] *City of London v Wood* (1701) 12 Mod Rep 669 at 687–688.
[8] [2005] 1 WLR 1057.
[9] [1982] AC 768.
[10] [1976] 2 NZLR 476.
[11] [1979] 1 WLR 305.
[12] [2004] 1 WLR 707.
[13] [2003] 2 AC 541.
[14] [2005] 1 WLR 1057.

The principal judgment was given by Lord Bingham. He said that one cannot possess something that is not separate and distinct from oneself. Parliament might have created an offence of falsely pretending to have a firearm. But it did not do so.[15] He went on to say:[16] 5.12

> Rules of statutory construction have a valuable role when the meaning of a statutory provision is doubtful, but none where, as here, the meaning is plain. Purposive construction cannot be relied on to create an offence which Parliament has not created.

This was a case in which the court gave effect to the ordinary meaning of the words of the statute and refused to extend the scope of a clear statutory provision in order to find someone guilty of an offence, however culpable his conduct. In the next case, the court relied on the ordinary meaning of the words in order to find someone guilty of an offence, even though it might have been argued that, on the facts, the purpose of the legislation had not been infringed. 5.13

In *R v Boyesen*,[17] the respondent was charged with unlawful possession of 5 mg of cannabis resin contrary to section 5 of the Misuse of Drugs Act 1971. The relevant provision made it an offence 'for a person to have a controlled drug in his possession'. The respondent had a measurable quantity of the drug, but he argued that the amount was so small that it was not usable in the way that the Act was intended to prohibit. 5.14

The House of Lords decided that the respondent was nevertheless guilty of an offence. There was no express requirement that the amount of the drug should be usable, and it refused to imply one. The words were clear. They were not ambiguous and no absurdity was produced. 5.15

These are both examples of the court giving effect to the natural meaning of the words in context. The second case is particularly interesting because the purpose of the Act was to prevent the misuse of drugs, and it could therefore sensibly have been argued that possession was only unlawful if it enabled misuse to occur. If the amount involved could not be used because it was such a small amount, then it was arguable that the purpose of the Act had not been contravened. But the court refused to accept this argument. It gave effect to the ordinary meaning of the words, even though that led to a conviction. 5.16

The result in *Boysen* can be contrasted with the decision of the New Zealand Court of Appeal in *Police v Emirali*.[18] The facts in *Emirali* were very similar to those in *Boysen*. The defendant was found in possession of measurable quantities of cannabis, but the amounts were so small that they were not usable. The New Zealand Court of Appeal took the opposite approach to that of the House of Lords in *Boysen*, deciding that the defendant could not be convicted where the amount of the drug in his possession was not usable. 5.17

The judgment of the court was given Woodhouse J. He said[19] that although the court should give every proper support to those who have the responsibility of controlling the serious problem of drug abuse, the point was to understand the purpose of the statute. He continued: 5.18

15 ibid, [8] and [9].
16 ibid, [10].
17 [1982] AC 768.
18 [1976] 2 NZLR 476.
19 ibid, 480.

> [The] real purpose of the statute is not to proscribe the existence of narcotics as an end in itself. Instead it is to prevent their illicit use. That general purpose indicates the sort of test that can and should be applied in a case such as this.

5.19 It is suggested that the judgment of the New Zealand Court of Appeal makes more sense than that of the House of Lords. The purpose of the legislation was to prevent the use of drugs, and it can certainly be argued that the decision of the New Zealand Court of Appeal gave better effect to that purpose than that of the House of Lords.

5.20 Sometimes, the precise application of the natural meaning of the words of the statute can prevent an odd result from occurring. On other occasions, it can create an odd result. This dichotomy can be illustrated by two cases involving Customs and Excise.

5.21 In *Customs and Excise Commissioners v Mechanical Services (Trailer Engineers)*,[20] a company that manufactured and distributed lightweight trailer equipment sold trailer couplings and winches for various purposes, including for use in connection with boats. The couplings were standard fittings capable of linking any trailer to a towing vehicle. There was nothing intrinsically in their design or construction that particularly fitted them for the purpose of a boat trailer.

5.22 Section 17 of the 1975 Finance Act introduced a higher rate of VAT on certain goods, including:

> 1 Boats … designed for use for recreation or pleasure; …
> 5 The following accessories to goods within item 1 … namely— … (f) trailers and trolleys …
> 6 Goods of a kind suitable for use as parts of goods within item 1 or item 5 …

5.23 The Commissioners of Customs and Excise decided that two couplings and two winches that the company sold were 'goods of a kind suitable for use as parts' of trailers when used as accessories for boats, and therefore that the higher rate of VAT was chargeable.

5.24 The Divisional Court, by a majority, held that 'suitable' must be given its ordinary meaning and that, since the couplings and winches supplied were suitable for use with boats and trailers, the goods supplied were chargeable at the higher rate of VAT.

5.25 This decision was overruled by the Court of Appeal. The principal judgment was given by Browne LJ. He accepted that the couplings and winches in question were suitable, in its ordinary meaning, for use as parts of trailers or trolleys that are accessories for pleasure boats. He continued:[21]

> This argument seemed to me for some time to be conclusive in favour of the commissioners, but in the end I have come to the conclusion that it fails to take into account all the words of Group 3, item 6. If the item had read 'Goods suitable for use as parts …', it would be difficult, if not impossible, to reject the commissioners' interpretation in spite of the anomalies which I think it would produce. But the item reads 'Goods *of a kind* suitable for use in boats …'. The words 'of a kind' must be intended to add something to the meaning of 'goods suitable' … It seems to me that 'goods of a kind' must refer to some class or category or genus of goods which has characteristics in common, and that it is necessary to identify

20 [1979] 1 WLR 305.
21 ibid, 312.

> the 'kind' to which the goods in question in any particular case belong. The question is then not whether the particular goods in question are 'suitable', but whether the 'kind' to which they belong is suitable. I cannot identify any 'kind' to which the couplings and winches here in question belong which is narrower than *all* couplings and winches. Many couplings and winches are not suitable for use as parts for pleasure boats or their accessories and I am therefore of the opinion that the couplings and winches with which we are concerned are not 'goods of a kind suitable for use as parts . . .' within Group 3, item 6.

This is a useful illustration of the way in which courts approach these issues. The court was clearly concerned that the meaning that the Commissioners put forward was unreasonably wide, and it was able to get round this by analysing the precise words in context. This case shows how important it is to adopt a forensic analysis of the actual words used rather than relying on generalities about the purpose of the legislation. It is an example of a court reaching a sensible result—not by doing violence to the words, but by careful reading of the words. **5.26**

Customs and Excise Commissioners v Zielinski Baker and Partners[22] was also concerned with VAT. The question was whether standard rate or zero rate VAT was payable on certain building works. The owners of a dwelling house, which was a listed building, constructed an indoor swimming pool and converted an existing barn into changing and games facilities. The barn was within the curtilage of the dwelling house and was itself a listed building. The owners claimed that the conversion of the barn was 'an approved alteration of a protected building' under the Value Added Tax Act 1994 and was therefore zero-rated. Customs and Excise assessed the work to VAT at the standard rate. **5.27**

The VAT Tribunal found in favour of the taxpayers, the judge in favour of the Commissioners, the Court of Appeal in favour of the taxpayers, and the House of Lords in favour of the Commissioners. **5.28**

Lord Hoffmann said that the case involved a point of statutory construction on which he did not feel the slightest doubt. To qualify for zero-rating, the outbuilding to which the alterations were made must have been a 'protected building'. This required it first to be 'a building which is designed to remain as or become a dwelling house' and secondly to be a 'listed building'. These two requirements were cumulative, being separated by the word 'and'. The actual building to which the alterations in this case were made was not designed to remain as or become a dwelling house. The claim to zero-rating therefore failed at the first hurdle.[23] **5.29**

Lord Hope said:[24] **5.30**

> The consequences of this approach to the definition may be to produce results which appear odd and unreasonable ... In my opinion the ordinary meaning of the words used, taken in the order in which they are set out in the definition, leads inevitably to the result contended for by the commissioners.

This is a relatively recent decision of the House of Lords that shows the importance of actually reading the words in the order in which they appear for the purpose of giving effect to their ordinary meaning. **5.31**

22 [2004] 1 WLR 707.
23 ibid, [9] and [10].
24 ibid, [21].

5.32 The final example is the decision of the House of Lords in *Actionstrength v International Glass Engineering*[25] that concerned an oral guarantee. Under section 4 of the Statute of Frauds 1677, an oral guarantee is unenforceable. The beneficiary of the guarantee tried to get round this problem by claiming estoppel. It argued that the guarantor should not be able to evade liability for the promise it had made for consideration. The House of Lords decided that an estoppel was not available because it would simply contradict the terms of the statute.

5.33 Lord Hoffmann expressed it this way:[26]

> The terms of the Statute therefore show that Parliament, although obviously conscious that it would allow some people to break their promises, thought that this injustice was outweighed by the need to protect people from being held liable on the basis of oral utterances which were ill-considered, ambiguous or completely fictitious. This means that while normally one would approach the construction of a statute on the basis that Parliament was unlikely to have intended to cause injustice by allowing people to break promises which had been relied upon, no such assumption can be made about the Statute.... [It] must not be construed in a way which would undermine its purpose.

5.34 This is a relatively modern illustration of the principle that the ultimate duty of the court is to give effect to what the statute says, and that it cannot avoid giving effect to the clear words of a statute just because it produces unfairness.

5.35 Most statutes contain definitions clauses, and the statutory words clearly need to be interpreted in accordance with those definitions. The Interpretation Act 1978 contains a number of definitions of words used generally and basic rules of interpretation for statutes of the kind that commonly appear in commercial contracts.

B. However Odd the Result

5.36 It will be seen in Principle 7 that there are limited circumstances in which the courts do override the ordinary meaning of the words where the result would otherwise be absurd. But the basic principle remains that the courts do, as a general rule, give effect to the ordinary meaning of the words even if the result is odd. There is clearly a tension between these two principles, but there is no doubt that the court will normally give effect to the natural meaning of the words, even if the result is surprising. This can be demonstrated by two tax cases, a corporate case and a case concerning industrial relations:

- *Collco Dealings v Inland Revenue Commissioners*;[27]
- *Vestey v Inland Revenue Commissioners*;[28]
- *Enviroco v Farstad*;[29] and
- *Esso Australia v Australian Workers' Union*.[30]

[25] [2003] 2 AC 541.
[26] ibid, [20].
[27] [1962] AC 1.
[28] [1980] AC 1148.
[29] [2011] 1 WLR 921.
[30] (2017) 263 CLR 551.

In *Collco Dealings v Inland Revenue Commissioners*,[31] the question was whether the words of a tax statute should be read in a particular way in order to comply with a treaty that had previously been entered into between the United Kingdom and Ireland. The issue was whether a particular company was 'a person entitled under any enactment to an exemption from income tax'. It was argued that if this was read literally, it would create a breach of the treaty. This would be inconsistent with the comity of nations and established rules of international law, and therefore the subsection had to be interpreted in order to avoid that result. **5.37**

The House of Lords rejected this approach. It gave effect to the natural meaning of the words. Viscount Simonds said:[32] **5.38**

> What, after all, is involved in the argument of the appellant? It is nothing else than that, when Parliament said 'under any enactment,' it meant 'any enactment except ...' ... It is said that the plain words of the statute are to be disregarded and these words arbitrarily inserted in order to observe the comity of nations and the established rules of international law ... But I would answer that neither comity nor rules of international law can be invoked to prevent a sovereign state from taking what steps it thinks fit to protect its own revenue laws from gross abuse, or to save its own citizens from unjust discrimination in favour of foreigners. To demand that the plain words of the statute should be disregarded in order to do that very thing is an extravagance to which this House will not, I hope, give ear.

Vestey v Inland Revenue Commissioners[33] is also a tax case. The apparent effect of a particular taxing provision was to tax a foreign resident on an amount that seemed excessive. At first instance, Walton J had inserted some words into the statute in order to give effect to what seemed to be a fairer meaning. The House of Lords held that this was impermissible. **5.39**

Lord Wilberforce said:[34] **5.40**

> My Lords, it is not necessary to enter upon objections of a detailed character to this emendation though some are formidable. For inspection of it unanswerably shows that the process involved is not one of construction, even one of strained construction, but is one of rewriting the enactment. The subsection says in the clearest terms that 'any income' of the foreign resident, etc, is to be deemed the income of the recipient of the capital sum. To say that what is to be deemed the recipient's income is not 'any income' but a portion of that income equal to the capital sum received would be a totally different fiscal approach—one which Parliament might certainly have taken, but which it has manifestly avoided in this instance.

Lord Wilberforce added:[35] '[The] subsection is clear beyond doubt in its terms ... From these words there is no escape.' **5.41**

What is interesting about this case is that it also involved the interpretation of another provision of the same taxing statute that the court accepted was ambiguous. In that instance, it was able to choose the fairer of the two competing interpretations (see Principle 6). But the same approach could not be applied to a provision the meaning of which was clear. There, **5.42**

31 [1962] AC 1.
32 ibid, 19.
33 [1980] AC 1148.
34 ibid, 1170.
35 ibid.

the court was unable to produce the fair result. It had no choice but to give effect to the unfair provisions of the section.

5.43 *Enviroco v Farstad*[36] involved a dispute between the owners of a vessel and a charterer, the outcome of which depended on whether or not a company described as the contractor was a subsidiary of a PLC. There was no doubt that the contractor was initially a subsidiary of the PLC. But the PLC then created security under Scots law over its shares in the contractor in favour of a bank as security for a loan. Under Scots law, the security had to be effected by the entry of the bank's nominee on the register of members of the contractor.

5.44 The owners accordingly argued that the contractor was no longer a subsidiary of the PLC because the relevant provisions of the Companies Act only applied where the PLC was a 'member' of the contractor, and the PLC had ceased to be a member of the contractor when it created security over the shares and the bank's nominee was entered on the register. That nominee was the member, not the PLC.

5.45 The charterer argued that on any sensible view of the facts, the charterer remained a subsidiary of the PLC even though it had created security over the shares in favour of the bank.

5.46 The House of Lords decided that the contractor was not a subsidiary of the PLC. The principal judgment was given by Lord Collins. Giving effect to the natural and ordinary meaning of the words of the relevant provisions of the companies legislation, he decided that the PLC was not a member of the contractor, and therefore that the contractor was not a subsidiary of the PLC.

5.47 Lord Collins accepted that it is usual, in commercial contracts, to incorporate the statutory definition of a subsidiary. He also accepted that it was likely that there had been an error in the drafting of the statute. Provisions that dealt with the problem in relation to subsidiary undertakings had not been applied to subsidiaries. Hence, although, in commercial substance, the contractor was a subsidiary of the PLC, it was not a subsidiary within the meaning of the companies legislation, and it was that provision that had been incorporated by reference into the definitions clause of the contract. A correction of the legislation would have been 'an impermissible form of judicial legislation'.[37]

5.48 Lord Clarke said[38] that he was initially attracted by the contractor's case because on any sensible view of the facts the contractor was throughout a subsidiary of the PLC. But the bank's nominee became the member of the contractor when the security was put in place and:

> [Try] as one might, there is no basis upon which it is legally possible to reach any other conclusion as a matter of construction [of the relevant sections]. While I agree ... that it looks likely that the omission from those sections of [a rectifying provision] was an error, I also agree ... that the correction of it would amount to impermissible judicial legislation.

5.49 *Esso Australia v Australian Workers' Union*[39] was concerned with an industrial dispute. The Fair Work Act 2009 protected industrial action in certain circumstances but one of the conditions of immunity was that the union 'must not have contravened any orders that apply to

[36] [2011] 1 WLR 921.
[37] ibid, [49].
[38] ibid, [72] and [73].
[39] (2017) 263 CLR 551.

them and that relate to, or relate to industrial action relating to, the agreement or a matter that arose during bargaining for the agreement'. The union had breached a particular order of this kind but, at the relevant time, it was no longer in contravention of it.

Esso's submission was that the natural and ordinary meaning of the words was clear. None of the limitations set out in the clause related to their time of application. The time of application was controlled by the present perfect conditional clause 'must not have contravened'. The clause therefore applied to past contraventions of orders relating to the agreement, and there was no requirement that the order was one that continued in operation at the relevant time. **5.50**

The union contended that it would be capricious and unjust to deny it protection where there was no longer a contravention. The provision should only apply where the contravention continued. **5.51**

The High Court of Australia found in favour of Esso. It gave effect to the natural and ordinary meaning of the words, although it also relied on the history and context of the provision. **5.52**

There is therefore plenty of recent authority at the highest level that the basic principle is that the courts will give effect to the natural and ordinary meaning of the words in context, however surprising the result. **5.53**

C. Context, Purpose and Mischief

Principle 5 requires the words of a statute to be read in context, taking account of the purpose of the statute. How does this affect the meaning of the words of the statute? **5.54**

It is first necessary to discuss the terminology. In contractual interpretation, the expression used most frequently is that the words of a contract need to be read in context. Statutory interpretation is sometimes described in the same way, but the more common expression is that statutes need to be read in the light of their purpose. **5.55**

Is there a difference in practice between contextual and purposive interpretation? **5.56**

There is no doubt that context and purpose have different meanings. The context of a document is its setting. The law defines the relevant context. For statutes, the context is narrower that it is for contracts. But, once the relevant context has been established, the role of the interpreter is to decide what the words of the document mean in the light of that context. **5.57**

Purpose is different. It is not concerned with the nature of the information that is available, but with the reason for its use. The essence of purposive interpretation is to give effect to the specific words of the statute in the light of the general purpose of the statute. In most cases, the purpose of a statute is clear from reading the text as a whole, although relevant context can also assist in identifying its purpose. **5.58**

Another expression frequently used is 'mischief'. The court needs to understand what the mischief was that the statute was intended to remedy—and then to read the particular words of the statute in the light of that. But this is just another way of saying that statutes need to be interpreted purposively. The purpose of the statute is to remedy the mischief. **5.59**

5.60 Although it is sometimes necessary to use background materials to establish the mischief concerned, this is very rarely required. It is nearly always the case that the mischief is perfectly obvious from the words of the statute itself. This is equally true of the purpose of the statute.

5.61 In *Black-Clawson International v Papierwerke Waldhof-Aschaffenburg*,[40] Lord Diplock said:

> As regards recourse to the report for the purpose of ascertaining the mischief for which Parliament intended to provide a remedy by the Act, this is based on the so-called 'mischief' rule which finds its origin in *Heydon's* case, 3 Co. Rep. 7a decided under the Tudor monarchy in 1584. The rule was propounded by the judges in an age when statutes were drafted in a form very different from that which they assume today ... Statutes in the sixteenth century and for long thereafter in addition to the enacting words contained lengthy preambles reciting the particular mischief or defect in the common law that the enacting words were designed to remedy. So, when it was laid down, the 'mischief' rule did not require the court to travel beyond the actual words of the statute itself to identify 'the mischief and defect for which the common law did not provide,' for this would have been stated in the preamble. It was a rule of construction of the actual words appearing in the statute and nothing else. In construing modern statutes which contain no preambles to serve as aids to the construction of enacting words the 'mischief' rule must be used with caution to justify any reference to extraneous documents for this purpose. If the enacting words are plain and unambiguous in themselves there is no need to have recourse to any 'mischief' rule. To speak of mischief and remedy is to describe the obverse and the reverse of a single coin. The former is that part of the existing law that is changed by the plain words of the Act; the latter is the change that these words made in it.

5.62 It is important not to carry the distinction between context and purpose too far. Contextual interpretation requires the statutory words to be read in the light of the statute as a whole and the relevant background. Purposive interpretation requires the statutory words to be read in the light of the broad objectives of the legislation. But those broad objectives are identified from the statute as a whole and the relevant background. In effect, what purposive interpretation does is to clarify the scope of the enquiry. The interpreter is not concerned with the background in general terms. The reason for using the context is to help to establish the purpose of the statutory provision concerned.

5.63 It is also important to appreciate that purposive interpretation is not confined to statutes. It applies to all documents. It is not an expression that is commonly used in relation to contracts, but there can be no doubt that in cases of difficulty contractual words are read in the light of the apparent purpose of the relevant contractual provision.

5.64 Both expressions—contextual and purposive—are used in the cases, and frequently in the same judgment. For instance, in the decision of the Supreme Court in *R v Lewisham London Borough Council*,[41] Lord Hodge, who gave the principal judgment, said that when ordinary words of the English language are used in a statute, their meaning depends on the context of the legislation in which they appear and they must be interpreted having regard to the purpose of that legislation.

[40] [1975] AC 591 at 637–638.
[41] [2015] AC 1259 at [44] and [45].

The cases frequently refer to the contextual nature of statutory interpretation. For instance, in *Maunsell v Olins*[42] Lord Wilberforce said: 'Before we try to interpret [an expression in a statute] we must look at its context.' 5.65

Even more frequently, the cases stress the paramount importance of giving statutes a purposive interpretation. As the House of Lords emphasised in *Barclays Mercantile Business Finance v Mawson*:[43] 5.66

> [The] modern approach to statutory construction is to have regard to the purpose of a particular provision and interpret its language, so far as possible, in a way which best gives effect to that purpose.

Section D considers what is meant in practice by contextual interpretation. Section E does the same for purposive interpretation. 5.67

D. Contextual Interpretation

A recent example of the contextual—and judgemental—nature of the exercise of statutory interpretation is the decision of the Supreme Court in *Shanks v Unilever (No 2)*.[44] The question at hand was whether an employee was entitled to compensation from his employer for an invention that it had patented. The employee would be entitled to compensation where 'having regard among other things to the size and nature of the employer's undertaking' it was 'of outstanding benefit to the employer'. 5.68

The claim was heard by a hearing officer at the Patent Office, who found that, having regard to the size and nature of the employer's business, the benefit provided by the patent fell short of being outstanding. That decision was upheld by Arnold J at first instance, and by the Court of Appeal. But the Supreme Court then reversed that decision, the principal judgment being given by Lord Kitchin. So, although the employee won the case, there were five judges who went one way and five the other. 5.69

The question at issue was what was meant by 'outstanding benefit'. There was no suggestion that it should be given anything other than its natural meaning in context. 5.70

Lord Kitchin stressed the contextual natural of the exercise. He said:[45] 5.71

> This is an ordinary English word meaning exceptional or such as to stand out and it refers here to the benefit (in terms of money or money's worth) of the patent to the employer rather than the degree of inventiveness of the employee. It is, however, both a relative and qualitative term and so I must now consider the context in which the question is to be asked and answered. Put another way, in relation to what was the benefit of the patent to be outstanding? Which factors may be taken into account in making that assessment?

When a word or phrase is interpreted in the context of the surrounding words or the relevant background facts, it may be given a meaning that would be considered surprising if the words were read in isolation. This can be illustrated by four cases: 5.72

[42] [1975] AC 373 at 385.
[43] [2005] 1 AC 684 at [28].
[44] [2019] 1 WLR 5997.
[45] ibid, [39].

- *Abrahams v Cavey*;[46]
- *Dixon v R*;[47]
- *YZ Finance Co v Cummings*;[48] and
- *Whitsbury Farm and Stud v Hemens*.[49]

5.73 In *Abrahams v Cavey*,[50] the Queen's Bench Divisional Court had to consider the meaning of section 2 of the Ecclesiastical Courts Jurisdiction Act 1860, by which:

> Any person who shall be guilty of riotous, violent, or indecent behaviour . . . in any place of religious worship . . . shall on conviction thereof . . . be liable to a penalty . . .

5.74 At the Labour Party Conference in 1966, there was a church service at which George Brown, the Foreign Secretary, and Harold Wilson, the Prime Minister, read the lessons. Their readings were interrupted by the defendants, and one of the defendants shouted, 'Oh, you hypocrites; how can you use the word of God to justify your policies?'

5.75 The defendants were charged with indecent behaviour in a place of religious worship. They argued that, in accordance with the normal meaning of the word 'indecent', they had not been involved in 'indecent behaviour'.

5.76 The court found them guilty. Lord Parker CJ said:[51]

> But the true meaning in any particular statute must naturally depend upon the context. It is quite clear here that indecency is not referring to anything in the nature of tending to corrupt or deprave; it is quite clearly used not with any sexual connotation whatsoever, but it is used in the context of 'riotous, violent or indecent behaviour' to put it quite generally, within the genus of creating a disturbance, in a sacred place.

5.77 Although the word 'indecent' would, in isolation, be given a narrower meaning, in the particular legislation in question it got its colour from the words 'riotous' and 'violent' and therefore connoted the creation of a disturbance.

5.78 In *Dixon v R*,[52] the Supreme Court of New Zealand decided that CCTV footage on a computer that was downloaded onto a USB stick constituted 'property' that had been obtained from accessing a computer system for a dishonest purpose. Although the conventional view is that information is not itself property, the court had no doubt that the digital files at issue were property, and not simply information. They had a value, they could be identified and they were capable of being transferred. They also had a physical presence, albeit one that could not be detected by means of the unaided senses.

5.79 The court accepted that the expression 'property' is not a term with one specific and precise meaning. Its meaning depends on the context. The context here was the dishonest acquisition of property from a computer system. In that context, the digital files were property, and not simply information.[53]

46 [1968] 1 QB 479.
47 [2016] 1 NZLR 678.
48 (1964) 109 CLR 395.
49 [1988] AC 601.
50 [1968] 1 QB 479.
51 ibid, 485.
52 [2016] 1 NZLR 678.
53 ibid, [25].

YZ Finance Co v Cummings[54] concerned the meaning of the word 'includes' when used in a definitions clause in a statute. If a definitions clause says *a* 'means' *x*, *y* and *z* it would generally be expected that *x*, *y* and *z* are exhaustive of the meaning of *a*; but where the clause says that *a* 'includes' *x*, *y* and *z*, then *x*, *y* and *z* form part of the definition of *a*, but do not limit its application. In principle, *a* would also include *b*, *c* and *d* if they fell within its ordinary meaning. But, in this case, the High Court of Australia read the word 'includes' more restrictively. **5.80**

Section 24 of the Moneylenders and Infants Loans Act 1941–1961 of New South Wales provided that if a moneylender took security for a loan, then the moneylender was restricted to recovering under the security. The moneylender was not able to recover under its personal claim against the debtor for the money lent. Subsection (2) provided: **5.81**

> In this section 'security' includes bill of sale, mortgage, lien, and charge of any real or personal property, and any assignment, conveyance, transfer or dealing with any real or personal property to secure the repayment of any loan.

A person borrowed money from a moneylender and, as security for the repayment of the loan, gave the moneylender a bill of sale over chattels, a second mortgage over land and a promissory note for the amount of the loan plus interest. The moneylender sued on the promissory note, and the borrower claimed that, having taken security by means of bill of sale and mortgage, the moneylender was precluded from suing on the promissory note. **5.82**

One of the arguments of the moneylender was that section 24(2) was merely inclusive, that in its ordinary and natural meaning a promissory note was a form of security for the repayment of the loan, and therefore recovery under the promissory note was allowed by the section. **5.83**

The High Court of Australia disagreed. It decided that recovery under the promissory note was precluded. Although, generally speaking, the word 'includes' does not exhaustively define the meaning of the expression concerned, in this case it did. **5.84**

The essential reason for this decision was that the words of the section had to be read in context. The purpose of the section was clear. It was to prevent claims being brought against a debtor personally where security had been taken. The only remedy was to enforce the security. To say that a promissory note is a separate asset from the liability to repay the loan (which it is) and that a promissory note is a form of security (which it is) was not to the point. The purpose of the section was clear. It was to preclude enforcement of the personal claim where security was taken. The expression 'security' can be used to refer to all forms of security for a debt, whether 'real' (such as a mortgage) or 'personal' (such as a guarantee). But in a different context it can mean real security only. All of the types of security referred to in section 24(2) were 'real' as opposed to 'personal' security. Although the legislature used the word 'include', section 24(2) indicated that it was thinking of real security when it used the expression 'security'. **5.85**

In essence, the court read the section in the context of the Act as a whole and in the light of the purpose of the section. The way the court reached its conclusion was by deciding that the word 'includes' was exhaustive. As Kitto J said, the element common to all of the types of security referred to in section 24(2) was that they were rights over property. If security were to include a promissory note, the policy of the Act would be subverted. There would be **5.86**

54 (1964) 109 CLR 395.

no sensible purpose in forbidding a moneylender from suing on the contract of loan whilst allowing it to sue on a collaterally created personal liability of the borrower under the promissory note and so obtain a judgment for the identical sum of money.

5.87 This case is a useful illustration of the contextual—and also judgemental—nature of the exercise of statutory interpretation. The word 'includes' has a normal meaning and in practically all cases it will be given that meaning. But, very occasionally, it is clear from the context that the legislature meant the definition to be restrictive even if it used the word 'includes'. In commercial practice, the word 'security' has two meanings. Sometimes it is used to describe the ways in which a proprietary interest is taken in an asset in order to secure a liability. Sometimes it has a wider meaning, and also encompasses personal obligations that secure a liability—for instance, guarantees. Here, the promissory note fell into the second category, but it was clear from the context of the definition that what the draftsman had in mind was security of the former nature. And, even though the draftsman used the word 'includes', the court decided that the word 'security' was intended to have the first (narrower) meaning because those were the only types of security that were described in the definition.

5.88 In *Whitsbury Farm and Stud v Hemens*,[55] the House of Lords gave a similarly restrictive meaning to the word 'includes' when used in the context of livestock. Lord Keith said:[56]

> It is true that what may be termed an inclusive definition is normally intended to widen the ordinary natural meaning of the word defined or at least to remove doubts as to the extent of that meaning.... Nevertheless, I think there can be no doubt that in some cases the language of an 'inclusive' definition, considered with the general context, can have the effect that the ordinary natural meaning of a word or expression is to some extent cut down.

5.89 It has been seen that reading words in context can sometimes require the court to give them a meaning that differs from their ordinary meaning. But sometimes the words are so clear that the context cannot alter their meaning. As Heydon J said in the High Court of Australia in *Victims Compensation Fund Corporation v Brown*:[57]

> To begin consideration of issues of construction by positing that a 'liberal', 'broad', or 'narrow' construction will be given tends to obscure the essential question, that of determining the meaning the relevant words used require.

5.90 In that case the New South Wales Court of Appeal had read the word 'and' disjunctively but the High Court of Australia overruled it—reading the word in its normal sense and therefore conjunctively.

5.91 Another illustration is the decision of the New Zealand Court of Appeal in *Commissioner of Inland Revenue v Alcan New Zealand*.[58] This was a tax case. If the words of the statute were read naturally, the taxpayer would have succeeded. The Revenue argued that words needed to be inserted into the relevant provision so that references to members of a group meant members of a group that were taxpayers in New Zealand. The court refused to imply these words. The statute needed to be given its natural and ordinary meaning.

5.92 The judgment of the court was given by McKay J. He said:[59]

55 [1988] 1 AC 601.
56 ibid, 613–614.
57 (2003) 77 ALJR 1797 at [33].
58 [1994] 3 NZLR 439.
59 ibid, 443–444.

> The first proposition ... is that words are to be given their ordinary meaning. This is fundamental to all statutory interpretation. There must be a strong and sufficient reason before words can be given some other meaning which they are capable of bearing in a particular context.

He continued:[60] **5.93**

> One should always have regard to the total context of the words used and to the purpose of the legislation in order to arrive at the meaning intended. This does not mean some forced meaning to fit a preconceived idea of purpose, but a proper approach to ascertain the true meaning. The true meaning must be consonant with the words used, having regard to their context in the Act as a whole, and to the purpose of the legislation to the extent that this discernible.

This case is a useful illustration of the continuing importance of establishing the natural and ordinary meaning of the words used without allowing context or purpose to intrude too far. **5.94**

It is nevertheless true that in many ways the defining characteristic of statutory interpretation is that it is purposive. And that is the subject of the next section of this chapter. **5.95**

E. Purposive Interpretation

The purposive interpretation of statutes has a long history. One of the most commonly cited judgments on statutory interpretation is the decision of the Court of Exchequer in 1584 in *Heydon's Case*:[61] **5.96**

> And it was resolved by them, that for the sure and true interpretation of all statutes in general ... four things are to be discerned and considered:—
> 1st What was the common law before the making of the Act.
> 2nd What was the mischief and defect for which the common law did not provide.
> 3rd What remedy the Parliament hath resolved and appointed to cure the disease of the commonwealth.
> And 4th The true reason of the remedy;
> and then the office of all the Judges is always to make such construction as shall suppress the mischief, and advance the remedy, and to suppress subtle inventions and evasions for continuance of the mischief, and *pro privato commodo*, and to add force and life to the cure and remedy, according to the true intent of the makers of the Act *pro bono publico*.

The same point was made with typical elegance by Learned Hand J in *Cabell v Markham*:[62] **5.97**

> Of course it is true that the words used, even in the literal sense, are the primary, and ordinarily the most reliable, source of interpreting the meaning of any writing: be it a statute, a contract, or anything else. But it is one of the surest indices of a mature and developed jurisprudence not to make a fortress out of the dictionary; but to remember that statutes

60 ibid, 444.
61 (1584) 3 Co Rep 7a.
62 148 F2d 737 at 739 (1945).

always have some purpose or object to accomplish, whose sympathetic and imaginative discovery is the surest guide to their meaning.

5.98 A more recent statement of the principle is contained in the judgment of Lord Steyn in *Attorney General's Reference (No 5 of 2002)*:[63]

> No explanation for resorting to purposive interpretation of a statute is necessary. One can confidently assume that Parliament intends its legislation to be interpreted not in the way of a black letter lawyer, but in a meaningful and purposive way giving effect to the basic objectives of the legislation.

5.99 More recently still, the Supreme Court has stressed the importance of reading statutory provisions purposively. In *Rittson-Thomas v Oxfordshire County Council*,[64] Lady Arden and Lord Burrows referred to 'the now well-settled view that the courts should adopt a purposive approach to statutory interpretation where possible'.

5.100 It is easy to say that statutes are to be interpreted purposively, but what does that mean in practice? This can be illustrated by four examples concerning company law and insolvency law:

- *Ex parte Walton, re Levy*;[65]
- *Re Mayfair Property Co*;[66]
- *Blue Metal Industries v Dilley*;[67] and
- *Re a Debtor (No 784 of 1991)*.[68]

5.101 The first example is *Ex parte Walton, re Levy*.[69] Section 23 of the Bankruptcy Act 1869 allowed a trustee in bankruptcy to disclaim onerous property, including leases. If he did so, that would be deemed to be a surrender of the lease. The question was whether or not this affected third parties. A literal interpretation would require it to do so. But the Court of Appeal decided that a literal interpretation was not appropriate.

5.102 The principal judgment was given by Sir George Jessel MR. He considered that the object of the legislature was plain. The purpose of a disclaimer was to release the bankrupt from their obligations in relation to the property, and to prevent the trustee from being liable for them. He said that it could never have been Parliament's intention[70] 'to confiscate the property of any man without urgent reason for doing so. A construction of the section which would lead to such a result might well be ... described as an absurdity.'

5.103 James LJ agreed that the purpose of the legislation was intended to affect the rights of the bankrupt and their creditors, and not third parties. It was therefore necessary to qualify the literal meaning of the words in order to prevent injustice and absurdity.

5.104 In the result, the word 'surrender' was given a qualified meaning. It applied between the parties, but did not affect third parties. This could be seen as an example of the application

63 [2005] 1 AC 167 at [31].
64 [2022] AC 129 at [33].
65 (1881) 17 ChD 746.
66 [1889] 2 Ch 28.
67 [1970] AC 827.
68 [1992] Ch 554.
69 (1881) 17 ChD 746.
70 ibid, 752.

of Principle 7—that the courts sometimes refuse to give effect to the natural meaning of the words in context where there is an absurdity. But it could equally well be seen as an example of Principle 5. The courts were interpreting the word 'surrender' in a limited sense in order to give effect to what must have been meant in the light of the purpose of the statute. Having regard to the purpose of the legislation, it was necessary to read the word in a limited way.

If *Ex parte Walton* is an example of a court reading the words of a statute in a limited way in order to give effect to the purpose of the legislation, *Re Mayfair Property Co*[71] is an example of the court giving a broad meaning to the words of a statute in order to give effect to its purpose. **5.105**

Re Mayfair Property Co[72] was concerned with the interpretation of the Companies Act 1879. Section 5 allowed a limited company to declare by special resolution that any portion of its uncalled capital was not capable of being called up except in a liquidation. The question was whether this prevented the company from charging that uncalled capital. **5.106**

The Court of Appeal held that it did prevent the uncalled capital from being charged. The principal judgment was given by Lindley MR. **5.107**

The debenture-holder had argued that a company can validly charge its uncalled capital and that there was no prohibition on creating charges in section 5. But, cogent as that argument was, Lindley MR was convinced that it was unsound and that to yield to it would defeat the purpose of the Act. In order to interpret any statute, it is necessary to consider the mischief for which the old law did not provide and the remedy provided by the statute to cure that mischief. The purpose of section 5 was to provide a fund for the general creditors of the company in liquidation. If a charge could be created over it, that object would be defeated. **5.108**

Lindley MR said:[73] **5.109**

> The prohibition against calling up the reserve capital in the case of limited companies is ... to preserve such capital for the general purposes of the company when wound up. To interpret the section so as to enable the company to defeat this object by pledging or otherwise disposing of its reserve capital is, in my opinion, entirely to miss the real meaning of the Legislature as expressed in the language it has used.

These two cases are important not just because they were decided by two of our greatest judges—Sir George Jessel and Sir Nathaniel Lindley—but because they illustrate the importance of understanding what the legislation is driving at in order to interpret its particular provisions. The interpreter needs to look at the broader picture, as well as the detail. Of course, it is the precise words of the detail that need to be interpreted, but this must be done in the context of the legislation as a whole and in the light of its purpose. The interpreter needs to see the wood as well as the trees. **5.110**

Blue Metal Industries v Dilley[74] involved the compulsory acquisition provision of the then New South Wales Companies Act, which allowed an offeror for the shares of a company which had obtained 90 per cent of the shares compulsorily to acquire the remaining 10 per cent. **5.111**

71 [1898] 2 Ch 28.
72 ibid.
73 ibid, 37.
74 [1970] AC 827.

5.112 What happened in this case was that a joint offer was made by two companies for the shares of the target company. The question was whether the Act applied where there was more than one offeror. The relevant section applied where there was a scheme involving the transfer of shares 'in a company . . . to another company'. The first 'company' clearly meant just one company, but could the second 'company' be more than one?

5.113 The New South Wales Interpretation Act contained a similar provision to that in the UK legislation that, unless the contrary intention appears, words in the singular include the plural. So the question was whether the context otherwise required.

5.114 The Privy Council decided that the section only applied where one company was acquiring the shares. It thought that it was important to look at the issue in the context of the Act as a whole and in the light of the purpose of the section. The purpose of the section was to allow a company that had acquired 90 per cent of the shares to acquire the rest, so that the target became a wholly owned subsidiary of the offeror. It followed that the section was only intended to apply where the offeror was a single company.

5.115 In this case, reading the words of the statute in the light of its purpose led to the conclusion that the second reference to 'company' in this particular provision was to a single company.

5.116 In *Re a Debtor (No 784) of 1991*,[75] the question at issue was what was meant by the expression 'carry on business' for the purpose of the Insolvency Act 1986. Those words had been given a broad meaning in cases decided under the Bankruptcy Act 1914, and the question was whether the same meaning should be taken to apply for the purpose of the Insolvency Act 1986.

5.117 Hoffmann J cautioned against assuming that the policy behind the new legislation was necessarily the same as that in the earlier legislation. One should not uncritically carry over meanings from one statute to another. He considered whether there was anything in the new Act that suggested that Parliament was intending the words to have a different meaning from those that they had held under the old Act. He could see no difference between the policy of the Acts on this point, and therefore accepted that the words 'carry on business' had the same meaning in the 1986 Act as they did in the 1914 Act.

5.118 When interpreting criminal statutes, there can sometimes be a tension between the understandable wish not to extend criminal liability beyond its proper bounds and the wish to give effect to the purpose of the legislation. These days, the wish to give effect to the purpose of the legislation normally overrides the desire to limit the scope of penal statutes. This can be illustrated by three cases:

- *R v Clayton*;[76]
- *R v Salmond*;[77] and
- *Smith v Hughes*.[78]

5.119 In *R v Clayton*,[79] the New Zealand Court of Appeal had to consider when a person could properly be described as 'driving' a motor vehicle.

75 [1992] Ch 554.
76 [1973] 2 NZLR 211.
77 [1992] 3 NZLR 8.
78 [1960] 1 NWLR 830.
79 [1973] 2 NZLR 211.

The defendant was convicted by a jury of driving a motor vehicle while disqualified from holding a driving licence. He had been sitting beside his wife, who was in the driving seat, and he had one or both of his hands on the steering wheel and at times he was in fact steering the vehicle. He was in a position to operate the clutch and foot brake, but not the accelerator. 5.120

The defendant argued that he had not actually been driving the vehicle in the sense of making it go. It would have been perfectly open to the New Zealand Court of Appeal to have given a more limited meaning to the word 'driving' and thereby to acquit the defendant. But it rejected that approach. It was necessary to determine the purpose of the legislation. Its primary purpose was to protect the public from the frailties of the driver concerned. And the defendant had sufficient control of the vehicle to make him guilty of driving it whilst disqualified. 5.121

McCarthy J, giving the judgment of the court, said:[80] 'The purpose of the legislation being clear, we should not seek to give the section a strict interpretation, merely because it has penal consequences.' In this case, the tension between giving the defendant the benefit of the doubt and giving effect to the purpose of the legislation was resolved in favour of purpose. 5.122

A similar approach was taken—again by the New Zealand Court of Appeal—in *R v Salmond*[81]. It concerned the use that could be made of blood taken from someone involved in a fatal car crash. The question for the court was whether the analysis of the blood taken from a person involved in the crash could be used to establish whether he was driving the car rather than to measure the amount of alcohol in his blood. The identification of the blood group would have been relevant to the former question. 5.123

The words of the legislation itself did not expressly restrict the use for which the sample was to be used. But, reading the relevant part of the Act as a whole, there was a strong argument that the intention of Parliament was to use the sample for the purpose of establishing the amount of alcohol in the blood, and not for any other reason. Indeed, this was the view of two of the judges in the Court of Appeal. 5.124

But the other three judges took a broader approach. They accepted that the framers of the Act probably had nothing more in mind than analysis for alcohol content. But the object of the legislation was road safety, and its purpose would be achieved if the blood sample were used to establish who was driving the car at the time. 5.125

It would have been open to the court to decide that the purpose of the blood samples was to establish alcohol content, and therefore that they could not be used more broadly. But, instead, it decided—albeit by a bare majority—that it should give effect to the natural meaning of the words—untrammelled by the possible contextual limitation—because that would further the purpose of the Act. A purposive interpretation trumped a contextual one. 5.126

This process also requires the interpreter to exercise common sense when interpreting the words. This principle is illustrated in *Smith v Hughes*.[82] It was, again, a criminal case. The question was whether the defendants did 'solicit in a street ... for the purpose of prostitution' contrary to section 1(1) of the Street Offences Act 1959. The defendants were not physically 5.127

80 ibid, 214.
81 [1992] 3 NZLR 8.
82 [1960] 1 WLR 830.

in the street, but were in a house adjoining the street, from which they encouraged men into the house.

5.128 The Queen's Bench Divisional Court decided that the defendants were guilty even though they were not physically in the street. Lord Parker CJ gave the principal judgment. He approached the matter by considering the mischief aimed at by the Act. He decided that it was to enable people to walk along the streets without being molested or solicited. It mattered little whether the defendants were soliciting while in the street or standing in a doorway or on a balcony or at a window. In each case, the solicitation was projected to someone walking in the street.

5.129 The court did not do undue violence to the actual words. What it did do was to read them in the light of the mischief of the Act. Identifying the mischief did not require detailed references to reports, committees or Hansard. All that was required was to apply a bit of common sense to the words of the statute itself. It was perfectly clear what the purpose of the legislation was, and the court gave effect to it.

5.130 The search for the purpose of the legislation is perhaps the defining element in the modern approach to statutory interpretation. But it cannot be carried too far. The words may be too clear to permit of any meaning other than their natural one. It is not always possible to establish a clear purpose and, in any event, the starting point is always the actual words used rather than some general notion of what their purpose might have been.

5.131 It is often relatively straightforward to establish the purpose of a new piece of legislation that deals with a particular issue. But much of our legislation now consists of consolidations and amended legislation where the purpose of the legislation—or even of particular provisions—is often more difficult to judge.

5.132 In *Avel v Attorney-General for New South Wales*,[83] Kirby P in the Court of Appeal of New South Wales described the difficulties involved in trying to find the purpose of a particular piece of gaming legislation in New South Wales. He described the legislation in the following terms:[84]

> It is a jumble of ill-matched and poorly integrated enactments. If there is now to be found a common thread through it all, it would seem to be nothing more than revenue raising.
>
> This conclusion suggests that the only safe approach to the construction the web of applicable legislation is an attention to the literal words of the legislation. A 'purposive' approach founders in the shallows of a multitude of obscure, uncertain and even apparently conflicting purposes.

5.133 Even where it is easier to establish the overall purpose of legislation, the nature of the legislative process means that the purpose is often only intended to be achieved in part. Different interests will be balanced, and the resultant legislation will constitute a comprise between conflicting approaches. This point was made very clearly by Gleeson CJ in the High Court of Australia in *Carr v Western Australia*.[85]

[83] (1987) 11 NSWLR 126.
[84] ibid, 127.
[85] (2007) 232 CLR 138.

In *Carr v Western Australia*, Gleeson CJ said:[86] **5.134**

> In the interpretation of a provision of an Act, a construction that would promote the purpose or object underlying the Act is to be preferred to a construction that would not promote that purpose or object.... That general rule of interpretation, however, may be of little assistance where a statutory provision strikes a balance between competing interests, and the problem of interpretation is that there is uncertainty as to how far the provision goes in seeking to achieve the underlying purpose or object of the Act. Legislation rarely pursues a single purpose at all costs. Where the problem is one of doubt about the extent to which the legislation pursues a purpose, stating the purpose is unlikely to solve the problem.

One example of this difficulty is tax legislation. Its underlying purpose is to raise revenue for the government. But, as Gleeson J said, no one would suggest that all tax legislation must be interpreted to advance that purpose. Interpretation of tax legislation commonly raises questions about how far the legislation goes in pursuit of the purpose of raising revenue.[87] **5.135**

Gleeson J continued:[88] **5.136**

> [The] general purpose of legislation of the kind herein in issue is reasonably clear [it was about police interviews]; but it reflects a political compromise. The competing interests and forces at work in achieving that compromise are well known. The question then is not: what was the purpose or object underlying the legislation? The question is: how far does the legislation go in pursuit of that purpose or object?

Issues of this kind are rarely clear-cut, and it is ultimately a question of judgement when deciding how the purpose of the legislation can affect the words used. There is an obvious tension between giving effect to the meaning of the words and giving effect to the apparent purpose of the legislation. It is ultimately a matter of judgement whether the words are sufficiently flexible to enable the purpose to override the apparently natural meaning. This point can be illustrated by comparing two cases on the Rent Acts: **5.137**

- *Remon v City of London Real Property Co*;[89] and
- *Harrison v Hammersmith and Fulham London Borough Council*.[90]

Remon v City of London Real Property Co[91] concerned the meaning of the word 'let' in section 12(2) of the Increase of Rent and Mortgage Interest (Restrictions) Act 1920. The Act extended the protection of tenants because there was a shortage of property at the end of the First World War. Mr Remon had been a tenant, but his tenancy had been determined by a notice to quit. The landlords argued that the property was not 'let' to him at the relevant time, and therefore that the protection afforded by the Act did not apply to him. **5.138**

The Court of Appeal disagreed. Scrutton LJ said:[92] **5.139**

> The object of the various Rent Restrictions Acts is clear. It was intended to prevent the tenant from having his rent raised against him, or from being turned out, though his

86 ibid, [5].
87 ibid, [6].
88 ibid, [7].
89 [1921] 1 KB 49.
90 [1981] 1 WLR 650.
91 [1921] 1 KB 49.
92 ibid, 57.

tenancy by agreement had expired, so long as he was willing to pay the rent authorised by statute.

5.140 Scrutton LJ went on to say:[93]

> I feel that I am straining language in speaking of a person whose tenancy has expired, and who stays in against the active protest of the landlord, as a 'tenant', and of the landlord's relation to him as a 'letting'; but such a person appears to be within the clear intention of the Legislature, and where the statute has forbidden any process of Court to be used to eject him, I think it must have intended and to be taken to forbid ejection by the private action of the landlord without the aid of the Court.

5.141 The Court of Appeal in this case stressed the importance of considering the purpose of the legislation, particularly where it is badly drafted. In context, the word 'let' in the statute had a broader meaning than it would normally have. But it is not always thus. This point is illustrated in the next case.

5.142 In *Harrison v Hammersmith and Fulham London Borough Council*,[94] the landlords had served notices to quit on the tenants, but the tenants claimed security of tenure under the provisions of the Housing Act 1980. Under that Act, the court was not able to give possession to the landlords in the circumstances of this case if the premises were 'let under a secure tenancy'.

5.143 The landlords argued that valid notices to quit had been served and therefore the flats were not let by the landlords to the tenants at all, let alone on secure tenancies. They relied on the ordinary and natural meaning of the words. The tenants argued that the expression was 'an elastic one' and applied where there was previously a tenancy that had now expired. The tenants relied on the *Remon* case.

5.144 In this case, the Court of Appeal took a different approach to that in the *Remon* case. They gave effect to the natural meaning of the words, and therefore found in favour of the landlord. Brandon LJ said:[95]

> [There] is no policy reason of any kind why the court should seek, by giving a strained and unnatural meaning to certain expressions in the Act, to give retrospective effect to the provisions of that [part of the Act].... [Gaps] in the express provisions of the kind which existed in the earlier Rent Acts do not exist in the Act of 1980, and do not therefore require to be filled up by the kind of process of strained and unnatural construction to which the Court of Appeal was admittedly driven in *Remon's* case.

5.145 This case illustrates the limits of the purposive principle. The tension between the words and the purpose will not always be resolved in favour of the purpose.

5.146 Another important example of the application of a purposive approach to statutory interpretation is a line of tax cases frequently referred to as the *Ramsay* doctrine. They will be discussed in the next section of this chapter.

93 ibid, 59.
94 [1981] 1 WLR 650.
95 ibid, 662.

F. The *Ramsay* Principle

In *Ramsay v Inland Revenue Commissioners*,[96] the House of Lords had to deal with a tax avoidance scheme that involved a series of steps that ultimately cancelled each other out, leaving the taxpayer in the same position as at the beginning. The question was whether each step should be considered separately from a tax point of view. The taxpayer argued that all of the steps were genuine (in the sense that they were not shams) and therefore the court had to take account of them. The House of Lords accepted this point. It could not simply ignore genuine transactions. But it nevertheless found in favour of the Inland Revenue on the basis that it was entitled to look at the series of transactions as a whole, rather than individually. **5.147**

This was a departure from the previous approach of the courts to tax avoidance schemes. Lord Wilberforce rejected the idea that a change of approach of this kind should be left to Parliament. Capital gains tax was created to operate in the real world. It is a tax on gains not on arithmetical differences:[97] **5.148**

> To say that a loss (or gain) which appears to arise at one stage in an indivisible process, and which is intended to be and is cancelled out by a later stage, so that at the end of what was bought as, and planned as, a single continuous operation, there is not such a loss (or gain) as the legislation is dealing with, is in my opinion well and indeed essentially within the judicial function.

The House of Lords therefore recognised that although all of the steps were genuine, the scheme nevertheless had to be considered as a whole for the purpose of the tax legislation. **5.149**

At the time it was decided, it was considered that this case was peculiar to tax legislation, and that it established a particular way of interpreting tax legislation. In fact, that was not what the House of Lords said in the *Ramsay* case, and subsequent cases have demonstrated that it did not involve a departure from the normal principles of statutory interpretation but, rather, a return to them. The court recognised that tax legislation operates in the real world and that the particular provisions have to be read in the context of the overall purpose of the legislation. In the result, *Ramsay* is not a doctrine peculiar to tax. It is an illustration of the principle that statutes need to be read in a purposive way. **5.150**

Ramsay was followed in quick succession by *Inland Revenue v Burmah Oil Co*[98] in which the House of Lords (and particularly Lord Diplock) made it clear that the *Ramsay* case did mark a significant change in the approach to tax avoidance schemes. **5.151**

The approach was then clarified two years later by the House of Lords in *Furniss v Dawson*.[99] In that case, the House of Lords emphasised that tax avoidance transactions had to be viewed as a whole. Lord Fraser said that:[100] **5.152**

> The true principle of the decision in *Ramsay* was that the fiscal consequences of a preordained series of transactions, intended to operate as such, are generally to be ascertained by considering the result of the series as a whole and not by dissecting the scheme and considering each individual transaction separately.

96 [1982] AC 300.
97 ibid, 326.
98 [1982] STC 30.
99 [1984] 1 AC 474.
100 ibid, 512.

5.153 Perhaps the fullest exposition of the principles underlying the *Ramsay* doctrine is contained in the judgment of the House of Lords in *Barclays Mercantile Business Finance v Mawson*.[101] In this case, there was a single judgment of a unanimous House of Lords (Lords Nicholls, Steyn, Hoffmann, Hope and Walker) that clarified the effect of the principle in the *Ramsay* case.[102]

5.154 The court explained that, before *Ramsay*, there were two features that allowed tax avoidance schemes to flourish. The first was the 'literal interpretation of tax statutes' and the second was 'the formalistic insistence on examining steps in a composite scheme separately'.[103] Far from *Ramsay* setting out a new principle that was applicable to tax statutes, all it did was to bring the interpretation of tax statutes into line with the interpretation of other statutes.

5.155 On the first point, the House of Lords recognised that:[104]

> [The] modern approach to statutory construction is to have regard to the purpose of a particular provision and interpret its language, so far as possible, in a way which best gives effect to that purpose.

5.156 As far as the second point was concerned, the House of Lords said that:[105]

> It is the task of the court to ascertain the legal nature of any transaction to which it is sought to attach a tax or a tax consequence and if that emerges from a series or combination of transactions, intended to operate as such, it is that series or combination which may be regarded.

5.157 The court went on to say:[106]

> The essence of the new approach was to give the statutory provision a purposive construction in order to determine the nature of the transaction to which it was intended to apply and then to decide whether the actual transaction (which might involve considering the overall effect of a number of elements intended to operate together) answered to the statutory description.

5.158 In the result,[107] the House of Lords decided that the *Ramsay* case did not introduce a new doctrine of tax law. On the contrary, it rescued tax law from being an island of literal interpretation and brought it within generally applicable principles of statutory interpretation.

5.159 More recently, in *UBS v Revenue and Customs Commissioners*,[108] the Supreme Court had to consider the *Ramsay* principle. It essentially adopted the approach in *Barclays Mercantile Business Finance v Mawson*.[109] The Supreme Court confirmed that the significance of *Ramsay* was, first, to read tax statutes in the same way as other statutes—in a purposive, rather than a literal, way—and, secondly, to identify the transaction that is to be taxed and, as a result, to treat a composite transaction as a single transaction where appropriate.

101 [2005] 1 AC 684.
102 ibid, [26] to [39].
103 ibid, [28].
104 ibid.
105 ibid, [30].
106 ibid, [32].
107 ibid, [33].
108 [2016] 1 WLR 1105.
109 ibid, [61].

Although the principle is clear, its application to the facts in this particular case was controversial. **5.160**

Ramsay and its successors were essentially concerned with establishing the amount of a profit or loss by reference to a series of transactions as a whole, rather than looking at each individual transaction in isolation. Later cases have carried this approach further. In *Inland Revenue Commissioners v Scottish Provident Institution*,[110] the House of Lords decided that a person did not have an 'entitlement' to gilts under a call option in respects of the gilts because it would effectively be cancelled out later in a linked series of transactions. **5.161**

The principle was carried yet further in *UBS v Revenue and Customs Commissioners*.[111] The particular issue was the meaning of a reference in a taxing statute to 'any contract, agreement, arrangement or condition which makes provisions to which any of sub-sections (2)–(4) applies'. The question was whether this had to be interpreted as being limited to provisions having a business or commercial purpose. **5.162**

The Court of Appeal read the words naturally, and refused to limit them in this way. But the Supreme Court read into the words a requirement that they must relate to a commercial purpose. Presumably these words were implied because it was assumed that Parliament would want to prevent tax avoidance. But it is not easy to see how—even with a purposive interpretation—an implication of this kind could be justified. In the earlier cases on the *Ramsay* principle, the court was treating a composite series of transactions as one transaction because Parliament must have intended tax to be payable on the basis of the overall transaction as it was effected. That is perfectly understandable. The *UBS* case goes further. It can only be justified on the basis of inserting words that do not appear in the statute. **5.163**

G. Common Sense

There is a strong link between the purposive approach to statutory interpretation and the requirement to use common sense when reading the words of a statute. **5.164**

In *Winfield v Secretary of State for Communities and Local Government*,[112] planning legislation defined 'advertisement' in a particular way and then said that 'it includes any hoarding or similar structure used or designed, or adapted for use ... for the display of advertisements ...' The question was whether a hoarding on which no advertisements were shown was itself an advertisement for those purposes. The Court of Appeal decided that it was not, relying on a common-sense interpretation. **5.165**

Maurice Kay LJ said:[113] 'I am satisfied that common sense can be accommodated within the cumbersome wording of the definition.' Sir Stephen Sedley agreed, but said:[114] 'It ought nevertheless to be acknowledged that our purposive construction ... has been required in order to make sense of [the provision]. This is not an ideal mode of legal reasoning.' **5.166**

[110] [2004] 1 WLR 3172.
[111] [2016] 1 WLR 1105.
[112] [2013] 1 WLR 948.
[113] ibid, [19].
[114] ibid, [29].

5.167 In *Exxon Corporation v Exxon Insurance Consultants*,[115] the question was whether the word 'Exxon' was an 'original literary work' within the meaning of the Copyright Act 1956. Graham J and the Court of Appeal decided that it was not. They agreed that it was necessary to read the three words together, not in isolation, and they gave them their natural meaning. 'Exxon' was original, and might possibly be a work, but it was not an original literary work, reading those words as a whole.

5.168 Oliver LJ said:[116]

> But that for which protection is sought in the instant case does not appear to me to have any of the qualities which commonsense would demand. It conveys no information; it provides no instruction; it gives no pleasure that I can conceive; it is simply an artificial combination of four letters of the alphabet . . .

5.169 These are salutary reminders that the natural and ordinary meaning of the words must be informed by common sense. In *Walker v Centaur Clothes Group*,[117] Lord Hoffmann had this to say about the necessity for common sense in interpretation:

> My Lords, a conclusion that a company which is liable to pay corporation tax is within the charge to corporation tax seems to me to be in accordance with the common sense which appealed to the special commissioner. It would be an extraordinary case of the tail wagging the dog if the provisions about accounting periods, which are mere machinery, could destroy the substantive right to recover the tax.

5.170 Lord Goddard summed it up in *Barnes v Jarvis*[118] when he said: 'A certain amount of commonsense [must be applied] in construing statutes.'

5.171 The way in which the requirement to use common sense in interpretation is used in practice can be illustrated by four examples:

- *Kay Green v Twinsectra*;[119]
- *Rank Xerox v Lane*;[120]
- *R v Lehair*;[121] and
- *Beswick v Beswick*.[122]

5.172 The problem in *Kay Green v Twinsectra*[123] was explained by Staughton LJ:[124]

> This is the most remarkable case of statutory interpretation that I have ever seen. It is as plain as can be what the purpose of Part I of the Landlord and Tenant Act 1987 was—to enable tenants of flats to buy their landlord's interest in the building if the landlord proposed to sell it to someone else, and to buy it from the purchaser if the landlord had actually done so. But nowhere does the statute say expressly that the tenants shall have that right against

115 [1982] 1 Ch 119.
116 ibid, 144.
117 [2000] 1 WLR 799 at 805.
118 [1953] 1 WLR 649 at 652.
119 [1996] 1 WLR 1587.
120 [1981] AC 629.
121 [2015] 1 WLR 4811.
122 [1968] AC 58.
123 [1996] 1 WLR 1587.
124 ibid, 1603.

> the new landlord. If that omission is fatal, Part I of the Act is not worth the paper which it is written on.

The problem was that section 12(1) allowed the tenants to serve a purchase notice on the new landlord requiring him to dispose of the freehold interest to the tenants' nominee, but it did not, in terms, instruct the landlord to comply with that notice. It provided for service of a notice in a particular form, but did not contain a requirement that a landlord who was served with a notice needed to comply with it. **5.173**

Hardly surprisingly, the Court of Appeal decided that the landlord did need to comply with the notice. In order to give effect to the obvious purpose of the section, it was necessary to require the landlord to do so. As Aldous LJ said, to decide otherwise would mean that the relevant section[125] 'had no purpose as a landlord could refuse to comply with a purchase notice which had been served. That is unreal.' **5.174**

This is an example of a badly drafted piece of legislation being interpreted by a court in a common-sense way in order to give effect to the obvious intention of the section. But the important point is that the intention was based squarely on the wording of the Act, not on anything extraneous. If legislation provides for the service of a notice on A to do *x*, then it must be implicit that A must do *x* if the notice is served. **5.175**

In *Rank Xerox v Lane*,[126] two companies entered into a contractual arrangement under which, for consideration, an amount was to be paid by one of the companies to the other. The undertaking to make the payment was made by deed, and it was argued that no chargeable gain accrued because it was an annual payment 'due under a covenant' and a covenant means an undertaking in a deed. **5.176**

The House of Lords held that a chargeable gain did arise. Although the primary meaning of the word 'covenant' meant a payment due under a deed, it did have other meanings, and one of those was an agreement for no consideration. In this context, what the legislation was concerned with was voluntary promises that would only be enforceable because they were by deed, rather than promises for consideration that would have been enforceable anyway. The undertaking in this deed was made for consideration, and so it was not due under a covenant within the meaning of the statute. **5.177**

It would have made no sense for the company to escape liability for tax merely because it had entered into an agreement by deed rather than under hand. The primary meaning of 'covenant' is a promise by deed but, in popular parlance, a covenant can mean a voluntary payment, and the court decided that it was this latter meaning that must have been intended. There was no real ambiguity here (as in Principle 6). Nor did the courts have to twist the meaning of the words in order to achieve a sensible result (as in Principle 7). There was only ever one sensible meaning of the word 'covenant' in this context—a voluntary payment. **5.178**

In *R v Lehair*,[127] the defendant robbed a bank and, later the same day, transferred some of the proceeds to her husband. Under section 77(5) of the Proceeds of Crime Act 2002, this amount would have been capable of being confiscated if 'it was made by the defendant at any time after . . . the date on which the offence was committed'. **5.179**

[125] ibid, 1597.
[126] [1981] AC 629.
[127] [2015] 1 WLR 4811.

5.180 The defendant argued that the section did not apply because the gift to her husband was made on the same day as the offence was committed and was therefore not made after that date. The legislation was clear and unambiguous. Date means date.

5.181 The Court of Appeal decided that, in this context, 'date' meant 'time'. It said:[128]

> We are satisfied that a literal interpretation of section 77(5)(a) is anomalous to the explicit purpose of the Act. It could not have been intended that criminals have a day's grace to dispose of their assets ...

5.182 The court continued:[129]

> We have no hesitation in endorsing the argument that there must be a purposive construction of the provision and in doing so, the sub-section must be read as though the *date* on which an offence is committed must refer to the actual *time* of commission ...

5.183 This is not as straightforward a case as the *Rank Xerox* case. There is no conceivable reason for giving bank robbers a day's grace, but the legislature should have got its drafting right. If it failed to do so, should the risk fall on the citizen? It is one thing to apply a purposive approach against the executive, another to do so against the citizen. But this was such an obvious anomaly that it is hard to disagree with the decision.

5.184 The final illustration is *Beswick v Beswick*,[130] a well-known decision of the House of Lords on third party rights under contracts. Its importance in this context is that the House of Lords had to consider the meaning of section 56(1) of the Law of Property Act 1925. Although its decision on this point was *obiter*, the case contains a useful discussion by a strong House of Lords on basic principles of interpretation.

5.185 It had been argued that section 56(1) allowed a person who was not a party to the contract to take a benefit under it if it was an 'interest in land, or other property'. The definitions section of the Law of Property Act said that, unless the context otherwise required, 'property' included choses in action. This argument would have cut across what was, at the time, a basic principle of contract law that a third party could not sue on a contract.

5.186 The court therefore started with a disinclination to believe that this section had the radical meaning that was proposed. But, faced with the definitions clause, how was it to avoid the result?

5.187 The House of Lords decided that the definitions clause did not apply because the context otherwise required. The members of the House of Lords used various means to reach that decision. The most convincing was that the relevant section was contained in a part of the Act that was concerned with property transactions, not with contracts. Reading the Act as a whole (Principle 3), this provision was not intended to create a general exception to the privity rule of contract. Allied to this was the necessity to give a common-sense meaning to the legislation, and that it could hardly have been intended by Parliament to make such a radical change to the law of contract by a side wind in a property law statute.[131]

128 ibid, [19].
129 ibid, [22].
130 [1968] AC 58.
131 ibid, 79 (Lord Hodson).

It is always a struggle to make sense of a statutory provision that appears to have a very odd result. But it can sometimes be achieved by a careful study of the precise words used. This can be illustrated by the decision of the Court of Appeal in *Customs and Excise Commissioners v Mechanical Services (Trailer Engineers)*,[132] that is discussed in Section A of this chapter. The court was clearly concerned that the apparent meaning of the provision was unreasonably wide, and it was able to avoid this problem by analysing the precise words in context. This case shows how important it is to adopt a forensic analysis of the actual words used rather than talking generalities about purposes. The court reached the sensible result, not by doing violence to the words, but by careful reading of the words. **5.188**

H. Always Speaking

The principle that words are given their ordinary meaning in context is a principle of general application. It applies to contracts as much as to statutes. But there is a difference between the two in relation to the time at which that meaning is established. Should the meaning be established at the time the document is issued, or at the time the question comes to be determined? **5.189**

The general position in relation to contracts is that the words of a contract are to be interpreted in the context of the relevant background at the time the contract was entered into. An example of this approach is the decision of the Supreme Court in *Lloyds TSB Foundation for Scotland v Lloyds Banking Group*.[133] Of course, this is subject to anything the parties may say about the issue in the contract; and contracts frequently do contain specific provisions dealing with potential changes to laws and regulations. But the starting point is to assume that, when the parties used particular words and expressions, they intended them to have their natural meanings at the time the contract was entered into. **5.190**

Statutes are different. They are expected to remain in force for a considerable period of time. Section 4 of the Statute of Frauds of 1677 is still in force almost 350 years after it was passed. Its terminology is not easy to grasp in the twenty-first century, and its words need to be understood in the light of how they were understood at the time it was passed. **5.191**

That might suggest that the starting point for statutes is the same as it is for contracts—that the words of a statute need to be understood by reference to their meaning at the time the statute was passed. There is certainly some authority for this proposition, as can be seen from the decision of the Court of Appeal in *The Longford*.[134] But the more prevalent view, particularly in recent times, is that the words of a statute are 'always speaking' and that the words they contain need to be read in accordance with their meaning at the time the question arises. So, if the meaning of the relevant words has changed since the statute was passed, then it is that new meaning that will be applied. **5.192**

The reason for this approach is essentially that it probably represents what the legislature intended. Parliament understands that, when it passes legislation, it may remain in force for a considerable time. It also understands that the meaning of words can change over time and that it is not normally practicable to require someone reading a statute to delve back into the **5.193**

132 [1979] 1 WLR 305.
133 [2013] 1 WLR 366.
134 (1889) 14 PD 34 at 36.

meaning of the words at the time it was passed—or, indeed, the time a predecessor statute was passed.[135] The basic constitutional principle is that citizens should be able to understand the laws that govern them by reading the words of the statute. It is just not practicable to require anyone reading a statute first to understand when the predecessor of the relevant statute was passed and then to consider whether the words used carried a different meaning at that time.

5.194 The starting assumption for statutes is therefore the opposite of that relating to contracts. But it is just an assumption, based on what the legislature is likely to have intended. The ultimate question in every case is what the legislature would reasonably have been expected to mean from the words it has used. It is therefore necessary to read the words in the relevant context in order to understand what the legislature must reasonably have intended in the case in hand.

5.195 In *R (Quintavalle) v Secretary of State for Health*,[136] the House of Lords had to deal with the meaning of words in a statute where scientific developments had resulted in a situation that had simply not been envisaged at the time the statute was passed. How should the words of the statute be interpreted in the light of these unanticipated developments? Lord Steyn had this to say:[137]

> That leads to the question whether it is appropriate to construe [the Act] in the light of the new scientific knowledge. In the case law two contradictory approaches are to be found. It reminds one of the old saying that the rules of interpretation 'hunt in pairs': that for every rule there is a rule to the contrary effect.... In the older cases the view often prevailed that a statute must be construed as if one were interpreting it on the day after it was passed: *The Longford* (1889) 14 PD 34, 36 ... But even in older cases a different approach sometimes prevailed. It was the idea encapsulated by Lord Thring, the great Victorian draftsman, that statutes ought generally to be construed as 'always speaking statutes'.

5.196 Lord Steyn went on to say[138] that it is a matter of interpretation whether or not the statute is 'always speaking'. Statutes dealing with a particular grievance or problem may sometimes require to be historically interpreted but, generally, they will be 'always speaking'.

5.197 In *R v Ireland*,[139] Lord Steyn explained why this is so:

> Bearing in mind that statutes are usually intended to operate for many years it would be most inconvenient if courts could never rely in difficult cases on the current meaning of statutes.

5.198 Perhaps the best discussion of the issues is in the judgment of Lord Hobhouse in *Morris v KLM*.[140] Under Article 17 of the Warsaw Convention of 1929 (which was brought into English law by the Carriage by Air Act 1961), an airline is liable for damage sustained in certain circumstances 'in the event of the death or wounding of a passenger or any other bodily

[135] See the observations of Leggatt J in *R (ZYN) v Walsall Metropolitan Borough Council* [2015] 1 All ER 165 at [45].
[136] [2003] 2 AC 687.
[137] ibid, [22].
[138] ibid, [23].
[139] [1998] 1 AC 147 at 158.
[140] [2002] 2 AC 628.

injury suffered by a passenger'. The main question in this case was whether 'bodily injury' included a psychiatric condition. The House of Lords held that it did not.

Lord Hobhouse said:[141] **5.199**

> First, the words used should receive an objective interpretation ... Therefore, it is the unadorned language of the article to which attention must be directed. It is again a descent into unprincipled subjectivism to use ... the absence of travaux preparatoires as a tool of construction.

Lord Hobhouse then considered the date to which the words had to be referenced. He said:[142] **5.200**

> Secondly it is also mistaken to interpret a convention such as the Warsaw Convention, or the various amended versions of it, as if they were intended to be historical documents frozen in time. They are intended to provide an enduring uniform code which will govern contractual and, where relevant, delictual relationships not just for a finite time but for the future as the transactions to which they apply are entered into ... Notionally to relate them back to a supposed state of affairs existing in 1929 is not only wrong but wholly impractical.

Lord Hobhouse continued:[143] **5.201**

> It is not necessary in order to understand this point to have regard to the principles applicable to 'always speaking' constitutional documents. The principle is more simple. Words have a meaning which does not change but the application of those words to the decision of any question depends on the facts and circumstances of the case in which that question arises. It is the facts and circumstances of the cases that change, not the meaning of the contractual words.

This last comment raises an important point. In many cases, it is not the meaning of words that change, but the way we understand those words to relate to particular circumstances. *Morris v KLM* was a case in point. The meaning of the word 'bodily injury' had not changed between 1929 and 2002. What had changed was our understanding of when an injury could be sensibly described as 'bodily'. **5.202**

It is therefore suggested that there are two reasons why it is normally appropriate for interpreters to read words according to their current understanding of the words. **5.203**

- First, if the meaning of the words has changed, we need to read them in accordance with their current meaning.
- Secondly, even if the meaning of the words has not changed, we need to read them in accordance with our current understanding of how they relate to the facts and circumstances of the relevant case.

These are not immutable rules. They are simply methods of trying to give effect to what the legislature is reasonably likely to have meant. Sometimes the context may lead the interpreter to decide that the legislature must reasonably have intended the words to be set in stone at the time the statute was passed. The practical problems of that approach make it unlikely that this will often be the case, but it can happen. **5.204**

[141] ibid, [148].
[142] ibid, [149].
[143] ibid.

5.205 The principle that a statute is normally 'always speaking' can be illustrated by five cases:

- *Barker v Wilson*;[144]
- *Aid/Watch Inc v Commissioner of Taxation*;[145]
- *Baker v Quantum Clothing Group*;[146]
- *Fitzpatrick v Sterling Housing Association*;[147] and
- *R (Quintavalle) v Secretary of State for Health*.[148]

5.206 *Barker v Wilson*[149] is a straightforward case decided in 1980. The question was whether bank records held on microfilm were 'bankers' books' within the meaning of the Bankers' Books Evidence Act 1879. The court held that microfilm was a 'book' for this purpose because it was necessary to read the Act in the light of current procedures at the time the case was decided.

5.207 Bridge LJ said:[150]

> The Bankers' Books Evidence Act 1879 was enacted with the practice of bankers in 1879 in mind. It must be construed in 1980 in relation to the practice of bankers as we now understand it. So construing the definition of 'bankers' books' and the phrase 'an entry in a banker's books,' it seems to me that clearly both phrases are apt to include any form of permanent record kept by the bank of transactions relating to the bank's business, made by any of the methods which modern technology makes available, including, in particular, microfilm.

5.208 The question in *Aid/Watch Inc v Commissioner of Taxation*[151] was whether Aid/Watch was entitled to tax relief on the basis that it was charity. Aid/Watch was an organisation that sought to promote the more efficient use of Australian and multinational foreign aid directed to the relief of poverty. Its activities included research and public campaigns intended to generate public debate and bring about changes in government policy and activity relating to the provision of foreign aid.

5.209 The Federal Court of Australia held that Aid/Watch was not a charitable institution because its main purpose was political—to bring about change in government activity and policy. The appeal to the High Court of Australia essentially required the court to decide two things. First, should the definition of a charity be widened to cover the types of activity that Aid/Watch carried out? Secondly, if so, when the tax legislation referred to charitable purposes, did it mean those purposes that were charitable at the time the legislation was passed, or those that had become charitable at the time the decision had to be made?

5.210 The High Court of Australia decided that the generation by lawful means of public debate about the efficiency of foreign aid directed to the relief of poverty was a purpose beneficial to the community and therefore charitable.[152] It then had to decide 'an important principle of statutory construction'.[153] Where a revenue statute gives tax relief for charitable trusts, is that

144 [1980] 1 WLR 884.
145 (2010) 241 CLR 539.
146 [2011] 1 WLR 1003.
147 [2001] 1 AC 27.
148 [2003] 2 AC 687.
149 [1980] 1 WLR 884.
150 ibid, 887.
151 (2010) 241 CLR 539.
152 ibid, [47].
153 ibid, [19].

relief limited to those trusts that would have been charitable at the time the legislation was passed, or did it extend to charities the purposes of which were held to be charitable at the time the issue arose?

The High Court of Australia decided that the legislation was 'always speaking'. It said:[154] **5.211**

> Where a statute picks up as a criterion for its operation a body of the general law, such as the equitable principles respecting charitable trusts, then, in the absence of a contrary indication in the statute, the statute speaks continuously to the present, and picks up the case law as it stands from time to time.

Baker v Quantum Clothing Group[155] is not as straightforward. One of the issues in the case was the meaning of section 29(1) of the Factories Act 1961, which provided: **5.212**

> There shall, so far as is reasonably practicable, be provided and maintained safe means of access to every place at which any person has at any time to work, and every such place shall, so far as is reasonably practicable, be made and kept safe for any person working there.

The question was whether the risks to which this section applied included the risk of employees suffering hearing loss as a result of continued exposure to noise levels. It was accepted that, at the time the legislation was passed in 1961, Parliament would not have considered this as an issue. But it was an issue at the time of the hearing in 2011. The Supreme Court interpreted the legislation so that it applied to the changed circumstances. **5.213**

The members of the Supreme Court recognised that section 29(1) was enacted without any appreciation that it could cover noise-induced hearing loss. There was therefore considerable force in the argument that it did not cover it. But, ultimately, the members of the court reached the conclusion that liability under section 29(1) is relative, depending in particular on knowledge about, and attitudes towards, safety from time to time.[156] **5.214**

Although Parliament did not have noise-induced hearing loss in contemplation when it passed the Act in 1961, the mischief of noise-induced hearing loss had been recognised by 2011. The court decided that the Act needed to be read in the light of understanding about safety at the time of the hearing, rather than at the time the statute was passed. **5.215**

This is an example of the point made by Lord Hobhouse in *Morris v KLM*. It is not that 'safety' had a different meaning in 1961 than in 2011. What had changed was our understanding of how noise can affect safety. But, in any event, it is reasonable to assume that when Parliament requires places of work to be safe, it would expect the interpreter to give effect to it by reference to the current understanding of what safety requires. The policy of section 29 is to ensure that workplaces are safe. Now we know that noise can be unsafe, it would run directly counter to Parliament's intention to exclude noise from the safety requirement.[157] **5.216**

It is not simply that Acts of Parliament are 'always speaking'. The real position is more nuanced. An Act will continue to speak if that can be seen to be the likely intention of Parliament when passing the legislation; and that will depend on the legislative purpose—which is determined from the words used in context. Ultimately, the court accepted that Parliament must have intended to legislate for safety by using words that had to be read at the relevant **5.217**

[154] ibid, [23].
[155] [2011] 1 WLR 1003.
[156] ibid, [61] (Lord Mance).
[157] ibid, [176] (Lord Kerr).

time by reference to the circumstances in existence at that time. If Parliament legislates for safety in workplaces, and that legislation may continue for many years, it is not unreasonable to assume that Parliament would expect the words to be given their ordinary meaning at the time the incident occurs.

5.218 *Fitzpatrick v Sterling Housing Association*[158] is a more difficult case. The question concerned a protected tenancy under the Rent Act 1977. The plaintiff had lived with the protected tenant of a flat in a stable and permanent homosexual relationship between 1976 and the tenant's death in 1994. The plaintiff applied to take over the tenancy but the defendant (who was the landlord of the flat) refused. The plaintiff would have been entitled to the tenancy if he were 'a member of the original tenant's family' within paragraph 3(1) of Schedule 1 to the Rent Act 1977. The House of Lords, by a majority of three to two, decided that he was entitled to the tenancy.

5.219 One of the questions was the meaning of the word 'family'. Should it be interpreted by reference to the meaning of the word in the 1990s (which was when the tenant died) or its meaning in the 1920s (which was when the first antecedent of the Rent Act had been enacted)?

5.220 The majority decided that the statute had to be read by reference to the facts existing at the time the dispute arose, not by reference to the time the legislation was originally passed. Lord Nicholls[159] accepted the defendant's submission that homosexual relationships have always existed and that, in the 1920s, a homosexual partner would not have been regarded as being a member of the tenant's family. But he decided that the underlying legislative purpose was to provide a secure home for those who share their lives together with the original tenant, and that this purpose would be at risk of being stultified if the courts could not have regard to changes in the way in which people live together and changes in the perception of relationships.

5.221 Lord Clyde[160] took a similar approach. He considered that it would be a rare case in which Parliament intended the language to be fixed at the time the original Act was passed. He said: '[The] rule of contemporary exposition should be applied only in relation to very old statutes . . . The general presumption is that an updating construction is to be applied . . .'

5.222 The majority also recognised that the word 'family' may not have altered as a matter of language. What had changed were the precise personal associations to which the concept is now applied. The essential meaning of the words had not changed, but those who are capable of falling within the words had changed.[161]

5.223 Perhaps the most difficult case is *R (Quintavalle) v Secretary of State for Health*.[162] It concerned the meaning of section 1 of the Human Fertilisation and Embryology Act 1990. Section 1(1) defined embryo as 'a live human embryo where fertilisation is complete'. A decade on, it was possible for embryos to be created without fertilisation that had not been envisaged when the Act was passed. How was the reference to fertilisation to be dealt with? To what extent must account be taken of changes in science since the Act was passed? Did the Act regulate embryos that had been created without fertilisation?

158 [2001] 1 AC 27.
159 ibid, 45.
160 ibid, 49–50.
161 ibid, 39 (Lord Slynn).
162 [2003] 2 AC 687.

The House of Lords decided that the Act did regulate embryos that had been created without fertilisation. Account needed to be taken of changes in science since the Act was passed. Lord Bingham did this whilst considering that the relevant provisions needed to read in the historical context of the situation that led to its enactment.[163] He could see 'no inconsistency between the rule that statutory language retains the meaning it had when Parliament used it and the rule that a statute is always speaking . . .'[164] He gave the example that the meaning of 'cruel and unusual punishments' has not changed since 1689, but many punishments that were not thought to fall within that category would now be held to do so. **5.224**

Lord Bingham therefore adopted the same approach as Lord Hobhouse in *Morris v KLM*. Even if the meaning of a word does not change, its application to current facts and circumstances can alter the outcome. **5.225**

Lord Steyn approached the problem from the other direction. He considered that the normal principle was that statutes are 'always speaking' and that only in rare cases must a statute be interpreted as if one were interpreting it on the day after it was passed.[165] Statutes dealing with a particular grievance or problem may sometimes require to be historically interpreted but, generally, they will be 'always speaking'. He went on to say:[166] **5.226**

> Here there was no drafting mistake. But in order to give effect to a plain parliamentary purpose a statute may sometimes be held to cover a scientific development not known when the statute was passed. Given that Parliament legislates on the assumption that statutes may be in place for many years, and that Parliament wishes to pass effective legislation, this is a benign principle designed to achieve the wishes of Parliament.

The most interesting judgment is that of Lord Millett. He was able to sidestep this whole debate by a careful reading of the words of the statute. He said:[167] **5.227**

> The search in every case is for what Parliament did intend, not what would it have intended had it foreseen later developments . . . The question is whether Parliament intended to legislate only for embryos created by a process which does involve the use of a fertilised egg or whether it intended to legislate for embryos by whatever process they are created.

Applying the statutory scheme of the Act (Principle 3), Lord Millett considered that Parliament intended to make comprehensive provision for the protection of human embryos however created. He then turned to section 1(1). The purpose of the opening words 'a live human embryo' was to limit the legislation to an embryo that is live and human. These are the essential characteristics that it must possess if it is to be given statutory protection. They are concerned with what an embryo is, not how it is produced.[168] But the words 'where fertilisation is complete' have a different function. They do not describe the essential characteristics of an embryo and do not form part of the definition of the word embryo. They merely indicate the stage of development that it must reach before it qualifies for protection. They are obviously inapplicable to embryos created by a process that does not involve fertilisation.[169] **5.228**

163 ibid, [8].
164 ibid, [9].
165 ibid, [22].
166 ibid, [25].
167 ibid, [39].
168 ibid, [45].
169 ibid, [46].

5.229 Lord Millett illustrates why much else said in the case was irrelevant to its conclusion:[170]

> This construction does not require words to be written into the section. There is no gap to be filled by implication. Nor is it a matter of updating the meaning of the word embryo by reference to subsequent developments. It is simply a matter of giving the opening words of paragraph (a) their natural meaning, recognising the function of the concluding words, and confining their operation to the case where they are capable of application. Once it is accepted that the embryo is defined by reference to what it is and not by reference to the process by which it is created, all need for updating falls away.

5.230 There was disagreement between the members of the House of Lords on whether the statute was, or was not, 'always speaking'. This is not surprising. It is not a straightforward question, and there is no simple answer. Ultimately the question is to establish what the legislature must reasonably have intended from the words it used. That requires the words to be understood in context. In some cases, that may require an understanding of the context at the time the statute was passed. But, because statutes are understood to last for a considerable time, it is not unreasonable that the starting point for the discussion is that Parliament probably intended the words it used to be interpreted in their natural context at the time the dispute arises. A requirement to look back to their meaning at the time the statute was passed will simply add to uncertainty and to the time and expense of litigation.

5.231 But ultimately there is no way of getting away from the fact that the answer to the question depends on the actual words used and the context in which they appear. Lord Millett's judgment demonstrates how important it is to conduct a close examination of the words used in the order in which they appear.

5.232 Although the general principle is that statutes are 'always speaking', the question is ultimately one of the interpretation of the words in issue, and they may point to a conclusion that the reference was intended to be to the position as it was at the time the legislation was passed. For instance, the Court of Appeal took this approach in *The Longford*[171] as did the High Court of Australia in *Attorney-General for the State of New South Wales v The Brewery Employees Union of New South Wales*.[172] These cases were both decided over a century ago, and it is now less common to find cases where a statute is interpreted in this way, but it can still occur. A more recent example is a decision of the Australian courts in 2007.

5.233 In *Forsyth v Deputy Commissioner of Taxation*,[173] the question was whether a particular Australian court had the jurisdiction to hear a particular matter. The case therefore involved the interpretation of the legislation by which jurisdiction had been conferred on the relevant court. The taxpayer argued that the relevant legislation was 'ambulatory' in character. The Deputy Commissioner of Taxation argued that it spoke at the fixed time when it was passed. If the Deputy Commissioner were correct, then the court did have jurisdiction. If the taxpayer were correct, then it did not.

5.234 The High Court of Australia decided that the particular legislation only spoke at the date it was passed, and did not have an 'ambulatory' effect. It did so on the basis of a detailed examination of the words of the relevant statute.

170 ibid, [49].
171 (1889) 14 PD 34 at 36.
172 (1908) 6 CLR 469.
173 (2007) 231 CLR 531.

This case is a useful illustration of the principle that the ultimate requirement of the interpreter of legislation is to establish the objective intention of the legislature from the words it has used. Although there is a strong presumption that the statute is 'always speaking', the question is always one of interpretation of the words used in the light of the relevant context and of the purpose of the legislation. **5.235**

I. Canons of Construction: Introduction

It is characteristic of lawyers that they try to establish rules to help them to decide cases. This is as true of the interpretation of documents as it is of any other legal endeavour. In the case of interpretation, they are known as 'canons of construction'; and they are used in the interpretation of all types of document. **5.236**

There has been quite a debate about canons of construction in relation to contractual interpretation. Some judges (for instance, Lord Hoffmann) consider that they can be a distraction from the real task at hand—which is to establish what the particular words used mean in their particular context.[174] Other judges believe that they can create more certainty in the interpretation process. If that were true, it would be an obvious advantage. The real question is whether these canons of construction really do increase certainty. **5.237**

These differences of opinion carry over into statutory interpretation. **5.238**

A degree of scepticism about the value of canons of construction can be seen in the judgment of Lord Reid in *Maunsell v Olins*:[175] **5.239**

> Then rules of construction are relied on. They are not rules in the ordinary sense of having some binding force. They are our servants, not our masters. They are aids to construction, presumptions or pointers. Not infrequently one 'rule' points in one direction, another in a different direction. In each case we must look at all relevant circumstances and decide as a matter of judgment what weight to attach to any particular 'rule'.

A more positive approach to canons of construction can be seen in the judgment of Lord Neuberger in *Cusack v Harrow London Borough Council*:[176] **5.240**

> It was suggested on behalf of the council that this case represented an opportunity for this court to 'make it clear that canons of construction should have a limited role to play in the interpretation' of statutes (and indeed contracts). In my view, canons of construction have a valuable part to play in interpretation, provided that they are treated as guidelines rather than railway lines, as servants rather than masters. If invoked properly, they represent a very good example of the value of precedent.
>
> Interpretation of any document ultimately involves identifying the intention of Parliament, the drafter, or the parties. That intention must be determined by reference to the precise words used, their particular documentary and factual context, and, where identifiable, their aim or purpose. To that extent, almost every issue of interpretation is unique in terms of the nature of the various factors involved. However, that does not mean that the court

[174] *Bank of Credit and Commerce International v Ali* [2002] 1 AC 251 at [51]–[62].
[175] [1975] AC 373 at 382.
[176] [2013] 1 WLR 2022 at [57] and [58].

> has a completely free hand when it comes to interpreting documents: that would be inconsistent with the rule of law, and with the need for as much certainty and predictability as can be attained, bearing in mind that each case must be resolved by reference to its particular factors.

5.241 A similar point was made by Lord Diplock in *Prestcold v Minister of Labour*:[177]

> Modern statutes are drafted by professional legal draftsmen and intended to be read and understood by professional lawyers. As they create legal rights and liabilities, their meaning should be unambiguous and precise, and to aid precision certain habits of composition have been acquired by Parliamentary draftsmen which are familiar to professional lawyers and to the courts. These habits obtain recognition in the canons of statutory construction, though many of them are general rules of composition which any writer seeking clarity of expression is likely to follow, such as *expressio unius exclusio alterius*, *eiusdem generis* and *noscitur a sociis* though, unlike lawyers, he does not express them in the arcane obscurity of the Latin tongue. As regards rules of composition of this kind the main difference between a professional legal draftsman and any other kind of writer is that the Parliamentary draftsman is less likely to depart from them.

5.242 The purpose of the canons of construction is to provide a starting point for the analysis of a particular provision of a statute. To say that they are presumptions probably carries their effect too far: they are easy to rebut. And it is often said that they hunt in pairs: for every canon that points in one direction, there will be another that points in the other. Some are more important in practice than others, and a number of these will be discussed in the ensuing sections of this chapter. But, first, there are a number of preliminary points that should be made.

5.243 First, one of the most common canons of construction in relation to contractual interpretation is the *contra proferentem* rule. But this is of little importance in relation to statutory interpretation. The purpose of the *contra proferentem* rule is to ensure that the person who drafted the relevant document or who benefits from a particular provision must draft clearly. Where there is any ambiguity, the benefit of the doubt will go to the other party.

5.244 None of this is relevant to statutory interpretation. A statute is a unilateral act. It is always drafted on behalf of the legislature. And it has never been suggested that ambiguities have to be interpreted against the legislature. The only equivalent is the suggestion made by some judges (such as Lords Steyn and Hope), that the rule in *Pepper v Hart* is a type of quasi-estoppel against the executive.[178] But, this aside, the *contra proferentem* rule has no part to play in statutory interpretation.

5.245 Secondly, there is often less to the canons of construction than meets the eye. Many apparent canons of construction fade away when they are analysed closely. This point will be illustrated in the following sections of this chapter.

5.246 The third general comment is that, even when a court does recognise that a canon of construction exists, it may decide not to follow it. This happens quite frequently in practice. An example is the decision of the Court of Appeal in *Dean v Wiesengrund*.[179] After the death of

177 [1969] 1 WLR 89 at 96.
178 This issue is discussed in Chapter 4.
179 [1955] 2 QB 120.

the tenant of a rent-controlled flat, her executor claimed to recover rent that had been overpaid to the landlord by the tenant. The relevant section of the Act concerned said that where a sum had been overpaid 'the sum so paid shall be recoverable from the landlord ... who received the payment or his legal personal representative by the tenant ... by whom it was paid ...'

The landlord argued that because the landlord's personal representatives were specifically referred to, but not the tenant's personal representatives, it followed that the claim could only be brought by the tenant and not by her executor. **5.247**

The landlord relied on a canon of construction: *expressio unius est exclusio alterius*. The Court of Appeal rejected this this argument. Jenkins LJ said:[180] **5.248**

> The argument for the landlord is summed up in the maxim *expressio unius exclusio alterius*, which, applied to the present case, is said to compel the conclusion that the express reference to the legal personal representative of one of the parties excludes any implied reference to the legal personal representative of the other. But this maxim is, after all, no more than an aid to construction, and has little, if any, weight where it is possible, as I think it is in the present case, to account for the '*inclusio unius*' on grounds other than an intention to effect the '*exclusio alterius*'.

This is important in practice because it is often possible to construct arguments that slight changes in the words used show an intention to do something different. The reality is that the draftsman probably intended nothing of the kind. Draftsmen are rarely entirely consistent, and this case illustrates that the courts are well aware of that. **5.249**

The following sections of this chapter will consider five canons of construction that are of particular relevance to statutory interpretation: **5.250**

- J: preserving the common law;
- K: limiting criminal legislation;
- L: limiting retrospective legislation;
- M: *eiusdem generis*; and
- N: profiting from one's own wrong.

J. Canons of Construction: Preserving the Common Law

There are many dicta of eminent judges that indicate that there is a presumption that legislation is not intended to change the common law unless it does so clearly and explicitly. An example of this approach is *National Assistance Board v Wilkinson*.[181] **5.251**

National Assistance Board v Wilkinson[182] concerned the interpretation of the National Assistance Act 1948. The National Assistance Board (which paid assistance to those in need) had a power under section 43(1) to recover some or all of the money it had paid from any person 'who for the purposes of this Act is liable to maintain the person assisted'. Section **5.252**

[180] ibid, 130–131.
[181] [1952] 2 QB 648.
[182] ibid.

42(1) provided that: 'For the purposes of this Act ... a man shall be liable to maintain his wife and his children ...'

5.253 The Board brought a claim against a husband to defray the cost of providing assistance to his wife. It looked like a clear case. Under the statute, the husband was liable to maintain his wife and therefore the Board had a right of recovery against him. But the Court of Appeal decided that the Board was not entitled to recover from the husband because the wife had deserted the husband and, at common law, a husband had no duty to maintain a wife who had deserted him.

5.254 The court relied on a presumption that a statute will not be taken as effecting a fundamental alteration in the general law unless it uses words that point unmistakably in that direction. It also relied on the principle that the court leans against an interpretation that produces unjust and arbitrary consequences.[183]

5.255 In the result, the court held that the words 'a man shall be liable to maintain his wife' did not mean what they said. They were limited to the circumstances where that was the case at common law, even though the section started: 'For the purposes of this Act ...'

5.256 One could be forgiven for thinking that the effect of this decision was simply to reverse that which the legislature had intended. The whole purpose of legislation is to amend the common law, and to deny that it is intended to have this effect is as unhelpful as to suggest that King Canute could stop the tide.

5.257 In reality, the presumption against altering the common law is more honoured in the breach than in the observance, as can be illustrated by two decisions of the High Court of Australia:

- *Malika Holdings v Stretton*;[184] and
- *Gifford v Strang Patrick Stevedoring*.[185]

5.258 In *Malika Holdings v Stretton*,[186] McHugh J considered this canon of construction in some detail:[187]

> Courts have long held that a statute should not be construed as amending fundamental principles, infringing common law rights or departing from the general system of law unless it does so with 'irresistible clearness'....
>
> But times change. What is fundamental in one age or place may not be regarded as fundamental in another age or place. When community values are undergoing radical change and few principles or rights are immune from legislative amendment or abolition, as the case is in Australia today, few principles or rights can claim to be so fundamental that it is unlikely that the legislature would want to change them. No doubt there are fundamental legal principles—a civil or criminal trial is to be a fair trial, a criminal charge is to be proved beyond reasonable doubt, people are not to be arrested or searched arbitrarily, laws, especially criminal laws, do not operate retrospectively, superior courts have jurisdiction to prevent unauthorised assumptions of jurisdiction by inferior courts and tribunals are examples. Clear and unambiguous language is needed before a court will find that the

183 ibid, 661 (Devlin J).
184 (2001) 204 CLR 290.
185 (2003) 214 CLR 269.
186 (2001) 204 CLR 290.
187 ibid, [27] and [28].

> legislature has intended to repeal or amend these and other fundamental principles. But care needs to be taken in declaring a principle to be fundamental. Furthermore, infringement of rights and departures from the general system of law are in a different category from fundamental principles.

This issue was put to the test two years later in *Gifford v Strang Patrick Stevedoring*.[188] One of the questions was whether section 4(1) of the Law Reform (Miscellaneous Provisions) Act 1944 of New South Wales limited the extent of common law liability for vicarious liability of a negligent employee. Where a person had been killed or injured as a result of the negligence of an employee, the section extended the liability of the employer to family members who suffered psychiatric injury because the event occurred within their sight or hearing. The issue was whether this impliedly prevented family members recovering from the employer for psychiatric injury incurred as a result of having been told about the accident. **5.259**

It is often the case in statutes, as in contracts, that an express statement that liability is incurred if certain conditions are satisfied has the implicit meaning that there is no liability if those conditions are not satisfied. But it all depends on the particular words used in their context. In this case, the High Court of Australia decided that there was no such implicit limitation. **5.260**

The most interesting judgment was again that of McHugh J. He grappled directly with the presumption that statutes are not intended to alter the common law unless they do so clearly. He rejected that approach but nevertheless decided that the particular legislation did not restrict liability at common law because of the way in which the provisions had been drafted. He said[189] that the legislature regularly enacts laws that infringe the common law rights of individuals. There is a strong presumption of non-interference when the right is a fundamental right but, where it is not, 'the presumption of non-interference with those rights is inconsistent with modern experience and borders on fiction. If the presumption still exists in such cases, its effect must be so negligible that it can only have weight when all other factors are evenly balanced.'[190] **5.261**

The right to bring an action for psychiatric injury is not a fundamental right. Whether or not it is excluded has to be determined by interpreting the legislation in its natural and ordinary meaning, having regard to its context and purpose. Here, the words of the statute indicated that it was intended to expand the scope of the common law in a particular way, but otherwise to maintain the existence of the common law action. **5.262**

These cases illustrate how limited is the presumption that statutes are intended to preserve the common law. **5.263**

K. Canons of Construction: Limiting Criminal Legislation

It is sometimes said that there is a presumption that *mens rea* is required for a criminal offence. But, although statements of this kind can be found in the cases, there is little evidence that it is of much value in practice. Where there is no express reference to *mens rea* as an **5.264**

[188] (2003) 214 CLR 269.
[189] ibid, [36]–[39].
[190] ibid, [36].

ingredient in a criminal offence, the court has to decide from the words of the statute as a whole whether or not it is implicitly required. The nature of the particular legislation concerned and the precise way in which the offence is drafted may mean that there is no requirement for *mens rea*.[191]

5.265 An illustration of this point is the well-known decision of the House of Lords in *Sweet v Parsley*.[192] Ms Sweet let out rooms to tenants who smoked cannabis. She was convicted of being concerned in the management of premises used for the purpose of smoking cannabis. She was not aware of the fact that the rooms were being used for this purpose. The House of Lords held that she was not guilty.

5.266 Lord Reid considered that there is a presumption in a criminal statute that *mens rea* is required and that it can only be excluded by express words or necessary implication.[193] But the reason Ms Sweet got off was not because of a presumption of this kind but because, in order to be concerned in the management of premises used for the purpose of smoking cannabis, she would need to have known that the premises were being used for that purpose; and she did not. In other words, the natural and ordinary meaning of the words meant that knowledge was necessary. No presumption was required. That was the view of Lords Morris,[194] Pearce,[195] Wilberforce[196] and Diplock.[197]

5.267 The presumption of the requirement for *mens rea* is nevertheless frequently prayed in aid. The Supreme Court has recently decided in *Pwr v Director of Public Prosecutions*[198] that there is a strong presumption that *mens rea* is a requirement of a criminal offence, although it can be rebutted expressly or by necessary implication (that is, an implication that is compellingly clear).[199] But it nevertheless decided that the statutory words led inexorably to the conclusion that the presumption was rebutted and that the offence was one of strict liability.[200]

5.268 Nor is there any general presumption that the benefit of the doubt is given to the accused in a criminal case. An example of the way the courts deal with issues of this kind is provided by the decision of the Privy Council on appeal from New Zealand in *R v Karpavicius*.[201] The case was concerned with the interpretation of the Misuse of Drugs Act 1975, which categorised drugs into three classes—A, B and C. Section 6(2A) provided for maximum sentences for particular types of drugs—fourteen years for Class A, ten years for Class B and seven years 'in any other case'.

5.269 The question was whether the words 'in any other case' only covered Class C drugs, or whether they could cover cases that involved Class A or B drugs but could not be prosecuted under the earlier provisions. In this case, it was established that the drugs involved were either Class A or B but it was not clear which.

191 *Gammon v Attorney-General of Hong Kong* [1985] 1 AC 1.
192 [1970] AC 132.
193 ibid, 148.
194 ibid, 156.
195 ibid, 159.
196 ibid, 160–161.
197 ibid, 165.
198 [2022] 1 WLR 789.
199 ibid, [34].
200 ibid, [35].
201 [2004] 1 NZLR 156.

The New Zealand Court of Appeal concluded that the section was 'intended to cover the field, leaving no gaps'. The Privy Council agreed. The opinion of the Privy Council was given by Lord Steyn. He said:[202] **5.270**

> Their Lordships are content to assume that linguistically the arguments are finally balanced ... In a more literalist age it may have been said that the words of s6(2A)(c) are capable of bearing either a wide or narrow meaning and that the fact that a criminal statute is involved requires the narrower interpretation to be adopted. Nowadays an approach concentrating on the purpose of the statutory provision is generally to be preferred.

The idea that a criminal statute is to be interpreted restrictively flies in the face of the overriding principle of giving effect to the natural meaning of the words in the light of the purpose of the statute. This point was discussed by Kirby J in the High Court of Australia in *R v Lavender*.[203] **5.271**

Kirby J said:[204] **5.272**

> In the past, including in this Court, it has been conventional to say that, where one has been left in real doubt as to the meaning of a penal provision, that provisions will be construed strictly and in favour of the person potentially affected by the provision.... In recent times the rule of strict interpretation has 'lost most of its importance' and is generally regarded as a rule of 'last resort'. It comes into operation when the normal principles of interpretation have 'run out' ... The ordinary rules of construction are now first applied, including in the ascertainment of the meaning of penal and taxing legislation. In such categories, as much as anywhere else, it is the duty of a court to ascertain and give effect to the purpose of the legislature as expressed in the language enacted by Parliament.

More recently, in *Aubrey v R*[205] Kiefel CJ and Keene, Nettle and Edelman JJ had to consider the principle that where there is doubt about the meaning of a penal statute, it should be resolved in favour of the subject; and they confirmed that it is a rule of last resort. Penal statutes should be construed in accordance with the ordinary rules of construction. **5.273**

L. Canons of Construction: Limiting Retrospective Legislation

The same is true of the presumption against retrospectivity. It is sometimes said that there is a presumption against legislation having retrospective effect. But the cases show that it all depends on the precise wording of the relevant statute in its context. **5.274**

In *Wilson v First County Trust (No 2)*,[206] a loan agreement had been entered into that did not comply with the Consumer Credit Act 1974 and was therefore unenforceable. The question in the case was whether the Human Rights Act 1998 had any effect on this outcome. For this purpose, the main issue was whether the 1998 Act had any effect on a loan agreement entered into before it came into force. The House of Lords decided that it did not. **5.275**

202 ibid, [15].
203 (2005) 222 CLR 67 at [87]–[94].
204 ibid, [88], [93] and [94].
205 (2017) 260 CLR 305 at [39].
206 [2004] 1 AC 816.

5.276 Lord Scott made this comment:[207]

> There is, therefore, a common law presumption that a statute is not intended to have a retrospective effect. This presumption is part of a broader presumption that Parliament does not intend the statute to have an unfair or unjust effect … The presumption can be rebutted if it sufficiently clearly appears that it was indeed the intention of Parliament to produce the result in question. The presumption is no more than a starting point.

5.277 Lord Nicholls expressed the principle in slightly different terms. He approved statements by Lord Mustill and Staughton LJ that he considered established the point of principle.

5.278 In *L'Office Cherifien des Phosphates v Yamashita-Shinnihon Steamship Co*,[208] Lord Mustill said:

> The subject matter of statutes is so varied that these generalised maxims are not a reliable guide. As always, therefore, the underlying rationale should be sought.

5.279 In *Secretary of State for Social Security v Tunnicliffe*,[209] Staughton LJ said:

> [The] true principle is that Parliament is presumed not to have intended to alter the law applicable to past events and transactions in a manner which is unfair to those concerned in them, unless a contrary intention appears. It is not simply a question of classifying an enactment as retrospective or not retrospective. Rather, it may well be a matter of degree—the greater the unfairness, the more it is to be expected that Parliament will make it clear if that is intended.

5.280 It is suggested that the real question in every case is whether or not the particular words of the statute in their context establish that the relevant provision is intended to be retrospective. Statutes commonly state when they will take effect, but if they do not it is a question of judgement whether or not they are intended to be retrospective.

5.281 In the case in hand, the House of Lords decided that the 1998 Act did not apply to causes of action occurring before the section came into force. They did so because to apply it in such cases, and thereby alter the effect of existing legislation, might well produce an unfair result for one party or the other; and this was unlikely to have been the intention.

5.282 Seen in this light, the presumption against retrospectivity is simply an example of the reluctance by the courts to interpret words in a way that will produce a manifestly unfair or unreasonable result, and that clear language is therefore required in order to do so. This is Principle 7. The issues involved are more subtle than can be achieved by just applying a presumption. So much depends on the individual circumstances. What did the legislature really mean in the case in hand, reading the statute as a whole in the light of the relevant context?

5.283 Sometimes the legislation can so clearly establish an intention to act retrospectively that the presumption is of little relevance. An example is the decision of the New South Wales Court of Appeal in *Durham Holdings v New South Wales*.[210]

[207] ibid, [153].
[208] [1994] 1 AC 486 at 524–525.
[209] [1991] 2 All ER 712 at 724; and see judgment of Spigelman CJ in the New South Wales Court of Appeal in *Attorney General of New South Wales v World Best Holdings* (2005) 63 NSWLR 557 at [59].
[210] (1999) 47 NSWLR 340.

Legislation in New South Wales provided for the compulsory acquisition of coal in consideration of a certain amount of compensation. The legislation was amended to provide that the arrangements concerning compensation could differentiate between the persons to whom compensation was payable by providing that specified persons were not to be entitled to be paid more than a specified sum, irrespective of the amount of coal they owned immediately before the commencement of the Act (which was about ten years previously). There was then a specific statutory provision relating to Durham Holdings, which provided that if that company had made claims for compensation and the total amount would, apart from this clause, exceed a certain amount then, irrespective of the other provisions, the total amount of compensation was limited to that amount. **5.284**

Durham Holdings claimed that two relevant presumptions meant that they were not restricted in the manner in which the legislation appeared to provide. The first was the presumption against retrospectivity (which is expressly provided for in the Australian Interpretation Act). The second was the presumption that property would not be compulsory acquired without compensation. **5.285**

The New South Wales Court of Appeal decided that neither of these presumptions applied. The provisions of the legislation were too clear, and the presumptions were rebutted by evidence to the contrary. The words of the statute 'were clear and unambiguous'.[211] **5.286**

M. Canons of Construction: *Eiusdem Generis*

The *eiusdem generis* principle is applied in the interpretation of all types of document. The rule was explained by Cockburn CJ in *R v Cleworth*:[212] **5.287**

> [According] to a well-established rule in the construction of statutes, general terms following particular ones apply only to such persons or things as are eiusdem generis with those comprehended in the language of the Legislature.

The principle was discussed in detail by the Court of Appeal in *Quazi v Quazi*.[213] The case concerned the meaning of the words 'juridical or other proceedings' in the Recognition of Divorces and Legal Separations Act 1971. **5.288**

Lord Diplock explained the principle in this way:[214] **5.289**

> As the Latin words of the label attached to it suggest, the rule applies to cut down the generality of the expression 'other' only where it is preceded by a list of two or more expressions having more specific meanings and sharing some common characteristics from which it is possible to recognise them as being species belonging to a single genus and to identify what the essential characteristics of that genus are. The presumption then is that the draftsman's mind was directed only to that genus and that he did not, by his addition of the word 'other' to the list, intend to stray beyond its boundaries, but merely to bring within the ambit of the enacting words those species which complete the genus but which have been omitted from the preceding list either inadvertently or in the interests of brevity. Where, however, . . ., the

211 ibid, [44].
212 (1864) 4 B&S 927 at 932.
213 [1980] AC 744.
214 ibid, 807–808.

> word 'other' . . . is preceded by one expression only that has a more specific meaning . . . there is no room for the application of any *eiusdem generis* rule; for unless the draftsman has indicated at the very least two different species to which the enacting words apply there is no material on which to base an inference that there was some particular genus of proceedings to which alone his mind was directed when he used the word 'other' . . .

5.290 Viscount Dilhorne expressed the point more pithily when he said:[215] 'In my opinion this rule does not apply for there is no genus.'

5.291 Even if the *eiusdem generis* rule is not relevant, the word 'other' may still be cut down by the context of the surrounding words.[216]

5.292 Although the *eiusdem generis* principle was not relevant in *Quazi v Quazi*, it is applied in practice, as can be illustrated by two cases:

- *Re Latham*;[217] and
- *Palmer v Snow*.[218]

5.293 *Re Latham*[219] concerned the meaning of the words 'trustee, guardian, committee or other person' in the Finance Act 1894. The question was whether the words 'or other person' should be interpreted *eiusdem generis*. Wilberforce J held that they should. This was because:

- 'trustee, guardian, committee' were clearly of a genus—fiduciaries;
- there might be other fiduciaries who were not encompassed by the words 'trustee, guardian, committee';
- there were other provisions in the section that indicated that the reference was to people in whom the management of trust property was vested;
- in context, this list was of a second group of people and, if given a broad meaning, the words 'or other person' could include those in the first category, which would clearly not be what was intended.

5.294 This is a sensible application of the *eiusdem generis* principle. In this context, it was quite likely that the reference to 'other persons' was intended to be read in the light of the earlier words.

5.295 In *Palmer v Snow*,[220] a barber was charged with working on a Sunday contrary to an Act that applied to a person who was a 'tradesman, artificer, workman or labourer, or other person whatsoever'. The Queen's Bench Divisional Court decided that the barber did not fall within the description. In the light of the earlier words, a barber was not any 'other person whatsoever'.

5.296 It is sometimes suggested that the addition of the word 'whatsoever' will prevent the *eiusdem generis* rule from applying.[221] But here the court gave effect to the *eiusdem generis* rule

215 ibid, 809.
216 *Quazi v Quazi* [1980] AC 744 at 808 (Lord Diplock); and see the decision of the New Zealand Court of Appeal in *Civil Aviation Authority of New Zealand v Witschke-Rudd* [2015] 2 NZLR 749, which is discussed in Section C of Chapter 3.
217 [1962] 1 Ch 616.
218 [1900] 1 QB 725.
219 [1962] 1 Ch 616.
220 [1900] 1 QB 725. Counsel for the respondent were Dickens QC and W. Shakespeare.
221 See eg the judgment of Devlin J in *Chandris v Isbrandtsen-Moller Co* [1951] 1 KB 240 at 245.

anyway. This does illustrate that there are really no rules. The guiding principle is to establish what the legislature must reasonably have meant from what it has said. In many cases, where general words follow a list, the legislature will objectively intend the general words to be qualified by the list. But not always. The context may make it clear that the words are intended to apply more generally.

Like the other canons of construction, the *eiusdem generis* rule does have its detractors, and it is often easy to find a reason not to apply it. **5.297**

In *James Buchanan & Co v Babco Forwarding & Shipping*, Lord Salmon said:[222] **5.298**

> The *eiusdem generis* rule is nothing but a guide, and sometimes an uncertain guide, to the proper construction of a statute. I can find no reason why the words 'other charges in respect of the carriage of the goods' should be held to be *eiusdem generis* with 'carriage charges' or 'customs duties'.

This disinclination to rely on *eiusdem generis* can also be found in the Australian cases. In *Mattinson v Multiplo Incubators*,[223] Mahoney JA in the New South Wales Court of Appeal said:[224] **5.299**

> The *eiusdem generis* process of reasoning has had a long but varied history; is based upon a doubtful premise; operates by a mechanism which is uncertain; and, to the extent that it presently operates, in my opinion, has real effect to determine the construction of a statute only in a limited area.

Mahoney JA did not think that the *eiusdem generis* rule was of any real value. The important principle was to give the words—including general words—their ordinary meaning. **5.300**

A similar approach was taken by the Supreme Court of Victoria in *Gas & Fuel Corporation of Victoria v Comptroller of Stamps*.[225] This was a stamp duty case. The legislation referred to the 'total amount payable under the agreement for or by way of interest or insurance or other charge'. One of the questions was whether the words 'other charge' should be read *eiusdem generis* with 'interest or insurance'. The first instance judge applied the *eiusdem generis* principle, but the Full Court overruled him. They thought that the *eiusdem generis* rule afforded no assistance to the interpretation of the words 'other charge'. **5.301**

The court considered that the *eiusdem generis* rules should not automatically be applied. It is a rule that may, by reason of context and subject matter, be of assistance. They thought that the more modern view was that the prima facie general words should be taken in the larger sense unless in the particular case it is necessary to apply *eiusdem generis*. To apply *eiusdem generis* was thought by the court to be 'mere conjecture as to the intention of Parliament'.[226] On the facts of the case, it decided that the application of the principle would be quite arbitrary. There was no reason to limit the general words by reference to the two preceding words. **5.302**

222 [1978] AC 141 at 160.
223 [1977] 1 NSWLR 368 at 373–377.
224 ibid, 373.
225 [1964] VR 617.
226 ibid, 620.

N. Canons of Construction: Profiting From One's Own Wrong

5.303 It is sometimes said that a court will interpret a document so that a person will not be able to benefit from his or her own wrongdoing.[227] But the real position is more nuanced. A court will doubtless try to avoid interpreting legislation so it has this effect, but the question is always what the words mean in context. It is not so much a rule, as something to bear in mind in the process of interpretation.

5.304 The issue can be illustrated by four cases:

- *Glamorgan County Council v Carter*;[228]
- *Governors of the Peabody Donation Fund v Higgins*;[229]
- *R (Best) v Chief Land Registrar*;[230] and
- *Welwyn Hatfield Borough Council v Secretary of State for Communities and Local Government*.[231]

5.305 *Glamorgan County Council v Carter*[232] involved the interpretation of a provision of the Town and Country Planning Act 1947. Planning permission was required under the Act for the development of land except in certain circumstances. One of the exceptions was that planning permission was not required if, when the Act came into force, the land was unoccupied—in which event it could be used 'in respect of the use of the land for the purpose for which it was last used'. Mrs James had kept a caravan on the land and she claimed that she could continue to do so in reliance on that provision.

5.306 The local planning authority contended that Mrs James had done this illegally under the law that was then in force and therefore planning permission was still required. The court accepted this, and Salmon J said:[233]

> It seems to me plain on principle that Mrs James could not acquire any legal right by the illegal use to which she was putting the land. In my view it is plain that the use referred to in section 12(5)(c) of the Town and Country Planning Act 1947, must mean lawful use, at any rate in this sense, that it cannot include use which constitutes the commission of a criminal or quasi-criminal offence.

5.307 Salmon J said that this did not require a rewriting of the legislation. It simply involved[234] 'the well-known principle that it is impossible to acquire a right by committing a quasi-criminal offence'.

5.308 What this meant in this case was that it was necessary to read the words 'in respect of the use of the land for the purpose for which it was last used' so that it only applied where that use was lawful. It is possible that Parliament would have contemplated that someone could

[227] See eg *JRTT v Haycraft* [1993] BCLC 501 (Chadwick J).
[228] [1963] 1 WLR 1.
[229] [1983] 1 WLR 1091.
[230] [2016] QB 23.
[231] [2011] 2 AC 304.
[232] [1963] 1 WLR 1.
[233] ibid, 5.
[234] ibid, 6.

obtain rights by use of land illegally. But the presumption would be against it, and clear words would be needed to establish it.

This case can be contrasted with *Governors of the Peabody Donation Fund v Higgins*.[235] A tenant had a secure tenancy under the Housing Act 1980. In breach of the terms of the lease, he assigned the tenancy to his daughter. The daughter would herself become a secure tenant if, in accordance with section 37(1) of the Housing Act 1980, the secure tenancy were 'assigned'. One of the questions in the case was whether the assignment in breach of the lease was an assignment for this purpose. **5.309**

The court accepted that the assignment was valid, even though it was in breach of the terms of the lease. But it was argued that the reference to 'assigned' in the section must have meant a lawful assignment, not an assignment in breach of the terms of the lease. May LJ said:[236] **5.310**

> The subsection does not say so. I see no reason why it could not have said so. I see less reason to read into the subsection any such words to give that effect.

Here, the Court of Appeal decided that the draftsman could have referred specifically to lawful assignments but did not. The words were clear and they meant what they said—no more, no less. **5.311**

This case illustrates that the principle that a person cannot take advantage of their own wrong will not always be applied when interpreting legislation. It might have been thought that the reference to assignment was likely to have meant a lawful assignment, not one in breach of the very lease that created the tenancy. But the Court of Appeal decided otherwise. What is ultimately much more important than presumptions is the necessity to interpret the words in the light of the purpose of the relevant legislation. The purpose of the Housing Act was to protect tenants and this may well have influenced the decision. **5.312**

The fragility of the presumption can also be seen from the decision in *R (Best) v Chief Land Registrar*.[237] Under section 144(1) of the Legal Aid, Sentencing and Punishment of Offenders Act 2012, certain types of trespass became criminal acts. The question in this case was whether that affected the rules concerning adverse possession of land. The Chief Land Registrar claimed that a person could not claim adverse possession if part of the period for which they were claiming it relied on action that was criminal. But the Court of Appeal decided that this provision did not have the effect of changing settled principles of the law adverse possession. **5.313**

The principal judgment was given by Sales LJ. He recognised that: 'In many contexts in the civil law, rights between persons are informed by the idea that a person should not benefit as a result of unlawful action taken by himself.'[238] But adverse possession is always founded on the tort of trespass to land, so the question was whether the fact that it was now a criminal offence as well made any difference. The Court of Appeal decided that it did not. Had Parliament intended to change the law of adverse possession, it would surely have dealt with it expressly. Since it did not, it was legitimate to decide **5.314**

[235] [1983] 1 WLR 1091.
[236] ibid, 1097.
[237] [2016] QB 23.
[238] ibid, [43].

that Parliament did not intend to produce a collateral effect on the settled law of adverse possession.[239]

5.315 In an appropriate case, the presumption will still be applied, as can be seen from the decision of the Supreme Court in *Welwyn Hatfield Borough Council v Secretary of State for Communities and Local Government*.[240] A builder obtained planning permission to construct a hay barn on open land within the green belt subject to the condition that it was to be used only for storage of agricultural products. In fact, he built something that had the external appearance of a hay barn but which was fitted out as a home, that he then lived in for four years. He then applied under the provisions of the Town and Country Planning Act 1990 for a certificate of lawfulness of the existing use. The purpose of these provisions was to legalise breaches of planning law where a certain amount of time (in this case four years) had elapsed.

5.316 The Supreme Court held that the builder was not entitled to rely on these provisions. In essence, this was because he had dishonestly prevented the council from detecting what it was that he had wrongfully done.

5.317 As Lord Brown said,[241] any other result would be a surprising outcome that decent law-abiding citizens would find incomprehensible. But he was clearly troubled by whether it was proper to import into an apparently self-contained legislative scheme the principle of public policy that one should not be allowed to profit from one's own wrong. One particular issue concerned him—which was that it would run counter to the plain intention of the legislative scheme as a whole. The whole purpose of the relevant section was to legitimise things that had been done in breach of the planning laws. He accepted that this argument was a serious one and that it would be impossible to superimpose upon the statutory scheme any sort of broad principle to the effect that no one guilty of wrongdoing could benefit. But this particular builder was involved in a deliberate, elaborate and sustained plan to deceive the council from first to last.

5.318 Lord Brown went on to say:[242]

> On any possible view the whole scheme was in the highest degree dishonest and any law-abiding citizen would be not merely shocked by it but astonished to suppose that, once discovered, instead of being enforced against, it would be crowned with success, with [the builder] entitled to a certificate of lawful use to prove it.

5.319 The cases demonstrate that there is no principle of interpretation that a person cannot take advantage of their own wrong. In each case, the duty of the court is to interpret the words of the statute in context. Whether such a principle can be implied—and, if so, its extent—is a question of interpretation of the particular words of the particular statute. This point is particularly well made by Lord Brown, who really does grapple with the propriety of imposing an interpretation that restricts the natural meaning of the words. And in the end he only allowed it do so because it would be absurd if there were any other conclusion. This is Principle 7.

239 ibid, [75].
240 [2011] 2 AC 304.
241 ibid, [72]–[81].
242 ibid, [80].

O. To Whom is the Statute Addressed?

When reading any document, it is important to understand to whom it is addressed. The first rule for writers is to know their audience. 5.320

Statutes are generally addressed to all citizens—and sometimes more widely still. With statutory interpretation, therefore, there is less ability to match the meaning of the words to the identity of the addressees than there is in relation to contractual interpretation. But, occasionally, it can be seen that statutes are addressed to a particular type of person, and that may affect the way in which they are interpreted. Two examples can illustrate this point. 5.321

In *Unwin v Hanson*,[243] justices of the peace had the statutory power to order trees growing near the highway to be 'lopped'. The question for the Court of Appeal was what was meant by 'lopped'. What had happened was that the surveyors had 'topped' the trees (that is, cut off their tops). The Court of Appeal held that they were not entitled to do this. Country-dwellers knew that to lop a tree means to cut off its branches laterally, not to cut off its top. 5.322

Lord Esher MR had this to say:[244] 5.323

> If the Act is directed to dealing with matters affecting everybody generally, the words used have the meaning attached to them in the common and ordinary use of language. If the Act is one passed with reference to a particular trade, business, or transaction, and words are used which everybody conversant with that trade, business or transaction, knows and understands to have a particular meaning in it, then the words are to be construed as having that particular meaning, though it may differ from the common or ordinary meaning of the words.

The second example is *Jenner v Allen West & Co*,[245] concerning the meaning of the words 'crawling boards' when used in building regulations. The Court of Appeal accepted that regulations of this kind are addressed to the building trade and must be interpreted in the light of that fact. As Lord Evershed MR said,[246] the expression 'crawling boards' must be understood in the way those versed in the appropriate trade would understand them, because that is what Parliament must have intended. 5.324

P. Technical Meanings

If a statute is concerned with a particular type of transaction, and a word used in that statute has a technical meaning in relation to that transaction, then it will often be necessary to give the word its technical meaning even if it may mean other things in other contexts. This was the case in *Jenner v Allen West & Co*,[247] which has just been discussed. There the relevant legislation was addressed to the building trade and it had to be interpreted in that light. 5.325

[243] [1891] 2 QB 115.
[244] ibid, 119.
[245] [1959] 1 WLR 554.
[246] ibid, 567.
[247] ibid.

5.326 In *Maunsell v Olins*,[248] Lord Simon said that where words have a technical meaning, they should presumptively being given that meaning because 'statutory language must always be given presumptively the most natural and ordinary meaning which is appropriate in the circumstances'. That was a dissenting judgment on the facts, but it does not alter the validity of the statement of principle.

5.327 An extreme example of the application of this principle can be seen in the decision of the Court of Appeal in *Fisher v Bell*.[249] A shopkeeper displayed a flick knife in his shop window with a price ticket. It was claimed that he committed an offence because he offered the flick knife for sale. The Court of Appeal held that he had not offered it for sale. Placing it in the window was an invitation to treat, and not an offer.

5.328 Lord Parker CJ put the position this way:[250]

> I confess that I think most lay people and, indeed, I myself when I first read the papers, would be inclined to the view that to say that if a knife was displayed in a window like that with a price attached to it was not offering it for sale was just nonsense. In ordinary language it is there inviting people to buy it, and it is for sale; but any statute must of course be looked at in the light of the general law of the country. Parliament in its wisdom in passing an Act must be taken to know the general law. It is perfectly clear that according to the ordinary law of contract the display of an article with a price on it in a shop window is merely an invitation to treat. It is in no sense an offer for sale the acceptance of which constitutes a contract.

5.329 It is difficult to believe that this was really Parliament's intention. In normal parlance, the knife was being offered for sale whether, in a contractual sense, it was an invitation to treat or not. The interpretation put on it by the Court of Appeal seems unduly technical. Surely what was needed was a bit more common sense.

5.330 The limits of the use of technical meanings can be illustrated by *Jones v Tower Boot Co*.[251] This was a case of racial abuse of an employee by other employees of the same company. For the employer to be liable for the acts of the other employees under the Race Relations Act 1976, those acts had to be done 'in the course of his employment'. The employer argued that 'in the course of employment' was an expression used in employment law and that the acts committed by the employees in this case were not 'in the course of their employment' within that meaning.

5.331 The Court of Appeal rejected this approach. It decided that the words in the context of the Race Relations Act 1976 did not have the same meaning as in the context of employment law.

5.332 The reason it took this view is apparent from the judgment of Waite LJ. He described how the race relations legislation broke new ground, and that it was necessary to interpret it in accordance with its purpose of eliminating the occasion for discrimination as well as compensating its victims or punishing its perpetrators.

5.333 Waite LJ went on to say:[252]

248 [1975] AC 373 at 391.
249 [1961] 1 QB 394.
250 ibid, 399.
251 [1997] ICR 254.
252 ibid, 262.

> A purposive construction accordingly requires [the relevant sections of the Race Relations Act 1976] to be given a broad interpretation. It would be inconsistent with that requirement to allow the notion of the 'course of employment' to be construed in any sense more limited than the natural meaning of those everyday words would allow.

The approach here is similar to that of the House of Lords in *Schuler v Wickman*[253] in relation to contractual interpretation. It is not always appropriate to assume that contracting parties or the legislature used words in a technical sense. Sometimes it is necessary to adopt a more common-sense approach to their interpretation. **5.334**

Q. Particular and General

Problems can be caused in any legal document if it contains both particular and general provisions dealing with the same type of issue. If, for instance, there is a particular provision that applies in certain circumstances, and then a more general provision that appears to apply in broader circumstances, it may very well be the case that the general provision is intended to be limited by the particular one. So, although on the face of it the general provision might seem to apply to the case in hand, it will be held not to do so if it would conflict with the particular provision. **5.335**

This principle was described by Sir John Romilly MR in *Pretty v Solly*:[254] **5.336**

> The general rules which are applicable to particular and general enactments in statutes are very clear, the only difficulty is their application. The rule is, that whenever there is a particular enactment and a general enactment in the same statute, and the latter, taken in its most comprehensive sense, would overrule the former, the particular enactment must be operative, and the general enactment must be taken to affect only the other parts of the statute to which it may properly apply.

An example of the application of this principle can be seen in the decision of the House of Lords in *R v J*.[255] The Sexual Offences Act 1956 contained two relevant offences. One, under section 6, concerned unlawful sexual intercourse with a girl under sixteen. The second, under section 14, concerned indecent assault. There was a one-year time limit on commencing a prosecution under section 6, but no such time limit under section 14. The Crown was unable in a particular case to bring a claim under section 6 because of the time limit, and it therefore brought a claim under section 14 based on the same facts. **5.337**

The House of Lords held that the Crown was unable to do so. The principal ground for the decision was that it cannot have been Parliament's intention that a prosecution could be brought under section 14 on the same facts as were relevant to a prosecution under section 6. Parliament must have intended the one-year time limit to have a purpose and it could not have intended the Crown to be able to bypass the time limit by bringing a prosecution under a different section. **5.338**

As Lord Bingham said,[256] any other reading is: **5.339**

253 [1974] AC 235.
254 (1859) 26 Beav 606 at 610.
255 [2005] 1 AC 562.
256 ibid, [18].

> an impossible reading, since Parliament must have intended the prohibition … to have some meaningful effect and this reading would deprive it of any meaningful effect whatever … Put another way, what possible purpose could Parliament have intended to serve by prohibiting prosecution under section 6 after the lapse of 12 months if exactly the same conduct could thereafter be prosecuted, with exposure to the same penalty, under section 14?

5.340 As with all these other canons and presumptions, this is simply a guide to what the legislature must objectively have intended. It is a starting point, no more. The ultimate aim in every case is to establish what the legislature is likely to have intended from the words it has used. And this generally requires the interpreter to give effect to the natural and ordinary meaning of the words in their context and in the light of the purpose of the statute.

6
Principle 6: Ambiguity

Principle 6: If the words of the statute are reasonably capable of more than one ordinary meaning, they are given the meaning the legislature is most likely objectively to have intended.

A. The Principle

Written texts are prone to ambiguity. We generally try to avoid ambiguity when drafting legal documents but, try as we will, we cannot eliminate it. **6.1**

Occasionally, when drafting contracts, provisions are deliberately left ambiguous because it proves impossible to reach agreement in any other way. This may also be true of legislation. In David Hare's play *Straight Line Crazy*, Robert Moses says:[1] **6.2**

> If you make things too explicit, too clear, when you draft a bill, then you may provoke unnecessary resistance. That's why a level of ambiguity is called for.

But in most cases ambiguity is unintentional. The longer the document, the more difficult it is to be consistent throughout. And the length of documents—both statutes and contracts—has increased exponentially over the last half-century. **6.3**

Where there is an ambiguity in a statute, the question for the interpreter is what the legislature would objectively have intended. It will often be clear from the rest of the statute what the ambiguous words are likely to mean. Failing that, the interpreter needs to fall back on common sense and fairness. It can be assumed that the legislature intended to act in a reasonable and fair way, and that can help in the choice between competing meanings. **6.4**

B. When is a Text Ambiguous?

Difficulty of interpretation is not the same thing as ambiguity. It is nearly always possible to cast some doubt on the meaning of any expression in a legal document. That does not make it ambiguous. It is normally reasonably clear what the expression means. An expression is only ambiguous for the purpose of statutory or contractual interpretation if it has two or more meanings each of which is reasonably possible in the circumstances. **6.5**

As Lord Simon said in *Farrell v Alexander*:[2] **6.6**

[1] D. Hare, *Straight Line Crazy* (Faber & Faber, 2022), Act 1, Scene 5.
[2] [1977] AC 59 at 86.

Principles of Statutory Interpretation. Richard Calnan, Oxford University Press.
DOI: 10.1093/oso/9780192864673.003.0007

> [Most] words in English are capable of more than one sense: for the words to be read in two possible senses does not make them ambiguous unless they can be fairly read in either sense in their context.

6.7 Lord Cooke made the same point in *R v Secretary of State for the Environment, Transport and the Regions, ex parte Spath Holme*:[3]

> 'Ambiguous' is a word not itself free from the quality which it purports to ascribe. The philosopher Sir William Empson famously identified seven types of ambiguity, none of which appears to correspond with ordinary legal usage. In ordinary legal usage, I think that a provision is ambiguous if reasonably open on orthodox rules of construction to more than one meaning.

6.8 Because it is ultimately a question of judgement whether or not something is ambiguous, it is not uncommon for different judges in the same case to have different views on this question. This point can be illustrated by two decisions of the House of Lords:

- *Black-Clawson International v Papierwerke Waldhof-Aschaffenburg*;[4] and
- *Maunsell v Olins*.[5]

6.9 In *Black-Clawson International v Papierwerke Waldhof-Aschaffenburg*,[6] the holder of a bill of exchange brought proceedings against the acceptor of the bill (which was a German company) both in Germany and in England. The German court held that the claim was time barred under the German limitation rules, which were shorter than the English rules. The main question for the English courts was whether section 8(1) of the Foreign Judgments (Reciprocal Enforcement) Act 1933 prevented the plaintiffs from proceeding with their claim in the English courts. Section 8(1) provided that certain judgments 'shall be recognised in any court in the United Kingdom as conclusive between the parties thereto in all proceedings founded on the same cause of action and may be relied on by way of defence or counterclaim in any such proceedings'.

6.10 The defendants argued that the German court had found that the defendants were not liable for the claim and therefore that the English courts should follow suit under section 8(1). The plaintiffs argued that section 8(1) only made the German judgment conclusive in relation to the matter that it had decided; and, since the court had only decided that the claim was time barred in Germany, it had not made any decision on the merits of the case, and therefore section 8(1) did not prevent the claim being made in England. The Court of Appeal accepted the defendants' argument. The House of Lords overruled them and, by a majority of four to one, found for the plaintiffs.

6.11 The majority in the House of Lords seemed to think that section 8 was ambiguous. Indeed, Lord Reid said as much.[7] Lord Diplock, on the other hand, thought that the words were clear.[8] In the event, they reached different decisions on what the words did actually mean.

[3] [2001] 2 AC 349 at 400.
[4] [1975] AC 591.
[5] [1975] AC 373.
[6] [1975] AC 591.
[7] ibid, 616.
[8] ibid, 638–639.

In *Maunsell v Olins*,[9] the question was whether a particular farm constituted part of 'premises' within the meaning of section 18(5) of the Rent Act 1968. By a majority of three to two, the House of Lords held that the farm was not part of 'premises' and therefore that the protections in the Rent Act did not apply. 6.12

The majority (Lords Wilberforce and Reid and Viscount Dilhorne) considered that the section was ambiguous. Lord Wilberforce said:[10] '[The] section is certainly one which admits, almost invites, opposing constructions.' But the minority (Lords Simon and Diplock) saw it differently. In ordinary legal parlance, 'premises' means the subject matter of the letting. The words were clear, and should be given effect. 6.13

Ambiguity, like beauty, is in the eye of the beholder. These cases illustrate the judgemental nature of the exercise of establishing whether something is ambiguous. The test is whether the expression is open to two or more sensible interpretations. Establishing whether or not that is the case is essentially a question of judgement. 6.14

C. If it is Ambiguous, More Context is Available

It has been seen in Principle 4 that the background against which a statute is interpreted is more limited than that for contracts. And in many cases external materials can only be consulted if the words of the statute are ambiguous when read in the context of the legislation as a whole. 6.15

The result is that it is not generally possible to use background materials to create ambiguity. This is in marked contrast to contractual interpretation, where it is now clear that relevant background material can create, as well as resolve, an ambiguity. 6.16

The requirement for ambiguity in the case of statutory interpretation can be illustrated by two cases concerning the legislative history of the statute concerned. They are: 6.17

- *Camden London Borough Council v Gunby*;[11] and
- *R v Secretary of State for the Environment, Transport and the Regions, ex parte Spath Holme*.[12]

In *Camden London Borough Council v Gunby*,[13] a council served an abatement notice under section 80 of the Environmental Protection Act 1990 on the managing agents of premises. The Act required the notice to be served on the 'owner' of the premises, and the managing agents argued that the notice had been served on the wrong people, because they were not the owners. In a different section of the Act, the word 'owner' was defined to include persons who were entitled to receive the rack-rent of the premises. The managing agent fell within that description, but that definition only applied for the purpose of a different section. 6.18

9 [1975] AC 373.
10 ibid, 385.
11 [2000] 1 WLR 465.
12 [2001] 2 AC 349.
13 [2000] 1 WLR 465.

6.19 The Court of Appeal decided that the fact that 'owner' was defined in one section and not the other created an ambiguity. In the words of Rose LJ:[14] 'That being so, a judge is entitled to resolve that ambiguity by recourse to the overwhelming legislative history [of the provision].'

6.20 *R v Secretary of State for the Environment, Transport and the Regions, ex parte Spath Holme*[15] concerned the extent of a power granted by section 31 of the Landlord and Tenant Act 1985. The Secretary of State could by order provide for 'restricting or preventing increases of rent for dwellings which would otherwise take place'. How wide a power was this, and was it impliedly restricted in any way?

6.21 One of the questions was whether it was appropriate to look back over the preceding provisions, tracing the section back to its original source. The court decided that this could only be done where the words were ambiguous, but that in this case they were ambiguous.

6.22 The same limitation applies to the use of ministerial statements under the rule in *Pepper v Hart*.[16] Information of this kind can only be used where the words of the statute are ambiguous. In *Ahmadi v Secretary of State for the Home Department*,[17] Sullivan LJ in the Court of Appeal said that[18] 'while Hansard may in certain limited circumstances be an aid to interpretation if there is ambiguity in an enactment, there is no ambiguity in [the relevant section]'.

D. Resolving Ambiguity

6.23 The resolution of an ambiguity involves broadly the same process whatever the nature of the text being interpreted.

- The first step is to consider the ambiguous words in the light of the document as a whole and in the context of its purpose. In practice, that will often resolve the ambiguity.[19]
- Failing that, the interpreter needs to rely on common sense and an understanding of which of the proposed interpretations produces the fairer result.[20]

6.24 These two points are illustrated by two cases:

- *Attorney-General's Reference (No 1 of 1988)*;[21] and
- *Re Marr*.[22]

6.25 In *Attorney-General's Reference (No 1 of 1988)*,[23] an individual had made a profit on the acquisition and subsequent sale of shares in a company on the basis of inside information that had been given to him. He was charged with insider dealing. In order for the offence to be made out, it had to be established that he had 'obtained' that inside information. He argued

14 ibid, 472.
15 [2001] 2 AC 349.
16 [1993] AC 593.
17 [2014] 1 WLR 401.
18 ibid, [31].
19 *Re Agricultural Sector (Wales) Bill* [2014] 1 WLR 2622.
20 *Ahmadi v Secretary of State for the Home Department* [2014] 1 WLR 401 at [28].
21 [1989] 1 AC 971.
22 [1990] 1 Ch 773.
23 [1989] 1 AC 971.

that the primary meaning of the word 'obtained' is to acquire by purpose and effort, and that he had not done this. He had not sought the information. He had simply been given it, and had then used it.

The first instance judge accepted this argument but the Court of Appeal and the House of Lords took the contrary view. They decided that 'obtained' had two meanings—a primary one of acquisition by purpose and effort, and a secondary, more general one, of receipt. Although the individual had not acquired the information by purpose and effort, he had received it, and therefore he had obtained it. 6.26

The judgment of the Court of Appeal was given by Lord Lane CJ. He decided that the word was capable of either meaning and that, looking at the Act as whole, the vice at which the Act was aimed was the exploitation of inside information. The vice was in the way the information was used, not in the method of its receipt. This conclusion was reinforced by looking at the White Paper on which the Act was based. The court held that it was permissible to use this because it helped to resolve an ambiguity. In the context of the purpose of the Act, 'obtained' meant 'received'. The House of Lords took the same approach. 6.27

Re Marr[24] concerned the interpretation of the Insolvency Act 1986. As a result of certain amendments, it contained two provisions within the same section that were inconsistent with each other. The question was whether a bankruptcy order could be made against two individual members of a partnership in circumstances where the partnership debt on which the petitioning creditor relied had been paid, but a winding-up order was in existence against the partnership. Section 271(1) of the Insolvency Act 1986 said that a bankruptcy order could not be made unless the petitioned debt was unpaid—and it had been paid. But section 271(2A) said that a bankruptcy order must be made against an individual member of a partnership if a winding-up order existed against the partnership—and it did. On the facts of the case, subsections (1) and (2A) of section 271 therefore led to opposite results. Which should prevail? 6.28

The Court of Appeal decided that subsection (1) prevailed. In essence, this was because the principle established in that subsection is a basic principle of insolvency law: 'no debt, no receiving order'. To read subsection (2A) as qualifying subsection (1), so that a bankruptcy order must be made even when the partnership debt on which the bankruptcy petition is founded has been paid, would be to negate this basic principle. 6.29

Here the court reached its conclusion in the light of the Act as a whole and its purpose and in the context of the underlying law. 6.30

[24] [1990] 1 Ch 773.

7
Principle 7: Unnatural Meaning

Principle 7:

7.1 **Very occasionally, it is clear that the legislature cannot objectively have intended the words it has used in the statute to have their ordinary meaning. If so, they are given the meaning that the legislature must objectively have intended.**
7.2 **The more unreasonable or unfair the result, the more unlikely it is that the legislature can have intended it.**
7.3 **Clear words are therefore needed to override a person's fundamental liberties.**

A. The Problem

Principle 7 needs to be understood in the light of the previous two principles. **7.1**

The starting point is Principle 5: words are nearly always given their ordinary meaning in context, taking account of the purpose of the statute. But Principle 5 recognises that it will not apply in every case. **7.2**

- Principle 6 is not an exception to Principle 5. Where an expression is truly ambiguous, the interpreter necessarily has a choice of ordinary meanings to make.
- Principle 7 is an exception to Principle 5. The ordinary meaning of words is displaced where it is necessary to prevent injustice. The difficult question is how frequently it should be used.

It is important to appreciate that Principle 5 is not some arcane rule that requires words to be given an entirely literal meaning. It is not a deterministic straightjacket from which the intelligent interpreter will want to escape. It requires words to be given their natural and ordinary meaning in the context of the legislation as a whole and in the light of the relevant background. It gives the interpreter the flexibility to match the outcome to the overall purpose of the legislation concerned. That cannot sensibly be described as arid literalism. **7.3**

It is for that reason that Principle 7 should rarely have to be applied. It only applies 'very occasionally' because it overrides the natural, contextual and purposive meaning of the words concerned. **7.4**

The courts recognise that it is necessary to read a contract contextually, and that the context can affect the meaning of the words written in the contract. In relation to contracts, the context can alter radically from case to case. The identity of the contracting parties can be very different. The nature and purpose of the contract can be very different. And the context in which the contract is set can be very different. The meaning of the words in the contract itself can take its colour from all three of those things. **7.5**

Principles of Statutory Interpretation. Richard Calnan, Oxford University Press. © Richard Calnan 2023.
DOI: 10.1093/oso/9780192864673.003.0008

7.6 This is much less of an issue in relation to statutory interpretation. A statute is a unilateral act which is always performed by the same person in the same way. The members of the legislature will change every so often, but it is the objective manifestation of the legislature—rather than the identity of any particular body of people—that is relevant to the interpretation exercise. The addressees of the legislation are broadly the same in most cases. The style of drafting is relatively uniform—especially when set against the various ways in which contracts can be drafted.

7.7 The result is that external context is of less relevance to the interpretation of statutes than contracts. Which might lead one to think that the courts will be less inclined to play fast and loose with statutory words than contractual words. This is because the more background is available in the interpretation process, the more likely it is that the court will find a way to use it to challenge the natural meaning of the words that have actually been used.

7.8 Another reason for thinking that statutes might be interpreted more strictly than contracts is that statutes tend to be better drafted than many contracts. In the realm of contractual interpretation, there is some acceptance of the idea that the more precise the drafting, the less room there is for manoeuvre in their interpretation.[1] That would suggest that statutes should generally be read quite strictly.

7.9 In practice, however, this has not been the case. Although statutes are professionally drafted and external context is of less relevance, the courts actually seem more inclined to interfere with the natural meaning of statutory words than contractual words. Why is that so?

7.10 Principle 5 describes the positivist view that Parliament is sovereign, that the words it uses mean what they say and that if a person has a grouse they can vote for someone else at the next election. But that positivist understanding of the law is tinged by an approach that has more to do with natural law. The social contract between Parliament and the people means that Parliament is there to legislate for the benefit of the people. When we interpret what Parliament says, we therefore need to do so in the light of an assumption that what it does will be done in a reasonable and fair way.[2] Hence Principle 7.

7.11 Lord Millett put it this way in *R (Edison First Power) v Central Valuation Officer*:[3]

> The Courts will presume that Parliament did not intend a statute to have consequences which are objectionable or undesirable; or absurd; or unworkable or impracticable; or merely inconvenient; or anomalous or illogical; or futile or pointless.
>
> But the strength of these presumptions depends on the degree to which a particular construction produces an unreasonable result. The more unreasonable a result, the less likely it is that Parliament intended it.

7.12 This is not a rule of law. It is a principle of interpretation. Parliament is sovereign. It can pass whatever laws it wants. But the effect of Principle 7 is that Parliament's words should be read—if they can—on the assumption that the outcome will be reasonable and fair.

[1] *Wood v Capita* [2017] AC 1173.
[2] *Inland Revenue Commissioners v Hinchy* [1960] AC 748 at 767 (Lord Reid).
[3] [2003] 4 All ER 209 at [116] and [117].

For this reason, the scope for intervention in statutory interpretation is greater than it is in relation to contractual interpretation. We do not expect all contracts to be fair. The law recognises that contracting parties have different bargaining powers and that they can enter into bad bargains. That necessarily limits the ability of a court to decide that something is unreasonable and therefore cannot have been what the parties objectively intended. But we do expect legislation to be reasonable and fair, and that gives a court greater scope to intervene. **7.13**

That can be dangerous. Unelected judges should not be able to put asunder what the elected Parliament has joined together. The difficult question is how far the courts can go, and that is a question of judgement. Different judges—and different lawyers—take different approaches. Some are much more likely to give effect to the natural and ordinary meaning of the words. Others will strain every sinew to find a way to establish a fair result. All lawyers fall somewhere along that spectrum. The real question is where the law draws the line. **7.14**

B. The Principle

Principle 7 has been described by a number of eminent judges. The following are some examples. **7.15**

In *Re British Concrete Pipe Association's Agreement*,[4] Sir John Donaldson MR said: **7.16**

> Our task, as I see it, is to construe the Act …, and in doing so the prima facie rule is that words have their ordinary meaning. But that is subject to the qualification that if, giving words their ordinary meaning, we are faced with extraordinary results which cannot have been intended by Parliament, we then have to move on to a second stage in which we re-examine the words and see whether they must in all the circumstances have been intended by Parliament to have a different meaning or a more restricted meaning.

In *Luke v Inland Revenue Commissioners*,[5] Lord Reid expressed the principle in this way: **7.17**

> To apply the words literally is to defeat the obvious intention of the legislation and to produce a wholly unreasonable result. To achieve the obvious intention and produce a reasonable result we must do some violence to the words. This is not a new problem, though our standard of drafting is such that it rarely emerges. The general principle is well settled. It is only where the words are absolutely incapable of a construction which will accord with the apparent intention of the provision and will avoid a wholly unreasonable result, that the words of the enactment must prevail.

In *Farrell v Alexander*,[6] Lord Simon said: **7.18**

> If a court of construction places itself in the position of the draftsman, acquires his knowledge, recognises his statutory objectives, tunes in to his linguistic register, and then ascertains the primary and natural meaning in their context of the words he has used, that will generally be an end of the task of construction. But occasionally something will go wrong. It may become apparent that the primary and natural meaning cannot be what Parliament

4 [1983] ICR 215 at 217.
5 [1963] AC 557 at 577.
6 [1977] AC 59 at 84.

intended: it produces injustice, absurdity, anomaly or contradiction, or it stultifies or runs counter to the statutory objective.

7.19 In *Stock v Frank Jones*,[7] Lord Simon described how limited the principle is. The following comments are particularly pertinent:

- '[In] a society living under the rule of law citizens are entitled to regulate their conduct according to what a statute has said, rather than by what it was meant to say.'
- '[What] strikes the lawyer as an injustice may well have seemed to the legislature as no more than the correction of a now unjustifiable privilege or as a particular misfortune necessarily or acceptably involved in the vindication of some supervening general social benefit.'
- '[An] unlooked-for and unsupportable injustice or anomaly can be readily rectified by legislation: this is far preferable to judicial contortion of the law to meet apparently hard cases with the result that ordinary citizens and their advisers hardly know where they stand.'
- 'All this is not to advocate judicial supineness: it is merely respectfully to commend a self-knowledge of judicial limitations, both personal and constitutional.'

7.20 Applying these principles to the facts of the case, Lord Simon went on to say:[8]

> [A] court would only be justified in departing from the plain words of the statute were it satisfied that: (1) there is clear and gross balance of anomaly; (2) Parliament, the legislative promoters and the draftsman could not have envisaged such anomaly, could not have been prepared to accept it in the interest of the supervening legislative objective; (3) the anomaly can be obviated without detriment to such legislative objective; (4) the language of the statute is susceptible of the modification required to obviate the anomaly.

7.21 Although it is generally accepted that it will take an extreme example to persuade a court to depart from the natural meaning of the words of a statute, there is not always unanimity about where the line should be drawn in practice. The judgment of the High Court of Australia in *Cooper Brookes (Wollongong) v The Commissioner of Taxation of the Commonwealth of Australia*[9] illustrates the judgemental nature of the exercise.

7.22 The *Cooper Brookes* case involved a deeming provision in tax legislation. Deeming provisions in statutes (as in contracts) are notoriously problematic. The taxpayer argued that the words of the statute should be given their natural meaning but, by a majority of four to one, the members of the High Court of Australia decided that it made no sense to read the deeming provision literally. Although they reached the same conclusion, the judges in the majority expressed their reasons rather differently.

7.23 Mason and Wilson JJ considered that, in some cases in the past, the rules of construction had been applied too rigidly.[10] They continued:[11]

> [When] the judge labels the operation of the statute as 'absurd', 'extraordinary', 'capricious', 'irrational' or 'obscure' he assigns a ground for concluding that the legislature could not

[7] [1978] 1 WLR 231 at 237.
[8] ibid.
[9] (1981) 147 CLR 297.
[10] ibid, 320.
[11] ibid, 321.

> have intended such an operation and that an alternative interpretation must be preferred. But the propriety of departing from the literal interpretation is not confined to situations described by these labels. It extends to any situation in which for good reason the operation of the statute on a literal reading does not conform to the legislative intent as ascertained from the provisions of the statute, including the policy which may be discerned from those provisions.

Gibbs CJ and Stephen J took a more limited approach to the circumstances in which the courts could intervene. In the words of Gibbs CJ:[12] **7.24**

> It is an elementary and fundamental principle that the object of the court, in interpreting a statute, 'is to see what is the intention expressed by the words used' ... And it is not unduly pedantic to begin with the assumption that words mean what they say ... Of course, no part of a statute can be considered in isolation from its context—the whole must be considered. If, when the section in question is read as part of the whole instrument, its meaning is clear and unambiguous, generally speaking 'nothing remains but to give effect to the unqualified words' ... There are cases where the result of giving words their ordinary meaning may be so irrational that the court is forced to the conclusion that the draftsman has made a mistake, and the canons of construction are not so rigid as to prevent a realistic solution to such a case ... However, if the language of a statutory provision is clear and unambiguous, and is consistent and harmonious with the other provisions of the enactment, and can be intelligibly applied to the subject matter with which it deals, it must be given its ordinary and grammatical meaning, even if it leads to a result that may seem inconvenient or unjust. To say this is not to insist on too literal an interpretation, or to deny that the court should seek the real intention of the legislature. The danger that lies in departing from the ordinary meaning of unambiguous provisions is that 'it may degrade into mere judicial criticism of the proprietary of the acts of the Legislature' ... ; it may lead judges to put their own ideas of justice or social policy in place of the words of the statute. On the other hand, if two constructions are open, the court will obviously prefer that which will avoid what it considers to be inconvenience or injustice. Since language, read in its context, very often proves to be ambiguous, this last mentioned rule is one that not infrequently falls to be applied.

Stephen J agreed, and explained why:[13] **7.25**

> Statute law, the direct product of the legislature, is perhaps the least appropriate field of all in which to indulge in judicial law-making. The corner of that field occupied by closely drafted statutes of high complexity should be particularly uninviting to the judicial law maker ... It can never be enough to justify judicial intervention that what has been enacted may seem to a court to lead to an irrational result ... Moreover, in the present circumstances, while the bare outcome of [the literal interpretation] is certainly unexpected and out of harmony with the legislative pattern which seems otherwise to emerge from these sections, it may not qualify for the epithet of irrational.

In *Attorney General's Reference (No 5 of 2002)*,[14] Lord Nicholls said that a statute should be interpreted so as to avoid a result that lacks rational justification, serves no useful purpose, achieves a bizarre effect or is unworkable. It has been seen that Lord Simon used a similar list **7.26**

[12] ibid, 304 and 305.
[13] ibid, 310.
[14] [2005] 1 AC 167 at [29].

of expressions in *Farrell v Alexander*[15] when he referred to injustice, absurdity, anomaly or contradiction.

7.27 Whichever word or phrase is used to describe the consequence that must be avoided, the overriding consideration is that the interpreter should try to avoid a result that is clearly unfair or unreasonable and therefore something that the legislature is unlikely objectively to have intended. The more unfair and unreasonable the result, the less likely it is that the legislature would have intended it.[16] And in considering these issues, it is important to bear to mind the qualifications described by Lord Simon in *Stock v Frank Jones*.[17] It is not up to unelected judges to say what Parliament has decreed. If the words are clear, then they must be applied, however unfair the result.

7.28 One of the issues that the interpreter has to face when applying this principle is to consider how much damage would have to be done to the statutory words in order to reach the desired result. In practice, it is normally much easier for a statutory provision to be 'read down' than 'read up'. In other words, it is easier to limit the scope of a statutory provision than to extend it.

7.29 It is not uncommon for a court to decide that the words of a statutory provision are subject to an unexpressed limitation. It is quite possible that when the legislature decided to provide for a particular matter, the provision was drafted broadly in order to capture the relevant mischief; but it may then—on its natural interpretation—go further than was intended. When drafting with a particular object in mind, it is not uncommon to overreach that objective unintentionally.

7.30 Extending the scope of a statutory provision is more problematical. It is possible that the provision has been drafted more narrowly than was intended, but it is more difficult to accept that this is so. If Parliament had intended the provision to cover a particular matter, why did it not say so? It is easier unintentionally to overstate than to understate.

7.31 As Spigelman CJ pointed out in the New South Wales Court of Appeal in *R v Young*,[18] it is easier to introduce words into a statutory provision where to do so will have the effect of reducing the scope of operation of the provision. That is not to say that words cannot be introduced to extend the scope of a provision, just that it is more difficult to do so. As the Victorian Court of Appeal demonstrated in *Director of Public Prosecutions v Leys*,[19] there are occasions when a court has found it necessary to read the words used in a statutory provision as if they had an extended operation, in order for the statutory purpose to be achieved.

7.32 The High Court of Australia expressed the principle this way in *Taylor v The Owners—Strata Plan No 11564*:[20]

> Consistently with this Court's rejection of the adoption of rigid rules in statutory construction, it should not be accepted that purposive construction may never allow of reading a provision as if it contained additional words (or omitted words) with the effect of expanding its field of operation.... The question whether the court is justified in reading a

[15] [1977] AC 59 at 84.
[16] *R (Edison First Power) v Central Valuation Officer* [2003] 4 All ER 209 at [117]; *Schuler v Wickman* [1974] AC 235 at 251.
[17] [1978] 1 WLR 231.
[18] (1999) 46 NSWLR 681.
[19] (2012) 44 VR 1 at [98].
[20] (2014) 253 CLR 531 at [37] and [38].

statutory provision as if it contained additional words or omitted words involves a judgment of matters of degree.

Never say never. But it is suggested that Spigelman CJ's instincts were correct when he cautioned against inserting words that would have the effect of extending the scope of operation of a statutory provision. It is more likely that the legislature inadvertently expressed a provision more widely than it intended. **7.33**

C. Examples

Six examples can illustrate how this principle is applied in practice: **7.34**

- *Re a Debtor (No 400—IO—1996)*;[21]
- *Re Lockwood*;[22]
- *Kammins Ballrooms Co v Zenith Investments (Torquay)*;[23]
- *R v Chief National Insurance Commissioner, ex parte Connor*;[24]
- *Agnew v Pardington*;[25] and
- *Federal Steam Navigation Co v Department of Trade and Industry*.[26]

In *Re a Debtor (No 400—IO—1996)*,[27] a husband and wife trading in partnership were insolvent. They proposed an individual involuntary arrangement with their creditors under the provisions of the insolvency legislation. Colonial was one of their principal creditors, but the debtors disputed the debt. When the notices were sent to creditors convening a meeting of creditors to vote on the proposal, no notice was sent to Colonial. But Colonial found out about the meeting and a representative of Colonial turned up at the meeting and voted. **7.35**

The question for the court was whether Colonial was entitled to do so. The relevant provision of the legislation provided that: 'every creditor who was given notice of the creditors' meeting is entitled to vote at the meeting'. The debtor's argument was that Colonial had not been given notice of the creditors' meeting and therefore it could not vote. **7.36**

Rimer J accepted that Colonial had not been given notice of the meeting, but he nevertheless decided that Colonial was entitled to vote. This was because, reading the insolvency legislation as a whole, an arrangement with creditors was an arrangement with all of the creditors; and therefore the rule concerning notices could not mean that only those creditors who had been given formal notice were entitled to vote. It would make no sense that a creditor who was erroneously not given notice, but who anyway learns of the meeting by other means, should not be entitled to attend and vote at it. **7.37**

Rimer J decided that the scheme of the relevant part of the Act and rules was that:[28] **7.38**

21 [1997] 1 WLR 1319.
22 [1958] 1 Ch 231.
23 [1971] AC 850.
24 [1981] 1 QB 758.
25 [2006] 2 NZLR 520.
26 [1974] 1 WLR 505.
27 [1997] 1 WLR 1319.
28 ibid, 1327–1328.

> [Individual] voluntary arrangements are intended to be put before all of the debtor's creditors and that notice of a ... meeting should be sent by the nominee to all of them. It is consistent with this that all such creditors should be entitled to attend and vote at a ... meeting of which they have actual notice, regardless of whether they were given notice of it ... It appears to me to make little sense of the legislation to interpret it as intended to achieve the result that a creditor who should have been given notice of such a meeting by the nominee, but was not, should be denied the right to vote at it if he is fortunate enough to have obtained sufficient notice of it by another route.

7.39 It is suggested that the result was justified—though perhaps for a different reason. In the context of the legislation, the reference to creditors who were 'given notice' would normally mean those who have been given notice in accordance with the rules. That is the natural meaning of those words. But this would mean that someone who should have been given notice and was wrongly omitted would have no vote even if they found out. That surely cannot have been intended. This problem can be avoided by reading the reference to those who were 'given notice' as being those who 'received notice', even if not as a result of a formal notice given in accordance with the rules. That is not the natural meaning of the words, but it is a legitimate—if strained—reading of the words in this context.

7.40 *Re Lockwood*[29] concerned the interpretation of section 47(5) of the Administration of Estates Act 1925. The problem was that a literal reading of the section indicated that the estate of a person who had died intestate would go to the Crown as *bona vacantia* if he or she did not have surviving primary issue, even if their deceased primary issue themselves had surviving issue.

7.41 Harman J refused to accept this. He said[30] that 'it is clear that so anomalous a result cannot have been intended by the legislature'. And he continued:[31] 'This is a result so capricious and absurd ... that the court is entitled to strain every nerve to avoid it.'

7.42 Harman J said:[32]

> [Counsel for the Crown] contended that to ignore words is only legitimate in order to make sense of what is otherwise nonsense, that here the subsection as it stands has an effect not absolutely repugnant to the rest of the statute, while, if the words be ignored, the subsection has no effect at all. Further, he says a treatment so drastic can only be justified where the court can see what the legislature did intend, whereas here no plain intention can be gathered. I feel the force of this line of reasoning, though it leads to a most lame and impotent conclusion ... On the whole, I have come to the conclusion that I am entitled to ignore the words 'or issue of any member of that class' or, rather, to treat them as not binding me to construe the word 'class' in the earlier part of the subsection as confined to the primary class of aunts and uncles. I take this course because I am convinced that Parliament, in laying down rules for ascertaining next-of-kin, cannot have intended to promote those more remote over those nearer in blood.

7.43 This is another case where what was really needed was common sense. Harman J was clearly concerned about simply ignoring a number of words in the subsection, but he was able to

29 [1958] 1 Ch 231.
30 ibid, 234.
31 ibid, 236.
32 ibid, 238.

reach the same result by a different method—which was to define the word 'class' in two different ways in the subsection. This would not normally be acceptable but, because the effect of not doing it would be to create an absurdity, he was able to do so.

Kammins Ballrooms Co v Zenith Investments (Torquay)[33] concerned the meaning of the following words of section 29(3) of the Landlord and Tenant Act 1954: **7.44**

> No application [for a new tenancy] under subsection 1 of section 24 of this Act shall be entertained [by the court] unless it is made not less two nor more than four months after the giving of the landlord's notice under section 25 of this Act . . .

The tenant made an application less than two months after the giving of the landlord's notice. The majority of the House of Lords nevertheless decided that the application was valid. The landlords could waive the time limit; and on the facts they had waived it. The court reached this conclusion because it did not believe that Parliament would have intended to have restricted the power of the court to entertain the claim. **7.45**

Lord Diplock applied what he described as a purposive, rather than a literal, approach to the task of statutory interpretation and decided that the words contained a procedural requirement imposed for the benefit of one party alone and that it could therefore be waived by them. **7.46**

Viscount Dilhorne, dissented. He said:[34] **7.47**

> Our task is to interpret section 29(3) 'according to the intent of them that made it' (Coke: 4 Inst: 330) . . .
>
> The appellants' contention here is that the words 'No application ... shall be entertained' must be interpreted as meaning that an application shall in certain circumstances be entertained notwithstanding that it is made to early or too late. That seems to me to involve implying something wholly inconsistent with the words expressly used.
>
> True it is that English is a flexible language but that does not mean that one can disregard the natural and ordinary meaning of the words used unless it is apparent that some other meaning was intended.

This may simply be a case in which the court used the context and purpose of the legislation in order to achieve a particular result. A person can waive a right that is solely for their benefit. But the clarity of the dissenting judgment shows how difficult it was do this in the light of the apparently clear words used. **7.48**

The fourth example is *R v Chief National Insurance Commissioner, ex parte Connor*.[35] Under the Social Security Act 1975, a woman was entitled to a widow's allowance if she had been widowed and certain conditions had been fulfilled. In the particular case concerned, all the conditions were fulfilled, but the woman had in fact killed her husband. She was not convicted of murder, but of manslaughter, and it was established that her act was deliberate, conscious and intentional. The question for the Queen's Bench Divisional Court was whether she was nevertheless entitled to the allowance. There was nothing in the wording of the Act that disentitled her by reason of the fact that she was responsible for her own widowhood. **7.49**

[33] [1971] AC 850.
[34] ibid, 869.
[35] [1981] 1 QB 758.

7.50 The court decided that she was not entitled to the allowance. The principal judgment was given by Lord Lane CJ. He indicated that it would not be in every case of manslaughter that the allowance would be denied, but here it was because of the deliberate, conscious and intentional nature of the act.

7.51 Lord Lane said:[36]

> [In] each case it is not the label which the law applies to the crime which has been committed but the nature of the crime itself which in the end will dictate whether public policy demands the court to drive the applicant from the seat of justice.

7.52 In this case, the court had to grapple with the principle that Parliament is expected to act reasonably and fairly. Would it have intended a widow to obtain the pension as a result of the deliberate, conscious and intentional killing of her husband? If one had asked Parliament whether it had intended someone to have an allowance if she had done away with her husband, it is reasonable to assume that the answer would have been no. Although there is no doctrine of implied terms in the law of statutory interpretation, there is an analogy here with the 'Oh, of course!' test of implied terms in contracts.[37]

7.53 *Agnew v Pardington*[38] is a New Zealand case in which the courts had to grapple with the meaning of section 30A of the Receiverships Act 1993. It provided:

> If property has been disposed of by a receiver, all security interests in the property and its proceeds that are subordinate to the security interest of the person in whose interests the receiver was appointed are extinguished on the disposition of the property.

7.54 The question in this case was whether section 30A had the effect of turning a subsequent secured creditor into an unsecured creditor. Creditor A had a first charge over a company's assets. Creditor B had a second charge over the same assets. Receivers were appointed by creditor A, and the assets were sold. The net proceeds of sale were sufficient to repay creditor A in full, and therefore there was a surplus for other creditors. Should it be paid to creditor B, as the subsequent secured creditor, or to the liquidator on behalf of all creditors *pari passu*?

7.55 Under the general law, the position was perfectly clear. Creditor B, as the holder of a second charge over the assets, was entitled to the remaining proceeds once creditor A had been paid. The receivers held the surplus proceeds on trust first for the second chargee and, thereafter, for the liquidator on behalf of the unsecured creditors.

7.56 But, on the face of it, section 30A seemed to have extinguished creditor B's right to be paid in priority to unsecured creditors. It provided that all subordinate security interests in the property 'and its proceeds' were extinguished when the property was sold. This indicated that creditor B had no right to the surplus proceeds in the hands of the receivers.

7.57 The problem with this interpretation was that it flew in the face of common sense. The sale of the charged assets by a receiver on behalf of creditor A must release the charged assets from the charges both of creditor A and of creditor B. Only by doing so, could the purchaser get good title free from encumbrances. But the net proceeds of sale should then be held on trust, first for creditor A, secondly for creditor B and thirdly for unsecured creditors.

36 ibid, 765.
37 Compare eg *Associated Japanese Bank v Credit du Nord* [1989] 1 WLR 255.
38 [2006] 2 NZLR 520.

The likely purpose of section 30A was to give effect to this principle, so that the charged assets would be released from the security, but not any surplus proceeds. The problem with this reading of the section was that it explicitly referred both to the property and to its proceeds—thereby, on the face of it, expressly extinguishing the rights of creditor B to both. 7.58

This led the first instance judge (Williams J) to conclude that Parliament intended to deprive creditor B of its security. But this decision was overruled by the New Zealand Court of Appeal, the judgment of the court being given by Glazebrook J. In order to avoid the problem of the express reference to 'proceeds', the court gave that expression a narrow meaning. It decided that the expression 'proceeds' in the section referred to any proceeds of a *subsequent* sale of the charged assets, not the proceeds of sale of the disposal by the receivers. That is definitely not the natural meaning of that expression, but it was the one which the Court of Appeal decided must have been intended by Parliament. It essentially did a rescue job on some very bad drafting. 7.59

This goes beyond a purposive interpretation of section 30A. It is hard to see how even a purposive interpretation could effectively read the words 'and its proceeds' out of all practical existence. It is suggested that the reason for the decision was that the alternative was so absurd that the court had to find a way to avoid it, and it was able to do so by reading the words 'proceeds' very restrictively. 7.60

The final example is *Federal Steam Navigation Co v Department of Trade and Industry*.[39] Section 1 of the Oil in Navigable Waters Act 1955 provided that if oil was discharged from a British ship into a prohibited sea area, 'the owner or master of the ship' was guilty of an offence. Both the owner and the master were convicted, and they appealed against conviction on the basis that only one of them could be convicted because the 'or' was disjunctive. 7.61

By a majority of three to two, the House of Lords dismissed the appeal. They were both guilty. 7.62

Lords Reid and Morris dissented. Essentially, they took the view that 'or' means 'or' and not 'and'. It would not be unreasonable, absurd or unjust to give the word 'or' its ordinary meaning. 7.63

Lords Wilberforce, Simon and Salmon were in the majority. They took the opposite approach. To give the word 'or' its natural meaning would be to produce an arbitrary result, contrary to legal principle. Lord Salmon said:[40] 7.64

> There is certainly no doubt that generally it is assumed that 'or' is intended to be used disjunctively and the word 'and' conjunctively. Nevertheless, it is equally well settled that if so to construe those words leads to an unintelligible or absurd result, the courts will read the word 'or' conjunctively and 'and' disjunctively as the case may be; or, to put it another way, substitute the one word for the other. This principle has been applied time and again even in penal statutes ...

This case is instructive in illustrating that, although the test is clear—and was accepted by all their Lordships—the application of the test to the facts of a particular case is essentially a matter of judgement on which reasonable people can hold differing views. 7.65

39 [1974] 1 WLR 505.
40 ibid, 524.

D. Extreme Examples

7.66 The examples that have been discussed so far show the courts grappling with a wish to do justice where the words of the legislation make it difficult for them to do so. Difficult, but not impossible. But there are cases where the courts carry this desire to breaking point, and beyond. In order to give an understanding of the types of circumstance in which this happens, a number of examples will be discussed. These are:

- *McMonagle v Westminster City Council*;[41]
- *Nokes v Doncaster Amalgamated Collieries*;[42]
- *Pollen Estate Trustee Co v Revenue and Customs Commissioners*;[43]
- *Gisborne v Burton*;[44]
- *R (Noone) v Governor of Drake Hall Prison*;[45]
- *Frucor Beverages v Rio Beverages*;[46]
- *R (UNISON) v Lord Chancellor*;[47] and
- *Yemshaw v Hounslow London Borough Council*.[48]

7.67 In *McMonagle v Westminster City Council*,[49] the council had the statutory power to license 'sex encounter establishments'. They were defined to mean premises at which certain types of performances 'which are not unlawful' were held. The defendant ran such an establishment, and was charged with using the premises without a licence. His defence was that the performances at the premises were unlawful at common law and therefore that the premises were not a 'sex encounter establishment' as defined, and so did not require a licence. Perhaps unsurprisingly, the Crown Court, a Divisional Court of the Queen's Bench Division and the House of Lords all found him guilty.

7.68 In the House of Lords, Lord Bridge gave the principal judgment. He commented that their Lordships found it both startling and unedifying that the defendant was in a position to dispute his guilt on the ground that he was guilty of a graver offence. The purpose of the legislation was for the London Borough Councils to be able to exercise more effective control over sex establishments in Greater London. He entertained no doubt that the court would be giving effect to the true intention of the legislature if it could avoid the absurdity by treating the phrase 'which are not unlawful' as mere surplusage. He recognised that it is a strong course to take, and one which displays an unusual degree of ineptitude in the drafting.

7.69 Lord Bridge said:[50]

> The presumption that every word in a statute must be given some effective meaning is a strong one, but the courts have on occasion been driven to disregard particular words or phrases when, by giving effect to them, the operation of the statute would be rendered insensible, absurd or ineffective to achieve its evident purpose.

41 [1990] 2 AC 716.
42 [1940] AC 1014.
43 [2013] 1 WLR 3785.
44 [1989] 1 QB 390.
45 [2010] 1WLR 1743.
46 [2001] 2 NZLR 604.
47 [2017] 3 WLR 409.
48 [2011] 1 WLR 433.
49 [1990] 2 AC 716.
50 ibid, 726.

The main object of the provision was to require premises of this kind to be licensed but, in order to avoid the frustration of that object, 'it is both necessary and legitimate that the words "which are not unlawful" should be treated as surplusage and as having been introduced by incompetent draftsmanship'.[51] 7.70

Nokes v Doncaster Amalgamated Collieries[52] concerned section 154 of the Companies Act 1929. This provided for the amalgamation of two companies by 'the transfer to the transferee company of the whole or any part of the undertaking and of the property or liabilities of any transferor company'. Overruling the Court of Appeal, the House of Lords decided by a majority of four to one that this section did not enable a contract of employment to be transferred. 7.71

The majority in the House of Lords relied on a fundamental principle of the common law—that a citizen is entitled to choose their employer—as a reason for not giving effect to the apparent meaning of the words of the statute.[53] 7.72

Lord Romer dissented. As a former Chancery judge, he understood what was involved and he explained why the legislation was there—in order to enable amalgamations to take place more easily. He went on to say:[54] 7.73

> My Lords, the more closely I examine the section the more I am convinced that the object of the Legislature was to enable the Court by an order to make a complete substitution of the transferee company for the transferor company as regards the whole the rights and liabilities of the latter without exception . . .

In the result, the court gave a limited interpretation to the legislation in order to ensure that it did not change the underlying law. On any measure, that is a curious approach to take. Surely the whole point of a statute is to change the law? The most cogent judgment was given by Lord Romer, and his is the approach that has been followed in subsequent legislation. It is hard to avoid the conclusion that the purpose of the statute was exactly as Lord Romer described and that the majority managed to subvert that purpose. 7.74

In *Pollen Estate Trustee Co v Revenue and Customs Commissioners*,[55] the question was whether a charitable institution that had contributed a proportion of the purchase price of property acquired by a non-charity was entitled to exemption from stamp duty land tax in relation to its proportion of the beneficial interest in the property. Under the relevant tax legislation, there was relief for charities from stamp duty land tax on land transactions if 'the purchaser is a charity' and certain other conditions were fulfilled. 7.75

The question in this case was whether, if a charity had an undivided beneficial interest in the property as a tenant in common, it was able to comply with the requirements of this section. The Revenue said that the conditions were not fulfilled because the purchaser was not a charity. The charity argued that stamp duty land tax was charged on each individual beneficial interest and therefore that, if one of the purchasers was a charity, it would get relief for its part of the beneficial interest. 7.76

[51] ibid, 727.
[52] [1940] AC 1014.
[53] ibid, 1022 (Viscount Simon) and 1033 (Lord Atkin).
[54] ibid, 1044.
[55] [2013] 1 WLR 3785.

7.77 In the Court of Appeal, the principal judgment was given by Lewison LJ. He agreed with the Revenue that where there are a number of people with beneficial interests in acquired property, there is only one equitable estate. The interest is held by tenants in common, but their shares are undivided and the equitable estate is not divided. The subject matter of the transaction was the entirety of the interest, and it is that interest by reference to which stamp duty land tax is levied.[56]

7.78 That would seem to have ended the matter in favour of the Revenue. But Lewison LJ went on to find for the taxpayer on a different ground. He said:[57]

> [It] seems to me that there is a sufficient 'policy imperative' to justify the reading I favour ... In substance what this means is that the exemption would apply as regards that proportion of the beneficial interest that is attributable to the undivided share held by the charity for qualifying charitable purposes ... In my judgment this reading is necessary in order to give effect to what must have been Parliament's intention as regards the taxation of charities. There has been no principled reason advanced why a charity should be exempt from [stamp duty land tax] in the situations to which I have referred ... ; but not be entitled to any relief at all on its proportionate undivided share in a jointly acquired property. Not to afford a charity relief in such circumstances would, in my judgment, be capricious.

7.79 The court therefore read the words:

> A land transaction is exempt from charge if the purchaser is a charity ...

as meaning:

> A land transaction is exempt from charge to the extent that a person who has contributed to the purchase price and accordingly holds a beneficial interest in the property is a charity ...

7.80 The court had clearly and compellingly demonstrated why the actual claim put forward by the charities was unsustainable: it simply did not fit with property law and the structure of the transaction. But the court then decided that Parliament must have made a mistake in the drafting and that there was a way of giving effect to what it must have intended. This is difficult to accept. There was absolutely no evidence that that was the policy. It was simply that the Revenue could not come up with a convincing reason why relief should not be available in this circumstance. That is not a justification for rewriting the statute. It may have been odd that it was only in certain circumstances that relief was available, but that is not unusual. Lines have to be drawn somewhere in tax legislation. We have to take the tax legislation as we find it. It is not up to a court to rewrite the legislation or move the lines.

7.81 *Gisborne v Burton*[58] is, it is suggested, another case in which the court went too far in giving effect to what it thought was the just result.

7.82 The Agricultural Holdings Act 1948 contained provisions to protect the tenancies of agricultural tenants. In essence, if they were given notice to quit by the landlord, they could serve a counter-notice that gave them protection from eviction. The protection applied to tenants, but not to sub-tenants.

[56] ibid, [40] and [41].
[57] ibid, [49].
[58] [1989] 1 QB 390.

In order to take advantage of this distinction between tenants and sub-tenants, a farmer granted a tenancy of his farm to his wife, who on the same day granted a sub-tenancy of the land to the intended tenant at the same rent. The sub-tenant was aware that this was the reason why the transaction was effected in this way. When the farmer died, his personal representatives gave notice to quit to his wife, the tenant. She did not serve a counter-notice, and the personal representatives then claimed possession of the land. **7.83**

By a majority of two to one, the Court of Appeal held that the farmer's personal representatives were not entitled to claim possession of the land. The effect of the scheme as a whole was that, by pre-ordained steps rather than by a single step, the landlord had granted an agricultural tenancy to the sub-tenant, and that therefore the sub-tenant could not be deprived of the power to stay the operation of a notice to quit if one had been given to him. The court recognised that the transaction was not a sham, but the majority nevertheless held that the scheme did not work. **7.84**

Dillon and Russell LJJ were in the majority. They considered[59] that the arrangement was an artificial device to disguise the grant of a tenancy to the sub-tenant and to evade the Agricultural Holdings Act 1948 by two pre-ordained steps. They therefore decided that the landlord had granted an agricultural tenancy to the sub-tenant. **7.85**

Ralph Gibson LJ dissented. The transactions were not shams, in the sense that the parties were saying one thing and doing something else. The court could not disregard the real transaction and treat the parties as having entered into some other transaction.[60] **7.86**

It is suggested that Ralph Gibson LJ gave the better judgment. Section 24(1) of the Agricultural Holdings Act 1948 said that where notice to quit an agricultural holding was given to the tenant, and the tenant served a counter-notice in accordance with the section, then the tenant could remain in occupation. The effect of this decision was that 'tenant' was held to include 'sub-tenant'. This collapsed the head lease/sub-lease structure and converted it into a single lease for the purpose of applying the words of the legislation. It is hard to think of any legal basis on which that could be done unless expressly provided for in legislation. **7.87**

In *R (Noone) v Governor of Drake Hall Prison*,[61] a statutory instrument provided that certain statutory provisions would not apply 'in relation to any sentence of imprisonment of less than 12 months (whether or not such a sentence is imposed to run concurrently or consecutively with another such sentence)'. The Court of Appeal decided that the words meant what they said, but the Supreme Court decided that they could not. The results were so absurd that the words could not mean what they said. **7.88**

Lord Phillips decided[62] that the words **7.89**

> (whether or not such a sentence is imposed to run concurrently or consecutively with another such sentence)

in fact meant:

> (other than a sentence which is imposed to run concurrently or consecutively with a sentence of 12 months or more).

59 ibid, 400 and 410.
60 ibid, 406.
61 [2010] 1 WLR 1743.
62 ibid, [32].

That appears to create substantially the opposite effect of what was written. Lord Mance came up with a different formulation which had broadly the same effect.[63]

7.90 This is quite a recent example of the absurdity principle. It had been argued that the words did not permit any other conclusion than that they meant what they said, but the Supreme Court disagreed. The adjectives that the court used to describe the outcome which had to be avoided included:

- absurd;
- irrational;
- indefensible;
- astonishing;
- incapable of contemplation;
- intolerable; and
- anomalous.

7.91 The best argument in favour of the decision of the Supreme Court in this case is that Parliament is assumed to act reasonably and fairly. The countervailing argument is that Parliament's intention must be judged from the words it has used. It may be that this a stronger argument when used against the executive and that here, when the argument is used in favour of the citizen, it is likely to have more traction.

7.92 In *Frucor Beverages v Rio Beverages*,[64] the question at issue was whether communications between patent attorneys and their clients were privileged. Whether or not they were privileged depended on the interpretation of section 34 of the Evidence Amendment Act (No 2) 1980 of New Zealand. That section prevented a patent attorney from disclosing relevant information without the client's consent, but it did not expressly provide for the relevant documents to be privileged in the hands of the client.

7.93 The issue was therefore whether the relevant section 'should be given its literal meaning or whether it is capable of a purposive construction which would depart from that meaning'.[65] The majority (Thomas and Blanchard JJ) give it a purposive meaning. McGrath J would have given it a literal meaning.

7.94 Thomas J accepted that, read literally, section 34 was not concerned with disclosure by the client but, having reviewed the legislative history of the enactment, he concluded that:[66]

> Parliament intended to confer a statutory privilege on both patent attorneys and their clients in respect of the defined 'protected information'. A literal reading of the section would deprive it of that purpose.

7.95 Thomas J then continued:[67]

> Once satisfied that Parliament intended to confer the privilege on both patent attorneys and their clients in respect of the defined protected communications, the Court should strive to arrive at a meaning which gives effect to that intention. The principles of interpretation

63 ibid, [73].
64 [2001] 2 NZLR 604.
65 ibid, [1] (Thomas J).
66 ibid, [21].
67 ibid, [28].

> which assist the Courts in that exercise are well established. They reflect commonsense propositions and should, therefore, be applied sensibly. Thus, it would be less than sensible to presume that Parliament intended to legislate in a manner which is absurd. Indeed, it would be uncharitable, if not presumptuous, for the Courts to approach the task of interpreting Parliament's legislation on any other basis. Thus, the courts have come to give the concept of 'absurdity' a wide meaning, using it to include virtually any result which is unworkable or impracticable, inconvenient, anomalous or illogical, futile or pointless, artificial, or productive of a disproportionate counter-mischief.

It had been argued that the wording was so plain as to be 'intractable', and that to adopt a purposive interpretation would be to depart from the text of the section. Thomas J accepted that 'it would require something in the nature of rewriting rather than the insertion of a word or phrase' to achieve Parliament's will,[68] but he continued:[69] **7.96**

> We regard this interpretation as permissible without finding it necessary to either fix on any particular wording or the omission of any particular wording. The necessary implication can be made. It would frustrate Parliament's intended purpose not to give effect to it merely because there are no particular words or phrases that are ambiguous or obscure to which the purposive interpretation can be attached.

Thomas J added:[70] **7.97**

> [There] is no inexorable logic about the distinction between interpretation and judicial legislation. It is all a question of degree. Different minds may differ as to when the boundary between interpretation and judicial legislation is reached and where the line is to be drawn.

This is an interesting case because of the very clear and persuasive judgment of Thomas J. Much of what he said is clearly correct. There is no inexorable logic in drawing a line between interpretation and legislation. It is ultimately a question of judgement. But here the court rewrote the legislation. It is an example of the courts finding the purpose from outside the statutory words and then rewriting the words to fit that purpose. **7.98**

There have been other cases where it is hard to avoid the conclusion that the court performed a legislative role rather than a judicial one. Two examples from the Supreme Court can illustrate the problem. **7.99**

R (UNISON) v Lord Chancellor[71] concerned section 42 of the Tribunals, Courts and Enforcement Act 2007. That section gave the Lord Chancellor power by Order to prescribe fees in relation to employment tribunals. An Order was made, and it went through the appropriate parliamentary procedure and was published. UNISON argued that the Order was unlawful. The Divisional Court and the Court of Appeal dismissed the claim, but UNISON's appeal was allowed by the Supreme Court. **7.100**

The principal judgment was given by Lord Reed, who said:[72] **7.101**

> In determining the extent of the power conferred on the Lord Chancellor by section 42(1) of the 2007 Act, the court must consider not only the text of that provision, but also the

68 ibid, [34].
69 ibid, [35].
70 ibid, [39].
71 [2017] 3 WLR 409.
72 ibid, [65].

> constitutional principles which underlie the text, and the principles of statutory interpretation which give effect to those principles. In that regard, there are two principles which are of particular importance in this case. One is the constitutional right of access to justice: that is to say, access to the courts (and tribunals ...). The other is the rule that 'specific statutory rights are not be cut down by subordinate legislation passed under the vires of a different Act ...'

7.102 The court decided that the fees order would reduce access to employment tribunals and therefore that it had not been authorised by the primary legislation. 'Even where a statutory power authorises an intrusion upon the right of access to the courts, it is interpreted as authorising only such a degree of intrusion as is reasonably necessary to fulfil the objective of the provision in question.'[73]

7.103 In the result, the court held that an Act that authorised the Lord Chancellor to prescribe fees in relation to employment tribunals did not allow him to do so if the effect of the fees he prescribed was to limit the practical likelihood of employees being able to have access to employment tribunals. The decision may owe something to the fact that the case concerned access to courts and tribunals, which is clearly a very sensitive issue for the Supreme Court.

7.104 In *Yemshaw v Hounslow London Borough Council*,[74] the question was whether a women was homeless within the meaning of the Housing Act 1996. That depended on whether she had been subject to 'violence' or the threat of it. In fact, she had not been subjected to physical violence.

7.105 The housing officers decided that she was not homeless as her husband had never actually hit her or threatened to do so. A review panel agreed, as did a first instance judge and the Court of Appeal. But the Supreme Court decided that 'violence' was not a term of art and was capable of including something that did not involve physical violence.

7.106 The principal judgment was given by Baroness Hale. She said[75] that although physical violence is a natural meaning of the word violence, it is not the only natural meaning. 'It is commonplace to speak of the violence of a person's language or of a person's feelings.'

7.107 Baroness Hale went on to say:[76]

> 'Violence' is a word very similar to the word 'family'. It is not a term of art. It is capable of bearing several meanings and applying to many different types of behaviour. These can change and develop over time ....
>
> That being the case, it seems clear to me that, whatever may have been the position in 1977, the general understanding of the harm which intimate partners or other family members may do to one another has moved on.

7.108 The *Shorter Oxford Dictionary* defines violence as the exercise of physical force so as to inflict injury on, or damage to, persons or property. Parliamentary draftsmen do not draft in metaphors. Humpty Dumpty might be expected to misuse words in this way,[77] but not lawyers,

[73] ibid, [80].
[74] [2011] 1 WLR 433.
[75] ibid, [19].
[76] ibid, [27] and [28].
[77] 'When *I* use a word,' Humpty Dumpty said in a rather scornful tone, 'it means just what I choose it to mean—neither more nor less' (Lewis Carroll, *Through the Looking-Glass* (Macmillan, 1866), ch 6).

and certainly not judges. The words of Tom Stoppard in *The Real Thing* seem apposite:[78] 'I don't think writers are sacred, but words are. They deserve respect.'

It is perhaps instructive that, in both of the last two cases, all the lower courts went one way and the Supreme Court went the other. They are both extreme cases of judicial intervention akin to judicial legislation. **7.109**

But they are not the norm. The true principle was expressed by Lord Reid in *Jones v Director of Public Prosecutors*:[79] **7.110**

> It is a cardinal principle applicable to all kinds of statutes that you may not for any reason attach to a statutory provision a meaning which the words of that provision cannot reasonably bear.

An example of the normal approach of our highest court to questions of this kind is the decision of the House of Lords in *Inland Revenue Commissioners v Hinchy*.[80] Section 25(3) of the Income Tax Act 1952 provided that: 'A person who neglects … to deliver … a true … return … shall … forfeit the sum of £20 and treble the tax which he ought to be charged under this Act … ' Mr Hinchy understated the interest that he had earned by £14 5*s*. The Inland Revenue claimed a penalty against him of £438—£20 plus treble the total amount of tax payable by him in the relevant tax year. **7.111**

Diplock J and the Court of Appeal considered that the section did not authorise this, and they gave judgment for £62 15*s* (that is, £20 + (3 × £14 5*s*)). The House of Lords unanimously decided that the words of the section were clear, and it allowed the Inland Revenue to recover the penalty of £438. **7.112**

Diplock J considered the Crown's contention to be absurd and unjust, and thought a reasonable meaning of the words 'the tax which he ought to be charged under this Act' was the tax which the taxpayer ought to have been charged but that he had not been charged by reason of the default. The Court of Appeal took the same approach. It considered that the Crown's contention was so extravagant and shocking as to be contrary to ordinary justice. **7.113**

The House of Lords disagreed. It considered that it had to apply the natural and ordinary meaning of the words, however unfair the result. **7.114**

Lord Reid said:[81] **7.115**

> Difficulties and extravagant results … caused Diplock J and the Court of Appeal to search for an interpretation which would yield a more just result. What we must look for is the intention of Parliament, and I also find it difficult to believe that Parliament ever really intended the consequences which flow from the appellants' contention. But we can only take the intention of the Parliament from the words which they have used in the Act, and therefore the question is whether these words are capable of a more limited construction. If not, then we must apply them as they stand, however unreasonable or unjust the consequences, and however strongly we may suspect that this is not the real intention of Parliament.

Lord Reid continued:[82] **7.116**

[78] Tom Stoppard, *The Real Thing* (Faber & Faber, 1982).
[79] [1962] AC 635 at 662.
[80] [1960] AC 748.
[81] ibid, 767.
[82] ibid, 768.

> One is entitled and indeed bound to assume that Parliament intends to act reasonably, and therefore to prefer a reasonable interpretation of a statutory provision if there is any choice. But I regret that I am unable to agree that this case leaves me with any choice.

7.117 It is suggested that this case illustrates the orthodox approach to statutory interpretation. The result of legislation might appear to be absurd, but nevertheless the words are so clear that the result cannot be avoided.[83] Some recent decisions of the Supreme Court might lead the observer to consider that the courts are now taking a more interventionist approach. But the way that the Supreme Court returned contractual interpretation to orthodoxy in *Arnold v Britton* gives some reason to believe that orthodoxy will also return to statutory interpretation.

E. Rectification

7.118 Rectification is one area where statutory interpretation differs from contractual interpretation in a material way. A contracting party who wants to challenge the natural meaning of the words of the contract has two quite distinct means of doing so. One approach is to argue, as a matter of interpretation of the words of the contract, that they do not mean what they appear to say because the result is so absurd that the parties cannot objectively have intended it; and therefore that they must mean something else. The other approach is to try to get the contract rectified on the basis that the contract as written does not represent what the parties had actually agreed at the time the contract was entered into. The evidential requirements are difficult to satisfy but, if they are, then, from the date of the order of rectification, the contract will be amended to reflect the true intention.

7.119 The first of these approaches is also available in relation to statutory interpretation. Indeed, in one sense it may be said to have more relevance to statutory interpretation. That is because we do not necessarily expect contracting parties to act reasonably. Parties have different bargaining powers, and people make bad bargains. Statutes, on the other hand, are always made by the same body, are drafted in a relatively consistent style and, most importantly, we are on stronger ground when we assume that the legislature is intending to act fairly and reasonably. That is its job. For all these reasons, it might be expected that the courts will intervene more frequently in statutory than in contractual interpretation.

7.120 But the second approach is not available when interpreting statutes. There is no doctrine of rectification in relation to statutes. If the legislature gets it wrong, then it has to amend the statute. If it gets it really wrong, it may have to do so retrospectively.

7.121 The result is that it is not possible to apply to a court and ask it to confirm that what the legislature really intended was something different from the words that it used and that, in the future, the words will be changed to reflect that intention. The courts are restricted to interpreting the words. But what they can do is to decide that the words as written cannot possibly mean what they appear to say, and therefore that they mean something else.

7.122 Three cases illustrate this point:

- *Inco Europe v First Choice Distribution*;[84]

[83] *Secretary of State for Media and Sport v BT Pension Scheme Trustees* [2014] EWCA Civ 958 at [77] to [83].
[84] [2000] 1 WLR 586.

- *Bogdanic v The Secretary of State for the Home Department*;[85] and
- *R (Confederation of Passenger Transport UK) v Humber Bridge Board*.[86]

Inco Europe v First Choice Distribution[87] involved the interpretation of a provision of the Supreme Court Act 1981, which had been amended by the Arbitration Act 1996. The section provided that 'No appeal shall lie to the Court of Appeal... (g) except as provided by Part I of the Arbitration Act 1996, from any decision of the High Court under that Part...' **7.123**

What had happened was that the High Court had given judgment under section 9 of the Arbitration Act 1996, which was contained in Part I of the Arbitration Act 1996. Relying on these amended words of the Supreme Court Act 1981, the successful party in the High Court argued that no appeal was available because nowhere in Part I was there any provision for an appeal from section 9. **7.124**

The Court of Appeal and the House of Lords decided that this cannot have been what was intended. A drafting mistake had been made when amending the legislation. It was clear from the amendments that had been made that what had been intended was to confine the limitation on appeals to cases where Part I itself provided for an appeal. Since Part I did not provide for an appeal in relation to section 9, it followed that the limitation contained in the Supreme Court Act 1981 did not apply. The words 'from any decision of the High Court under that Part' were to be read as meaning 'from any decision of the High Court under a section in that Part which provides for an appeal from such decision'.[88] **7.125**

Lord Nicholls (with whom all the other judges agreed) said:[89] **7.126**

> I freely acknowledge that this interpretation of [the section] involves reading words into the paragraph. It has long been established that the role of the courts in construing legislation is not confined to resolving ambiguities in statutory language. The court must be able to correct obvious drafting errors. In suitable cases, in discharging its interpretative function the court will add words, or omit words or substitute words...
>
> This power is confined to plain cases of drafting mistakes. The courts are ever mindful that their constitutional role in this field is interpretative. They must abstain from any course which might have the appearance of judicial legislation. A statute is expressed in language approved and enacted by the legislature. So the courts exercise considerable caution before adding or omitting or substituting words. Before interpreting a statute in this way the court must be abundantly sure of three matters: (1) the intended purpose of the statute or provision in question; (2) that by inadvertence the draftsman and Parliament failed to give effect to that purpose in the provision in question; and (3) the substance of the provision Parliament would have made, although not necessarily the precise words Parliament would have used, had the error in the Bill been noticed. The third of these conditions is of crucial importance. Otherwise any attempt to determine the meaning of the enactment would cross the boundary between construction and legislation...
>
> Sometimes, even when these conditions are met, the court may find itself inhibited from interpreting the statutory provision in accordance with what it is satisfied was the

85 [2014] EWHC 2872 (QB).
86 [2004] QB 310.
87 [2000] 1 WLR 586.
88 ibid, 592.
89 ibid, 592–593.

> underlying intention of Parliament. The alteration in language may be too far-reaching.... Or the subject matter may call for a strict interpretation of the statutory language as in penal legislation. None of these considerations apply in the present case. Here, the court is able to give effect to a construction of the statute which accords with the intention of the legislature.

7.127 It is important to appreciate the limits of what was being done in this case. There is no general power to rewrite the statute. That would clearly be stepping on legislative toes. All this case is doing is saying that where there is an obvious typographical error and it is clear what was intended, the court can read the statute in the way in which it was clearly intended.[90] It is equivalent to the principle of contractual interpretation that obvious typographical errors can be rectified as a matter of interpretation.[91]

7.128 In *Bogdanic v The Secretary of State for the Home Department*,[92] it was claimed that three clandestine entrants were found hiding in a lorry driven by Mr Bogdanic in the immigration control zone at Dunkirk. The Home Secretary imposed a penalty on Mr Bogdanic under the Immigration and Asylum Act 1999. Mr Bogdanic denied liability on the basis that the appropriate Commencement Order, which had brought into place certain amendments to the legislation, only applied to those who arrived in the United Kingdom, not to those held in the immigration control zones in France. On an ordinary reading of the Commencement Order, this was correct. It was expressed only to apply 'for the purposes of clandestine entrants who arrive in the United Kingdom'. But the Home Secretary argued that the Commencement Order had to be given a 'rectifying interpretation'. The purpose of the legislation was quite clear. It was clearly intended to apply both in relation to those who arrive in the United Kingdom, and to those who arrive in a prescribed immigration control zone.

7.129 Mr Bogdanic argued that this was penal legislation, and therefore that the principle should not apply. Sales J decided that the principle did apply, and read the legislation as if it applied to the immigration control zones in France.

7.130 Sales J said this:[93]

> [It] is only if the legislative instrument has a clear, objectively assessed meaning, having regard to all the circumstances and all indicators of the legislator's intention available to the person subject to the law (assisted as necessary by his legal advisers), and that meaning is contrary to the literal meaning of the text of the instrument, that it will be appropriate for the Court to give a rectifying interpretation to the instrument. Given the primacy ordinarily to be given to the language used in a legislative instrument as an indicator of the legislator's intention, the countervailing objective indicators that, despite the language being used, the legislator's intention was different need to be very strong... It must be clear that the true intention of the legislator, objectively assessed, was different from the language used by the draftsman. It is only if the Court has no doubt that the draftsmen 'slipped up'... i.e. that there was a mistake made in the language chosen by the draftsman to give effect to the intention of the legislator, that it can be confident that the proper interpretation of the provision is given by other objective indicators of the legislator's intention.

[90] For an example, see *Director of Public Prosecutions for Nauru v Fowler* (1984) 154 CLR 627.

[91] *Fitzgerald v Masters* (1956) 95 CLR 420 at 426–427; *East v Pantiles (Plant Hire)* [1982] 2 EGLR 111 at 112; *Chartbrook v Persimmon* [2009] 1 AC 1101 at [22]–[25].

[92] [2014] EWHC 2872 (QB).

[93] ibid, [42].

Sales J commented[94] that this was an approach relevant to contractual interpretation as well and that, although he referred to it as a rectifying interpretation, 'properly speaking a court does not rectify or amend the legislative instrument. It gives it its true meaning, arrived at by the process of objective interpretation described in the authorities referred to above.' **7.131**

R (Confederation of Passenger Transport UK) v Humber Bridge Board[95] concerned a statutory instrument under which tolls were levied for traffic crossing the Humber Bridge. The expression 'large bus' was defined in the Order, but there was no provision in the operative part that expressly levied a toll on large buses. The Court of Appeal nevertheless decided that the Order should be interpreted as including a provision for tolls to be levied on large buses. **7.132**

The principal judgment was given by Clarke LJ. He said that there was no doubt that the omission of the reference to 'large bus' was a mistake—not only because it had been defined (and was not used) but also because the explanatory note said that it did impose a toll on large buses.[96] **7.133**

Clarke LJ accepted that tolls could not be charged unless there was 'clear and distinct statutory authority to do so'.[97] He also accepted[98] that: **7.134**

> If the words of the Order are given their ordinary and natural meaning there is on the face of it no such authority because there is no reference to 'large bus' in the operative part of the Order despite the reference to 'large bus' in the definition section of it.

The court nevertheless decided[99] that 'on its true construction, the 1997 Order should be read as including the words "large bus" in class 4 of column 1 of the Schedule to the Order'. **7.135**

This is an extreme example of the use of this principle. There was clearly a mistake, but surely it is up to the government to get its words right. It is one thing for the citizen to be able to rely on absurdity in order to say that the statute cannot mean what it says. It is quite something else for the makers of the Order to be able to argue that they simply got the words wrong and that they can be rescued from their mistake. If they get the words wrong, then they should amend the legislation. A citizen should not be taxed on the basis of legislation which does not properly provide for it. That is judicial legislation. **7.136**

The dangers of carrying the *Inco* principle too far are illustrated in the judgment of Laws LJ in *R (Kelly) v Secretary of State for Justice*:[100] **7.137**

> As the law has developed since 1975 we have seen a growing acceptance of purposive constructions. They have their dangers; there is a price to be paid in the coin of legal certainty, and in a debasement, however marginal, of the constitutional truth that it is the legislature's will, found from the words of the Act, and not the executive's will, found from the promoter's intentions, that drives the meaning of statute law. A way often has to be found between an approach that is too lax and an approach that is too austere. In an appropriate case [*Inco*] will give the right direction, but its scope is tightly confined, as Lord Nicholls himself made clear.

94 ibid, [42] and [43].
95 [2004] QB 310.
96 ibid, [19].
97 ibid, [27].
98 ibid, [28].
99 ibid, [53].
100 [2009] QB 204 at [24].

7.138 It is important to appreciate that these cases do not create a separate doctrine. There is no doctrine of rectification in relation to statutes. These cases are simply examples of the general proposition of Principle 7 that the courts will very occasionally read the words of a statute in an unnatural way where to do otherwise would be absurd and it is clear what was really meant.

F. Overriding Fundamental Liberties

7.139 One important type of case in which the courts presume that the legislature has acted reasonably and fairly is in relation to fundamental liberties. The legislature is presumed not to intend to override the fundamental liberties of the citizen unless it does so clearly. General words are insufficient.[101]

7.140 This is sometimes known as the 'principle of legality', which is an unfortunate choice of words. It suggests that Parliament can only act if it does so 'legally'. But the sovereignty of Parliament means that anything which it enacts is legal. The principle of legality is not a limit on Parliament's powers. It is a principle of interpretation. If a statute appears to override a fundamental liberty, it will only be taken to do so if it does so clearly.

7.141 The principle was expounded by John Marshall, the Chief Justice of the United States Supreme Court in 1805. He said:[102]

> Where rights are infringed, where fundamental principles are overthrown, where the general system of the laws is departed from, the legislative intention must be expressed with irresistible clearness, to induce a court of justice to suppose a design to effect such objects.

7.142 More recently, the principle has been described by Lords Steyn and Hoffmann in *R v Secretary of State for the Home Department, ex parte Simms*.[103] The case concerned prisoners' rights—whether a particular rule made under the Prison Act 1952 prevented prisoners from exercising certain fundamental rights.

7.143 Lord Steyn gave the principal judgment. He said:[104]

> It is now necessary to examine the correctness of the interpretation of [the statutory provisions], involving a blanket ban on interviews, as advanced by the Home Secretary. Literally construed there is force in the extensive construction put forward. But one cannot lose sight that there is at stake a fundamental or basic right, namely the right of a prisoner to seek through oral interviews to persuade a journalist to investigate the safety of the prisoner's conviction and to publicise his findings in an effort to gain access to justice for the prisoner. In these circumstances even in the absence of an ambiguity there comes into play a presumption of general application operating as a constitutional principle . . . This is called 'the principle of legality . . .' Applying this principle I would hold that [the statutory provisions] leave untouched the fundamental and basic rights asserted by the applicants in the present case.

101 *Raymond v Honey* [1983] 1 AC 1.
102 *United States v Fisher*, 6 US 358 at 390 (1805).
103 [2000] 2 AC 115.
104 ibid, 130.

Lord Hoffmann put it this way:[105] **7.144**

> Parliamentary sovereignty means that Parliament can, if it chooses, legislate contrary to fundamental principles of human rights. The Human Rights Act 1998 will not detract from this power. The constraints upon its exercise by Parliament are ultimately political, not legal. But the principle of legality means that Parliament must squarely confront what it is doing and accept the political cost. Fundamental rights cannot be overridden by general or ambiguous words. This is because there is too great a risk that the full implications of their unqualified meaning may have passed unnoticed in the democratic process. In the absence of express language or necessary implication to the contrary, the courts therefore presume that even the most general words were intended to be subject to the basic rights of the individual. In this way the courts of the United Kingdom, though acknowledging the sovereignty of Parliament, apply principles of constitutionality little different from those which exist in countries where the power of the legislature is expressly limited by a constitutional document.

The principle was summarised by Gleeson CJ in the High Court of Australia in *Plaintiff S157/2002 v The Commonwealth of Australia*,[106] where he said: **7.145**

> [Courts] do not impute to the legislature an intention to abrogate or curtail fundamental rights or freedoms unless such an intention is clearly manifested by unmistakable and unambiguous language. General words will rarely be sufficient for that purpose. What courts will look for is a clear indication that the legislature has directed its attention to the rights or freedoms in question, and has consciously decided upon abrogation or curtailment.

This approach is very similar to that which used to be adopted for exclusion clauses in contracts. The courts recognised that it was possible to exclude liability, but made sure it could only be done if it was expressed very clearly and directly. Exclusion clauses are no longer interpreted in that way, but this approach does still apply to statutory interpretation as a result of the principle of legality. **7.146**

This approach certainly does seem to be more suited to statutory interpretation. The problem with treating an exclusion clause in a contract as subject to different principles of interpretation from the rest of the contract is that it offends against one of the fundamental principles of the interpretation of any type of document—that it must be read as a whole. There is no logical or practical justification for treating an exclusion clause any differently from any other clause in a contract. **7.147**

There is no such logical or practical difficulty in positing a principle of statutory interpretation that fundamental liberties will not be taken to have been overridden without clear wording. This can be justified on the basis that statutes are only issued by the legislature and we expect the legislature to act fairly and reasonably. In a parliamentary democracy, although Parliament is sovereign, certain liberties are so fundamental that Parliament must spell out what it is doing very clearly before they will be taken to have been overridden. **7.148**

Six examples can illustrate the way in which this principle is applied in practice: **7.149**

- *Secretary of State for the Home Department v GG*;[107]

[105] ibid, 131.
[106] (2003) 211 CLR 476 at [30].
[107] [2010] QB 585.

- *Morris v Beardmore*;[108]
- *Coco v R*;[109]
- *R (Ingenious Media Holdings) v Revenue and Customs Commissioners*;[110]
- *R (Morgan Grenfell) v Special Commissioner of Income Tax*;[111] and
- *R v Tower Hamlets London Borough Council, ex parte Chetnik Developments*.[112]

7.150 In *Secretary of State for the Home Department v GG*,[113] the question was whether sections 1(3) and 1(4) of the Prevention of Terrorism Act 2005 permitted the Home Secretary to require a person who was the subject of a control order to submit to personal searches.

7.151 Section 1(3) provided that:

> The obligations that may be imposed by a control order made against an individual are any obligations that the Secretary of State ... considers necessary for purposes connected with preventing or restricting involvement by that individual in terrorism-related activity.

7.152 Section 1(4) then went on to say: 'Those obligations may include, in particular—' and it then set out a series of particular obligations, which did not include personal searches.

7.153 Did the general words of section 1(3) allow personal searches to be required if the Secretary of State considered them necessary for the relevant purposes? The first instance judge and the Court of Appeal decided that the general words did not authorise the Secretary of State to require personal searches.

7.154 As a general matter of the interpretation of written documents, the provisions of section 1(3) were wide enough to include anything that the Secretary of State reasonably regarded as necessary for the relevant purposes. Subsection (4) contained certain specific provisions, but they were clearly not intended to limit the generality of subsection (3). The principle of *eiusdem generis* would not apply here, where the general statement comes first, and then particular examples are described.

7.155 So, in order to reach the conclusion which they did, the courts had to decide that the words in subsection (3) did not carry their ordinary meaning. And the basis on which they did this was that freedom from personal search is a fundamental liberty that can only be overridden by an express provision.

7.156 The result was that there must be a clear and unambiguous authorisation in a statute to override a fundamental liberty such as the liberty not to be searched. Sedley LJ said:[114]

> It is in my judgment axiomatic that the common law rights of personal security and personal liberty prevent any official search of an individual's clothing or person without explicit statutory authority.

7.157 Dyson LJ said:[115]

108 [1981] AC 446.
109 (1994) 179 CLR 427.
110 [2016] 1 WLR 4164.
111 [2003] 1 AC 563.
112 [1998] 1 AC 858.
113 [2010] QB 585.
114 ibid, [12].
115 ibid, [36].

> [General] words *without more* are insufficient to show that Parliament intended to take away fundamental rights. Something more is required.

Morris v Beardmore[116] concerned the interpretation of section 8(2) of the Road Traffic Act 1972. If a motor accident occurred, a constable in uniform could require any person to provide a specimen of breath if the constable had reasonable cause to believe that the person was driving or attempting to drive the vehicle at the time of the accident. What happened was that an individual was arrested at his home by policemen who were trespassing on his premises. The question was whether the arrest was lawful. The House of Lords held that it was not. **7.158**

This case raises an issue that is common in the interpretation of all types of legal document. The section laid down certain conditions that had to be fulfilled in order for the arrest to be made. Was that therefore exhaustive of the conditions, or was there also an implied condition that the constables were acting lawfully at the time? **7.159**

One possible approach is to say that if Parliament had intended to impose such a condition, it could have said so. The other approach is to say that it must surely be implicit that Parliament would only allow a constable to arrest someone if they were acting lawfully. **7.160**

There is merit in both approaches. The only way the conflict can be resolved is by reference to the context. And here the context was that the constables were requiring something to be done that was unlawful under the general law, and the court decided that Parliament cannot have intended them to be entitled to do this. If it had wanted to allow this, it would have said so expressly. **7.161**

As Lord Diplock said,[117] the statute provides for 'considerable inroads by the police upon rights and liberties of private citizens that are recognised and protected by the common law'. This was the context against which the legislation needed to be interpreted. In the circumstances, it was not right to decide the case on the basis that no express provision had been made. If Parliament intended to authorise the doing of an act that would otherwise constitute a tort, it had to say so expressly. **7.162**

Lord Diplock continued:[118] **7.163**

> I find it quite impossible to suppose that Parliament intended that a person whose common law right to keep his home free from unauthorised intruders had been violated in this way, should be bound under penal sanctions to comply with a demand which only the violation of that common law right had enabled the constable to make to him.

It was therefore necessary to imply a further condition—that the constables were acting lawfully. If Parliament gives the police powers to do things that they do not otherwise have the power to do, then it is a reasonable assumption that what it meant (even though it may not have said so) is that it can only be done where it is done lawfully. **7.164**

A similar approach was taken by the High Court of Australia in *Coco v R.*[119] The Invasion of Privacy Act 1971 made it an offence to use a listening device to record or listen to a private conversation. There were various exemptions, one of which was use by a member of the police force acting in the performance of his or her duty if they had been authorised in writing **7.165**

[116] [1981] AC 446.
[117] ibid, 454.
[118] ibid, 456.
[119] (1994) 179 CLR 427.

in accordance with an approval given by a judge of the Supreme Court in relation to a particular matter specified in the approval. When granting the approval, the judge had to have regard to the gravity of the matters being investigated, the extent to which the privacy of a person was likely to be interfered with and the extent to which the prevention or detection of the offence was likely to be assisted.

7.166 A judge gave the approval for a listening device to be used in a particular case in relation to a person suspected of having committed an offence. The approval authorised a police officer to enter the premises for the purpose of installing the device. The police gained entry to the premises by pretending they were investigating a fault in the telephone line and they installed the device. The Crown argued that they had obtained the necessary approval for the listening device. The defendant argued that the actions of the police constituted the tort of trespass and that the judge had no power under the relevant section to authorise something that would otherwise be a tortious act.

7.167 The majority judgment (Mason CJ and Brennan, Gaudron and McHugh JJ) contains an important discussion of the principle. They said:[120]

> Every unauthorised entry upon private property is a trespass, the right of a person in possession and entitled to possession of premises to exclude others from those premises being a fundamental common law right. In accordance with that principle, a police officer who enters or remains on private property without the legal licence of the person in possession or entitled to possession commits a trespass unless the entry or presence on the premises is authorised or excused by law. Statutory authority to engage in what otherwise would be tortious conduct must be clearly expressed in unmistakable and unambiguous language.... But the presumption is rebuttable and will be displaced if there is a clear implication that authority to enter or remain upon private property was intended....
>
> In England, Lord Browne-Wilkinson has expressed the view that the presence of general words in a statute is insufficient to authorise interference with the basic immunities which are the foundation of our freedom; to constitute such authorisation express words are required. That approach is consistent with statements of principle made by this Court.... An insistence on the necessity for express words is in conformity with earlier judicial statements in England which call for express authorisation by statute of any abrogation or curtailment of the citizen's common law rights or immunities.

7.168 They continued:[121]

> The insistence on express authorisation of an abrogation or curtailment of a fundamental right, freedom or immunity must be understood as a requirement for some manifestation or indication that the legislature has not only directed its attention to the question of the abrogation or curtailment of such basic rights, freedoms or immunities but has also determined upon abrogation or curtailment of them. The courts should not impute to the legislature an intention to interfere with fundamental rights. Such an intention must be clearly manifested by unmistakable and unambiguous language. General words will rarely be sufficient for that purpose if they do not specifically deal with the question because, in

120 ibid, 435–436.
121 ibid, 437.

> the context in which they appear, they will often be ambiguous on the aspect of interference with fundamental rights.

But their Honours accepted that the presumption could be rebutted by implication, as well as expressly. They said:[122] 7.169

> The need for a clear expression of an unmistakable and unambiguous intention does not exclude the possibility that the presumption against statutory interference with fundamental rights may be displaced by implication. Sometimes it is said that a presumption about legislative intention can be displaced only by necessary implication but that statement does little more than emphasise that the test is a very stringent one. As we remarked earlier, in some circumstances the presumption may be displaced by an implication if it is necessary to prevent the statutory provisions from becoming inoperative or meaningless. However, it would be very rare for general words in a statute to be rendered inoperative or meaningless if no implication of interference with fundamental rights were made, as general words will almost always be able to be given some operation, even if that operation is limited in scope.

The relevant section did not contain express words conferring power on a judge to authorise conduct that would otherwise be tortious; and the court decided that there was no clear expression in the legislation of an unmistakable and unambiguous intention to confer such a power. In the result, it could not be said that there was to be implied into the section a power in a judge to authorise conduct that would otherwise amount to a trespass. 7.170

The next example is *R (Ingenious Media Holdings) v Revenue and Customs Commissioners*.[123] Section 18 of the Commissioners for Revenue and Customs Act 2005 provided: 7.171

> (1) Revenue and Customs officials may not disclose information which is held by the Revenue and Customs in connection with functions of the Revenue and Customs.
> (2) But subsection (1) does not apply to a disclosure—
> (a) which—
> (i) is made for the purposes of a function of the Revenue and Customs, and
> (ii) does not contravene [certain specific restrictions].

What did the words 'for the purposes of a function of the Revenue and Customs' mean? The Revenue argued that they had a very wide meaning—including anything which in its view was necessary or expedient or incidental to the exercise of the functions of the collection and management of revenue. The Supreme Court disagreed. The principal judgment was given by Lord Toulson. He gave these words a narrower meaning—they only covered the disclosure of information reasonably necessary for the Revenue to fulfil its primary function of revenue collection and management. 7.172

The first reason for this conclusion was that there were a number of specific exceptions in subsection (2) that would have been rendered otiose if a broad meaning had been given to point (a). The second reason was more important. The court set the section against the background of the general duty of confidentiality of those in a public office (which was actually set out in subsection (1)). 7.173

122 ibid, 438.
123 [2016] 1 WLR 4164.

7.174 Lord Toulson said:[124]

> Secondly, and more fundamentally, [the Revenue's interpretation] means that the protection which would otherwise have been provided to the taxpayer by [the Revenue's] duty of confidentiality will have been very significantly eroded by words of the utmost vagueness. So to construe the words would run counter to the principle of construction known as the principle of legality.

7.175 In the result, the general words of the subsection did not to override the basic duty of confidentiality.

7.176 The principle is not always easy to apply in practice, as can be seen from the decision in *R (Morgan Grenfell & Co) v Special Commissioner of Income Tax.*[125] Section 20(1) of the Taxes Management Act 1970 allowed a tax inspector, by delivering a notice to a person, to require to be delivered to the inspector 'such documents as are in the person's possession or power'. The question was whether this overrode legal professional privilege. All the judges in the case adopted the same principles in deciding it, but they reached very different conclusions as to the application of those principles to the facts of the case.

7.177 All the judges accepted that a fundamental legal right can only be overridden by express provision or by necessary implication. All the judges agreed that legal professional privilege was such a fundamental legal right. The Divisional Court (two judges) and the Court of Appeal (three judges) nevertheless decided that the structure of the Act was such that legal professional privilege had been overridden by necessary implication. But the House of Lords decided that it had not. So, in the outcome, five judges went one way and five went the other.

7.178 All the judges in the case accepted that the relevant issue here was the principle of legality, and they all adopted the description of its scope given by Lord Hoffmann in *R v Secretary of State for the Home Department, ex parte Simms,*[126] which is discussed earlier. But the Divisional Court and the Court of Appeal decided that the provisions of the Act taken as a whole did demonstrate that legal professional privilege was excluded except where it was expressly preserved in the Act, whereas the House of Lords decided to the contrary. This is a classic illustration of the fact that statutory interpretation is a matter of judgement. Ten judges had to consider the case. They all adopted the same criteria for deciding it. Five went one way. Five went the other.

7.179 A further manifestation of this principle is concerned with discretions granted by the legislature to members of the executive. They are limited in the same way. As Lord Browne-Wilkinson said in *R v Secretary of State for the Home Department, ex parte Pierson:*[127]

> A power conferred by Parliament in general terms is not to be taken to authorise the doing of acts by the donee of the power which adversely affect the legal rights of the citizen or the basic principles on which the law of the United Kingdom is based unless the statute conferring the power makes it clear that such was the intention of Parliament.

7.180 An example of the application of this principle is *R v Tower Hamlets London Borough Council, ex parte Chetnik Developments.*[128] Section 9 of the General Rate Act 1967 gave a

124 ibid, [19].
125 [2003] 1 AC 563.
126 [2000] 2 AC 115.
127 [1998] AC 539 at 575.
128 [1988] 1 AC 858.

rating authority the power to refund money paid in various circumstances. It was a discretion, not a duty, but the House of Lords (the principal judgment being given by Lord Bridge) made it clear that statutory powers conferred for public purposes can only be exercised for the purposes which Parliament intended when conferring the power on them. The powers of public authorities are essentially different from those of private persons. They can only be exercised for the public good.

The purpose of the statute is a question of interpretation. As Lord Bridge said:[129] **7.181**

> Thus, before deciding whether a discretion has been exercised for good or bad reasons, the court must first construe the enactment by which the discretion is conferred. Some statutory discretions may be so wide that they can, for practical purposes, only be challenged if shown to have been exercised irrationally or in bad faith. But if the purpose which the discretion is intended to serve is clear, then discretion can only be validly exercised for reasons relevant to the achievement of that purpose.

The idea that powers are given for particular purposes and must be exercised in the light of those purposes is common in private law as well as in public law. For instance, it underlies one strand of case law on the duties of directors to their companies. There is therefore nothing particularly surprising about the courts limiting discretions in public law in this way. The key point is that the purpose of the discretion is established by interpreting the statute concerned. **7.182**

It is important to appreciate that the 'principle of legality' is a presumption—the starting point from which the words of the statute are to be interpreted. The ultimate object is always to interpret the words that Parliament has used. Sometimes the words are too clear to allow the presumption to operate. It is rebutted by evidence to the contrary. The clearer the words, the more difficult it is to apply the presumption. This can be illustrated by two Australian cases: **7.183**

- *Lee v New South Wales Crime Commission*;[130] and
- *Al-Kateb v Godwin*.[131]

Lee v New South Wales Crime Commission[132] concerned the interpretation of a provision of the Criminal Assets Recovery Act 1990 of New South Wales, which essentially provided for the confiscation of the proceeds of crime. Section 31D(1)(a) empowered the Supreme Court to make an order for examination on oath of a person in order to promote that object. It provided that the person being examined was not excused from answering any question or from producing any document on the ground that the answer or production might incriminate, or tend to incriminate, the person concerned. **7.184**

An application was made to have two people examined under this section. They objected, on the ground that the Act did not empower an examination about conduct in respect of which there were pending criminal charges. Essentially, the argument was that although the Act specifically removed the 'right to silence', it did not, in terms, express itself to apply to a case where criminal proceedings had yet to be brought in relation to the relevant facts. **7.185**

129 ibid, 873.
130 (2013) 251 CLR 196.
131 (2004) 219 CLR 562.
132 (2013) 251 CLR 196.

7.186 The defendants' argument was accepted by the first instance judge, but the New South Wales Court of Appeal (five judges) overruled him. The case then went to the High Court of Australia. There, it was a close-run thing. Of the seven judges, four did not accept the defendants' argument and three would have accepted it. So the defendants lost—but only just. This is yet another example of how judgemental this exercise is, and how difficult it can be to predict the outcome.

7.187 In the High Court of Australia, the majority (French CJ and Gageler, Keane and Crennan JJ) accepted that, if the legislature wants to achieve a result which overrides fundamental liberties, it must make its intention unambiguously clear. But the principle should not be extended beyond its rationale—which was the inadvertent and collateral alteration of fundamental freedoms. The principle did not exist to shield fundamental freedoms from being specifically affected in the pursuit of clearly identified legislative objects. It had no part to play where the object of the legislation made it plain that the legislature had directed its attention to the question and had decided to curtail those fundamental freedoms. In this case, the legislation was too clear to be implicitly limited.[133]

7.188 Hayne, Kiefel and Bell JJ dissented, essentially on the basis that the words were not clear enough to warrant the intrusion into such a fundamental immunity as the right to silence.

7.189 A further example of the limits of the principle is the decision of the High of Australia in *Al-Kateb v Godwin*.[134] The case concerned Australian migration laws, and the position of someone who was described as an 'unlawful non-citizen'.

7.190 Under section 189(1) of the Migration Act 1958, 'if an officer knows or reasonably suspects that a person in the migration zone ... is an unlawful non-citizen, the officer must detain the person'.

7.191 Section 196(1) went on to say:

> An unlawful non-citizen detained under section 189 must be kept in immigration detention until he or she is:
>
> (a) removed from Australia ...; or
> (b) deported; or
> (c) granted a visa.

7.192 Section 196(3) said:

> To avoid doubt, subsection (1) prevents the release, even by a court, of an unlawful non-citizen from detention (otherwise than for removal or deportation) unless the non-citizen has been granted a visa.

7.193 The case concerned a stateless person who arrived in Australia without a visa and was taken into immigration detention. He applied for a protection visa but his application was refused. He then asked to be removed from Australia, but his attempts to obtain the necessary international cooperation were unsuccessful, and it was found that there was no real likelihood or prospect of removal in the reasonably foreseeable future. He claimed to be entitled to be removed from detention.

133 See the judgment of Gageler and Keane JJ at (2013) 251 CLR 196 at [307]–[335].
134 (2004) 219 CLR 562.

By a majority of four to three, the High Court of Australia decided that he had to remain in detention. 7.194

The minority in the High Court (Gleeson CJ and Gummow and Kirby JJ) considered that section 196 ought to be read in a way that avoided detention where its essential purpose (removal or deportation) was not reasonably practicable. But the majority (McHugh, Hayne, Callinan and Heydon JJ) gave effect to what they regarded to be the clear words of the statute in overriding the fundamental liberty concerned. 7.195

McHugh J put it this way:[135] 7.196

> The words of the three sections are too clear to read them as being subject to a purposive limitation or an intention not to affect fundamental rights...
>
> The unambiguous language of s196—particularly sub-s (3)—indicates that Parliament intends detention to continue until one of the conditions expressly identified therein—removal, deportation or granting of a visa—is satisfied.

The interesting point here—from the point of view of the drafting of legislation—is subsection (3). This did make it abundantly clear what the intention was. Parliament was essentially saying 'and we really mean this'. 7.197

But, again, it was a close-run thing. The minority took the view that section 196 is based on the implicit assumption that the person concerned is capable of being removed and therefore that, if he is not, he can no longer be detained. 7.198

In recent years, the principle of legality has been bolstered by statutory intervention—section 3 of the Human Rights Act 1998. That is discussed in Section H of this chapter. But, before considering that, it is first necessary to discuss the European approach to statutory interpretation. This is because the interpretation of section 3 has been heavily influenced by the European approach. 7.199

G. European Influence

The civil law approach to both the drafting and the interpretation of documents is different from that used in the common law jurisdictions, although the difference can be overstated. In practice, the results are often the same even if the means of getting there is sometimes different. 7.200

In fact, the most important manifestation of this difference of approach is in relation to the legislation of the European Union. When the United Kingdom was part of the European Union, its judges had to interpret European legislation in accordance with European principles. And that applied not just to the European legislation itself, but also to UK legislation derived from European legislation. Now that the United Kingdom is no longer part of the European Union, the importance of this alternative approach to interpretation will wane, but it may continue to be relevant for some time in relation to the large amount of UK legislation that is derived from the European Union. 7.201

[135] ibid, [33] and [35].

7.202 In *Marleasing v La Comercial Internacional de Alimentación*,[136] the European Court described the European approach to interpretation as requiring the court to interpret the legislation 'as far as possible, in the light of the wording and the purpose of the directive in order to achieve the result pursued by the latter'. In terms, that is no different from the common law approach to interpretation. But there are definitely differences of emphasis between the common law and the civil law approach in relation to both statutory and contractual interpretation.

7.203 In *Vodafone 2 v Revenue and Customs Commissioners*,[137] Sir Andrew Morritt C had this to say about the approach to the interpretation of European legislation. He said:

> (a) it is not constrained by conventional rules of construction . . . ;
> (b) it does not require ambiguity in the legislative language . . . ;
> (c) it is not an exercise in semantics or linguistics . . . ;
> (d) it permits departure from the strict and literal application of the words which the legislature has elected to use . . . ;
> (e) it permits the implication of words necessary to comply with Community law obligations . . . ; and
> (f) the precise form of the words to be implied does not matter . . .
>
> The only constraints on the broad and far-reaching nature of the interpretative obligation are that: (a) the meaning should 'go with the grain of the legislation' and be 'compatible with the underlying thrust of the legislation being construed' . . . An interpretation should not be adopted which is inconsistent with a fundamental or cardinal feature of the legislation since this would cross the boundary between interpretation and amendment . . . ; and (b) the exercise of the interpretative obligation cannot require the courts to make decisions for which they are not equipped or give rise to important practical repercussions which the court is not equipped to evaluate . . .

7.204 In *British Gas Trading v Lock*,[138] the question at issue was whether UK regulations could be read in a manner that was consistent with the EU directive under which they had been made. On the face of it, they could not, and a normal interpretation of the provision would mean that the regulations did not comply with the directive. But, applying a 'conforming interpretation', the Court of Appeal decided that it was able to read the regulations in a manner that was consistent with the directive.

7.205 The European approach to interpretation can be illustrated by three cases:

- *Litster v Forth Dry Dock & Engineering Co*;[139]
- *Pickstone v Freemans*;[140] and
- *Re Olympus UK*.[141]

136 [1993] BCC 421 at [8].
137 [2010] Ch 77 at [37] and [38].
138 [2017] ICR 1.
139 [1990] 1 AC 546.
140 [1989] 1 AC 66.
141 [2014] Bus LR 816.

Litster v Forth Dry Dock & Engineering Co[142] concerned the interpretation of the Transfer of Undertakings (Protection of Employment) Regulations 1981, which were enacted to comply with an EU directive on safeguarding employees' rights on the transfer of a business. **7.206**

An insolvent company went into receivership. The receivers dismissed the workforce and, an hour later, sold the business to a purchaser. The issue was whether the employees had been unfairly dismissed, and the key point was the interpretation of regulation 5(3). This provided that a reference to a person employed in an undertaking is a reference 'to a person so employed immediately before the transfer'. The receivers argued that because the former employees had been dismissed an hour before the transfer, they were not employed 'immediately before the transfer'. **7.207**

The House of Lords decided that they needed to interpret legislation implementing EU directives in a different way from ordinary UK legislation. The words could not be read literally because that would enable the evasion of the purpose of the directive—which was to protect employees. In order to give effect to the general scheme of the regulations, and to fulfil the purpose of the directive, it was necessary to imply into regulation 5(3) words indicating that, where a person had been unfairly dismissed, he or she was deemed to have been employed in the undertaking immediately before the transfer. **7.208**

Pickstone v Freemans[143] concerned the interpretation of a provision of the Equal Pay Act 1970. The legislation derived from EU law, and the European Court of Justice had decided that the United Kingdom had not properly implemented a particular provision of EU law. The Act was therefore amended in order to deal with the problem that had been identified. But, on a normal interpretation of the legislation, the amendment had still not achieved the intended purpose. **7.209**

The House of Lords decided that the words should be read in a way that gave effect to the clear intention by reading them in a purposive manner. What is interesting about this case is that it did not carry the process too far. Here it was manifestly clear what was intended—it was to give effect to EU law—and the wording could be read in a manner consistent with EU law by reading the words in a particular way. The approach taken was not the natural meaning of the words, even in context, but it was not a wholesale departure from the words. **7.210**

The third example is *Re Olympus UK*.[144] It concerned the interpretation of the cross-border merger regulations, which implemented in the United Kingdom the EU directive on cross-border mergers. The particular circumstances are not relevant here, but what is interesting is the approach of Hildyard J to the interpretation of the regulations. He started with the directive, rather than the regulations, and spent a lot of time considering its various versions in different languages and the effect which it was intended to have as an autonomous matter. **7.211**

There are undoubtedly differences between the common law and civil law approaches to interpretation. As Lord Steyn said in *Shanning International v Lloyds TSB Bank*:[145] **7.212**

> [The] British doctrine of purposive construction is more literalist than the European variety, and permits a strained construction only in comparatively rare cases. Judges need to take account of this difference.

142 [1990] 1 AC 546.
143 [1989] 1 AC 66.
144 [2014] Bus LR 816.
145 [2001] 1 WLR 1462 at [24].

7.213 But, in the same case, Lord Hope emphasised that even the civil law approach has its limitations:[146]

> But I think it is necessary to bear in mind that the instrument which is binding in its entirety in terms of the Treaty is the regulation which was adopted by the Council of the European Communities at the end of the legislative process which the Treaty has identified. Moreover . . . [in an EU case], the court held that in view of the clear and precise terms of the article it was not necessary to look even at the preamble to the directive in order to determine the purpose or the scope of the provision.

7.214 The interesting question is the extent to which the courts will continue to adopt the European approach to interpretation of legislation that derives from European legislation. They no longer have a duty to do so under European law. They may consider it appropriate to continue this approach with legislation that does derive from Europe, but for how long?

7.215 It is likely, as time goes on, that the UK courts will increasingly decide to interpret UK legislation in accordance with normal UK principles even if it derives from EU legislation. An illustration is the recent judgment of the Supreme Court in *Balhousie Holdings v Commissioners for Her Majesty's Revenue and Customs*.[147] That was a Scottish case involving whether the Revenue was entitled to claw back the benefit of the zero-rating of VAT where the owner of a care home entered into a sale and lease-back of the building with a finance house. The clawback would have been triggered if the company had 'disposed of [its] entire interest in the relevant premises'.

7.216 On any sensible reading of those words, a sale and lease-back did not involve the disposal of the company's entire interest in the property. The sale constituted a disposal of the entire interest, but that was not the only element of the transaction. There was also the lease-back. Under the general law, a sale and lease-back is frequently regarded as being a single transaction for the purpose of priorities.[148] That is not determinative of the interpretation of a particular statutory provision, but it certainly adds weight to the argument that the company could not be said to have disposed of its entire interest where it continues in possession of the property as lessee rather than freeholder. The transaction needs to be understood as a whole. As Lord Briggs said,[149] a reasonably intelligent and well-informed reader of the relevant provision would be forgiven for thinking it tolerably clear that the clawback would only apply where the company no longer had any interest in the property—which was not the case.

7.217 That was the view of the First-Tier Tribunal, but the Upper Tribunal and the Inner House of the Court of Session decided that the sale itself was a disposal of the company's entire interest in the care home, notwithstanding the fact that the company continued in possession as lessee. The Supreme Court unanimously reversed that decision and decided that the company had not disposed of its entire interest in the property. The majority (Lords Hodge, Briggs, Sales and Carloway) reached this conclusion on the basis of normal UK principles of interpretation. Lady Arden reached the same conclusion, but in this case by reference to EU principles.

146 ibid, [34].
147 [2021] 1 WLR 2164.
148 *Abbey National Building Society v Cann* [1991] 1 AC 56.
149 [2021] 1 WLR 2164 at [6].

The majority accepted that there would be occasions where recourse might be appropriate to the jurisprudence of the European Court but they decided that this was not an appropriate case in which to do that. 7.218

It is suggested that this was the right approach. The statutory words could hardly have been clearer. The company was subject to a clawback of VAT if it disposed of its entire interest in the relevant property. On no sensible basis could it be argued that it had done so. It remained in possession of the property, running the business—albeit as tenant rather than as freeholder. It had not disposed of its entire interest in the premises. 7.219

Citizens should be able to understand the laws that govern them and by which they are taxed by reference to the words of the statutes concerned. The more the interpreter moves away from the natural meaning of the words in context, the more that principle is breached. The *Balhousie* case may well indicate the way in which these questions will be approached in the future. 7.220

It is suggested that the circumstances in which the courts will consider it appropriate to have recourse to European principles of interpretation when interpreting EU-derived legislation will become less frequent as time goes on. But the European approach to interpretation has had a considerable impact on the approach of the courts to another question—how to interpret section 3 of the Human Rights Act 1998. That is the subject of the next section of this chapter. 7.221

H. Section 3 of the Human Rights Act 1998

Section 3 of the Human Rights Act 1998 is concerned with the interpretation of legislation. It says: 7.222

> (1) So far as it is possible to do so, primary legislation and subordinate legislation must be read and given effect in a way which is compatible with the Convention rights.
> (2) This section—
> (a) applies to primary legislation and subordinate legislation whenever enacted;
> (b) does not affect the validity, continuing operation or enforcement of any incompatible primary legislation; and
> (c) does not affect the validity, continuing operation or enforcement of any incompatible subordinate legislation if (disregarding any possibility of revocation) primary legislation prevents removal of the incompatibility.

'Convention rights' are defined in section 1 to mean certain of the provisions of the Convention for the Protection of Human Rights and Fundamental Freedoms of 4 November 1950 as it has effect for the time being in relation to the United Kingdom.[150] Section 4 allows the court to make a declaration of incompatibility if it is satisfied that a provision of primary legislation is incompatible with a Convention right. 7.223

In June 2022, the Bill of Rights Bill was introduced into Parliament. If passed in the form in which it was introduced, it would repeal section 3. But, unless and until section 3 is actually repealed, it is necessary to consider its effect. Indeed, even if it is repealed, the issues 7.224

[150] Human Rights Act 1998, section 21(1).

discussed in this and the following section should continue to be of importance in practice because they go to the heart of the relationship between Parliament and the courts and the proper role of the courts when interpreting legislation.

7.225 On the face of it, section 3 looks as if it is a statutory recognition of the principle of legality, which is discussed in Section F of this chapter. The fundamental liberties protected by the principle of legality have much in common with the human rights protected by the Convention. The principle of legality requires legislation to be read in a way that preserves fundamental liberties if it is possible to do so. Section 3 requires legislation to be read in a way that is compatible with human rights so far as it is possible to do so. Both are principles of interpretation. Both recognise that the wording of the legislation may be too clear to permit the liberties or rights concerned to be protected.

7.226 As will be seen in Section I of this chapter, the Australian and New Zealand courts have interpreted their equivalents of section 3 in this way. But in the United Kingdom, the courts have read section 3 more broadly—giving themselves greater powers to override the words of a statute. And they have done so under the influence of the European approach to interpretation described in Section G of this chapter.

7.227 That is not to say that there has been unanimity in the approach of judges in the United Kingdom to the interpretation of section 3. There have been differences of approach. Some judges are more inclined to read section 3 widely than others. But the overall consensus is that section 3 gives the courts wider powers than they have at common law. Disagreements tend to be about the precise extent of those powers.

7.228 *Re S*[151] concerned the interpretation of the Children Act 1989. It is a cardinal principle of that Act that, when a court makes a care order, the local authority has parental responsibility for the child and that, whilst the care order is in force, the courts' powers are excluded. Where a care order is made, the responsibility for the child's care is therefore with the local authority rather than the court. For this reason, the House of Lords decided that the courts had no power to impose requirements on the local authority in order for the Act to comply with Convention rights. That would be inconsistent with the purpose of the Act, and was therefore an impermissible application of section 3. Even if the Children Act was incompatible with Convention rights, section 3 did not give the court the power to do this.

7.229 The principal judgment was given by Lord Nicholls, who made the following points about section 3:

- It is a powerful tool, not dependant on the existence of ambiguity; and it applies retrospectively.[152]
- But its reach is not unlimited. It is concerned with interpretation. Section 4 presupposes that not all provisions can be rendered compliant by the application of section 3.[153]
- 'In applying section 3 courts must be ever mindful of this outer limit. The Human Rights Act reserves the amendment of primary legislation to Parliament. By this means the Act seeks to preserve parliamentary sovereignty. The Act maintains the constitutional

[151] [2002] 2 AC 291.
[152] ibid, [37].
[153] ibid, [38].

boundary. Interpretation of statutes is a matter for the courts; the enactment of statutes, and the amendment of statutes, are matters for Parliament.'[154]

Lord Nicholls also made the following important point:[155] **7.230**

> Up to this point there is no difficulty. The area of real difficulty lies in identifying the limits of interpretation in a particular case ... Nowadays courts are more 'liberal' in the interpretation of all manner of documents. The greater the latitude with which courts construe documents, the less readily defined is the boundary. What one person regards as sensible, if robust, interpretation, another regards as impermissibly creative. For present purposes it is sufficient to say that a meaning which departs substantially from a fundamental feature of an Act of Parliament is likely to have crossed the boundary between interpretation and amendment ... The boundary line may be crossed even though a limitation on Convention rights is not stated in express terms.

Lord Nicholls emphasised the judgemental nature of the exercise, and that different lawyers will have different views on this. Although it is clear that the courts must not stray into areas of legislation, this is much easier to say than to apply in practice. **7.231**

A very broad view of section 3 was given by Lord Bingham in *Sheldrake v Director of Public Prosecutions*:[156] **7.232**

> First, the interpretative obligation under section 3 is a very strong and far reaching one, and may require the court to depart from the legislative intention of Parliament. Secondly, a Convention-compliant interpretation under section 3 is the primary remedial measure and a declaration of incompatibility under section 4 is an exceptional course. Thirdly, it is to be noted that during the passage of the Bill through Parliament the promoters of the Bill told both Houses that it was envisaged that the need for a declaration of compatibility would rarely arise. Fourthly, there is a limit beyond which a Convention-compliant interpretation is not possible ... In explaining why a Convention-compliant interpretation may not be possible, members of the committee used differing expressions: such an interpretation will be incompatible with the underlying thrust of the legislation, or would not go with the grain of it, or would call for legislative deliberation, or would change the substance of a provision completely, or would remove its pith and substance, or would violate a cardinal principle of the legislation ... All of these expressions, as I respectively think, yield valuable insights, but none of them should be allowed to supplant the simple test enacted in the Act: 'So far as it is possible to do so ...'

A difference of approach between the members of the House of Lords can be seen very clearly in *R v A (No 2)*.[157] Section 41 of the Youth Justice and Criminal Evidence Act 1999 prohibited the use of certain evidence in rape trials unless it was specifically permitted under the legislation. One of the issues in the case was whether this breached the right to a free trial under Article 6 of the European Convention on Human Right and, if so, what could be done about this under section 3. **7.233**

Lord Steyn gave a very broad reading of section 3. He said:[158] **7.234**

154 ibid, [39].
155 ibid, [40].
156 [2005] 1 AC 264 at [28].
157 [2002] 1 AC 45.
158 ibid, [44].

> [The] interpretative obligation under section 3 of the 1998 Act is a strong one. It applies even if there is no ambiguity in the sense of the language being capable of two different meanings ... Under ordinary methods of interpretation a court may depart from the language of the statute to avoid absurd consequences: section 3 goes much further ... It is a general principle of the interpretation of legal instruments that the text is the primary source of interpretation: other sources are subordinate to it ... Section 3 qualifies this general principle because it requires a court to find an interpretation compatible with the Convention rights if it is possible to do so ... In accordance with the will of Parliament as reflected in section 3 it will sometimes be necessary to adopt an interpretation which linguistically may appear strained. The techniques to be used will not only involve the reading down of express language in a statute but also the implication of provisions. A declaration of incompatibility is a measure of last resort. It must be avoided unless it is plainly impossible to do so.

7.235 Lord Steyn therefore considered that it was possible, under section 3, to read section 41 of the 1999 Act as subject to the requirement that evidence would be admissible if required to ensure a fair trial under Article 6 of the Convention.[159]

7.236 This is difficult to accept. The 1999 Act specifically—in terms—prohibited certain types of evidence from being used in rape trials. Lord Steyn would have turned that on its head by allowing evidence to be used that the 1999 Act specifically prohibited. That is not interpreting the Act; it is amending it.

7.237 Lord Hope took a different approach. He thought that it was neither necessary nor appropriate in this case to rely on section 3. He said:[160]

> I would find it very difficult to accept that it was permissible under section 3 of the Human Rights Act 1998 to read in to section 41(3)(c) a provision to the effect that evidence or questioning which was required to ensure a fair trial under article 6 of the Convention should not be treated as inadmissible. The rule of construction which section 3 lays down is unlike any previous rule of statutory interpretation. There is no need to identify an ambiguity or absurdity. Compatibility with the Convention rights is the sole guiding principle. That is the paramount object which the rule seeks to achieve. But the rule is only a rule of interpretation. It does not entitle the judges to act as legislators ... The compatibility is to be achieved only so far as this is possible. Plainly this will not be possible if the legislation contains provisions which expressly contradict the meaning which the enactment would have to be given to make it compatible. It seems to me that the same result must follow if they do so by necessary implication, as this too is a means of identifying the plain intention of Parliament ...

7.238 Lord Hope continued:[161]

> In the present case it seems to me that the entire structure of section 41 contradicts the idea that it is possible to read into it a new provision which would entitle the court to give leave whenever it was of the opinion that this was required to ensure a fair trial. The whole point of the section ... was to address the mischief which was thought to have arisen due to the width of the discretion which had previously been given to the trial judge.... Section 41(2)

159 ibid, [45].
160 ibid, [108].
161 ibid, [109].

forbids the exercise of such a discretion *unless* the court is satisfied as to the matters which that sub-section identifies. It seems to me that it would not be possible, without contradicting the plain intention of Parliament, to read in a provision which would enable the court to exercise a wider discretion than that permitted by section 41(2).

The other judges lent more towards Lord Steyn's approach than that of Lord Hope, but this case does illustrate two very different approaches to section 3, and it is not at all clear whether Lord Steyn's approach will, over time, prevail over that of Lord Hope. A more limited approach to section 3 may become more common as the courts move away from processes of interpretation influenced by European jurisprudence. **7.239**

Some examples of the application of the provision in practice can help to illustrate its scope. The examples are: **7.240**

- *Beaulane Properties v Palmer*;[162]
- *Ghaidan v Godin-Mendoza*;[163] and
- *Bellinger v Bellinger*.[164]

Beaulane Properties v Palmer[165] involved a claim for title to land based on adverse possession. The judge (Nicholas Strauss QC) decided that, under the general law, the claimant would have been entitled to claim title based on adverse possession. But the registered owner of the land claimed that this would breach the Human Rights Act, and the judge agreed. He was able to interpret the relevant provision of the Land Registration Act 1925 in a way that was consistent with the Convention. **7.241**

Nicholas Strauss QC emphasised that although the court had a broad power under section 3 to adapt the wording in order to comply with the Convention rights, this had to be done in accordance with the underlying thrust of the legislation and that the court could not, by using section 3, create a wholly different scheme. **7.242**

One of the most important discussions of section 3 is contained in the decision of the House of Lords in *Ghaidan v Godin-Mendoza*.[166] Paragraph 2 of Schedule 1 to the Rent Act 1977 allows 'a person who was living with the original tenant as his or her wife or husband' to take over a statutory tenancy from the original tenant on their death. In *Fitzpatrick v Stirling Housing Association*,[167] a few years earlier, the House of Lords had decided that those words did not extend to the survivor of a homosexual relationship. In this case, the question was whether the passing of the Human Rights Act 1998 made any difference. By a majority of four to one, the House of Lords held that it did. **7.243**

The court decided that to deny the claimant the right to a statutory tenancy was a breach of his Convention rights. They also decided that they could use section 3 in order to read the words 'a person who was living with the original tenant as his or her wife or husband' as including a homosexual couple. **7.244**

[162] [2006] Ch 79.
[163] [2004] 2 AC 557.
[164] [2003] 2 AC 467.
[165] [2006] Ch 79.
[166] [2004] 2 AC 557.
[167] [2001] 1 AC 27.

7.245 Lord Nicholls recognised that section 3 is itself not free from ambiguity—the difficulty lying in the word 'possible'. Parliament had made it clear that it would not always be possible to read a statute in a way that would comply with the Convention. Hence section 4. But the power of the courts under section 3 is a broad one—enabling them to read words in a way other than their natural meaning and thereby changing the meaning of the legislation. What could not be done was to adopt a meaning inconsistent with a fundamental feature of the legislation. Any changes must go with the grain of the legislation.[168]

7.246 Similarly, Lord Rodger emphasised that the precise adjustments to the words contained in the statute and the number of words that might have to be read into the statute were of far less importance than ensuring that the changes did not affect the underlying substance of the legislation.[169]

7.247 Lord Millett dissented on the section 3 point, taking the view that the essential feature of the relationship that Parliament had in contemplation was one between persons of the opposite sex. He therefore took the view that to do what was proposed would offend against a fundamental feature of the legislation. This, again, shows how difficult it often is to draw the line. Whether a proposed amendment is an acceptable reading of the statute in the light of the Convention rights or an unacceptable exercise of legislative powers by amending the legislation is often a hard line to draw.

7.248 The key point is that this is a limited power that needs to be exercised sparingly. This can be seen from the decision of the House of Lords in *Bellinger v Bellinger*.[170] At the time, section 11(c) of the Matrimonial Causes Act 1973 provided that 'A marriage … shall be void on the following grounds only, that is to say … that the parties are not respectively male and female … ' The court was asked to grant a declaration that a marriage was valid between a man and a person who had been classified and registered at birth as male but had undergone gender reassignment surgery and treatment. The court refused to read the 1973 Act in a manner that would validate the marriage, but it did declare under section 4 that the relevant section was incompatible with the Human Rights Act 1998.

7.249 The court distinguished three questions:

- What is the natural meaning of the words of the section?
- Can the words be read differently under section 3 of the Human Rights Act?
- If not, should a declaration of incompatibility be made?

Their Lordships spoke with one voice on all three issues.

7.250 On the first issue, Lord Hope said:[171]

> I need hardly say that … the words 'male' and 'female' in section 11(c) of the 1973 Act … are not technical terms and that they must be given their ordinary, everyday meaning in the English language … The fact is that the ordinary meaning of the word 'male' is incapable, without more, of accommodating the transsexual person within its scope.

168 [2004] 2 AC 557 at [27]–[33].
169 ibid, [122] and [123].
170 [2003] 2 AC 467.
171 ibid, [62].

Lord Rodger demonstrated[172] that section 11 made reference to some things that could change, in which event it specified that the test was 'at the time of the marriage'. But: **7.251**

> Section 11(c) is different ... ; a marriage is void if 'the parties are not respectively male and female'. Both the present tense and the omission of any reference to the time of the marriage indicate that, in relation to the validity of the marriage, Parliament regards gender as fixed and immutable.

On the second point, there was very little consideration given to whether it was possible to read down the words in section 11 by reference to section 3 of the Human Rights Act. It seems to have been generally acknowledged that they could not be. But Lord Hobhouse did discuss this point:[173] **7.252**

> The threshold question is whether, by applying section 3, it is possible, as a matter of interpretation, to 'read down' section 11(c) of the 1973 Act so as to include additional words such as 'or two people of the same sex one of whom has changed his/her sex to that of the opposite sex'. This would in my view not be an exercise in interpretation however robust. It would be a legislative exercise of amendment making a legislative choice as to what precise amendment was appropriate.

All the members of the House of Lords recognised that this was a matter for Parliament not for the courts. **7.253**

The third issue was whether the court should make a declaration of incompatibility with the Human Rights Act. It did but, of course, this does not affect the existing law. It is saying that although the law says *x*, it should say *y*. But that does not stop the law from being, and continuing to be, *x* until it is changed by Parliament. **7.254**

Bellinger demonstrates the broad way in which section 3 has been interpreted. The three questions described earlier show very clearly that the courts see section 3 as giving them stronger powers than they have at common law—even taking account of the principle of legality. **7.255**

But *Bellinger* also illustrates the limits of their power under section 3. Three further cases illustrate those limits: **7.256**

- *R v Lambert*;[174]
- *McDonald v McDonald*;[175] and
- *AS (Somalia) v Secretary of State for the Home Department*.[176]

In *R v Lambert*,[177] Lord Hope made two comments about the scope of section 3:[178] **7.257**

> The first point ... is that the effect of section 3(1) is that the interpretation which it requires is to be achieved only so far as this is possible ... Resort to it will not be possible if the legislation contains provisions, either in the words or phrases which are under scrutiny or elsewhere, which expressly contradict the meaning which the enactment would have to be

172 ibid, [83].
173 ibid, [78].
174 [2002] 2 AC 545.
175 [2017] AC 273.
176 [2009] 1 WLR 1385.
177 [2002] 2 AC 545.
178 ibid, [79].

> given to make it compatible. The same consequence will follow if legislation contains provisions which are to have this effect by necessary implication.... [It] is not for [the judges] to legislate. Section 3(1) preserves the sovereignty of Parliament. It does not give power to the judges to overrule decisions which the language of the statute shows have been taken on the very point at issue by the legislator.

7.258 Lord Hope's second point was that:[179]

> [Great] care must be taken, in cases where a different meaning has to be given to the legislation from the ordinary meaning of the words used by the legislator, to identify precisely the word or phrase which, if given its ordinary meaning, would otherwise be incompatible. Just as much care must then be taken to say how the word or phrase is to be construed if it is to be made compatible. The justification for this approach to the use of section 3(1) is to be found in the nature of legislation itself. Its primary characteristic, for present purposes, is its ability to achieve certainty by the use of clear and precise language. It provides a set of rules by which, according to the ordinary meaning of the words used, the conduct of affairs may be regulated. So far as possible judges should seek to achieve the same attention to detail in their use of language to express the effect of applying section 3(1) as the parliamentary draftsman would have done if he had been amending the statute. It ought to be possible for any words that need to be substituted to be fitted into the statute as if they had been inserted there by amendment. If this cannot be done without doing such violence to the statute as to make it unintelligible or unworkable, the use of this technique will not be possible. It will then be necessary to leave it to Parliament to amend the statute and to resort instead to the making of a declaration of incompatibility.

7.259 The importance of these points can be seen from the next two cases.

7.260 In *McDonald v McDonald*,[180] the question was whether the granting of a possession order to a private sector landlord under the Housing Act 1988 breached the tenant's rights under the Human Rights Act. The Supreme Court decided that those rights were not breached in the circumstances but, because the issue had been argued and was important, it also considered the question whether, if there had been a breach of the Human Rights Act, it would be possible to use section 3(1) to read down the legislation in a way that would be consistent with the Human Rights Act.

7.261 Lord Neuberger and Baroness Hale made a number of important general comments on the scope of section 3.[181] There are substantive limits to what the courts can achieve under section 3. It is possible to do a great deal with words, but there is a difference between interpretation and amendment. The former is a matter for the courts, the latter for Parliament—although they accepted that the boundary may not always be easy to discern. They also recognised the importance that the decision must 'go with the grain' of the legislation.

7.262 In this case, they decided that reading the words of the statute concerned in a way that would comply with the Convention rights would contradict the grain of the legislation, and therefore could not be done. Had it been incompatible with the Convention rights, the only remedy would therefore have been a declaration of incompatibility under section 4.

179 ibid, [80].
180 [2017] AC 273.
181 ibid, [68]–[70].

The decision in *AS (Somalia) v Secretary of State for the Home Department*[182] is to similar effect. The words of the statute were perfectly clear. When there was an appeal from a refusal to grant entry clearance, the appellate tribunal was only entitled to consider the circumstances appertaining at the time the original decision to refuse was made. It was not entitled to take account of matters arising subsequently. **7.263**

The Supreme Court decided that even if there might be cases where a decision to refuse to consider the up-to-date position could lead to an interference with Convention rights, the relevant words of the statute were unequivocal and unyielding, and reading them down would be to cross the boundary between interpretation and amendment of the statute.[183] **7.264**

I. Statutory Interpretation and Human Rights: The Future

In June 2022, a Bill of Rights Bill was introduced into Parliament. If passed in its form as introduced, it would repeal the Human Rights Act 1998 and replace it with a new Bill of Rights that does not contain a provision equivalent to section 3. The Bill prescribes how the European Convention on Human Rights should be interpreted in the United Kingdom but not how other statutes should be interpreted in relation to the Convention. **7.265**

The purpose of the Bill as introduced to Parliament in June 2022 can be seen clearly from clause 1(2): **7.266**

> [This] Act clarifies and re-balances the relationship between courts in the United Kingdom, the European Court of Human Rights and Parliament by ensuring—
>
> ...
>
> (b) that courts are no longer required to read and give effect to legislation, so far as possible, in a way which is compatible with the Convention rights ...

The Human Rights Act 1998 would be repealed by paragraph 2 of Schedule 5 to the Bill, and section 3 would not be replaced. **7.267**

The Bill is not yet law and it might never be passed. It is therefore appropriate to consider how the courts ought to approach the interpretation of section 3 in the light of the departure of the United Kingdom from the European Union and in the context of the way in which analogous provisions have been interpreted in other common law jurisdictions. **7.268**

Perhaps even more importantly, the issues discussed in this section go to the heart of the relationship between Parliament and the courts. They are crucial to an understanding of the proper approach to the interpretation of statutes, and they will continue to be relevant long after section 3 is a distant memory. **7.269**

The assumption which underlies the approach of the House of Lords—and now the Supreme Court—to the interpretation of section 3 of the Human Rights Act is that the principle that it espouses, although a principle of interpretation, gives the court greater freedom to interpret legislation than has traditionally been available in relation to UK statutes. The premise is that **7.270**

[182] [2009] 1 WLR 1385.
[183] ibid, [19].

the power of the courts under section 3 is greater than it was under the general law. Why else would Parliament have passed section 3?

7.271 This approach required the courts to establish the nature of that extended power. Searching around for an answer to this question, they alighted upon the body of case law that had developed since the United Kingdom joined the European Economic Community in 1972 concerning the way in which UK legislation based on European Union directives ought to be interpreted. It has been seen in Section G of this chapter that the approach to the interpretation of EU-derived legislation is different from—and broader than—the approach taken to the interpretation of UK statutes. And it is this approach that informed the courts' method of interpreting section 3. It is clear from *Ghaidan* and the cases that followed it that the courts have created a single method of dealing with these disparate issues. In short, they adopt the same approach to section 3 as they do to EU-derived legislation.

7.272 Now that the United Kingdom is no longer a member of the European Union, the European approach to interpretation of statutes will become less important. It will take some time to replace all of the EU-derived legislation, but the trend must be to move away from European-style interpretation to the traditional approach to the interpretation of UK statutes.

7.273 Which then leaves an important question to be answered. How will this affect the courts' approach to the interpretation of section 3? Will they continue to apply the broad European style of interpretation, or will they adopt a different approach?

7.274 In making this decision, it is important to appreciate that there is a different way in which section 3 can be understood. Rather than requiring the court to adopt a radically different approach to the interpretation of statutes, it can be read as a statutory confirmation of the principle of legality. It has been seen in Section F of this chapter that the courts have long adopted a particular approach to the interpretation of statutes which appear to impinge upon fundamental freedoms. It is presumed that statutes are not intended to override fundamental liberties unless they do so clearly. Many of those fundamental freedoms cover the same ground as the Convention rights which are protected under the Human Rights Act. The way in which section 3 is drafted is consistent with the conclusion that what Parliament was doing was recognising the principle of legality and giving it statutory effect. It is not uncommon for legislation to codify common law principles.

7.275 There is some support for this alternative approach to the interpretation of section 3 in the English cases, and a great deal of support in cases in Australia and New Zealand which have similar statutory provisions to section 3.

7.276 It is suggested that the withdrawal of the United Kingdom from the European Union will require the courts to reconsider their approach to section 3. When doing so, it is suggested that they should adopt this alternative approach to the interpretation of section 3.

7.277 In *R (Wilkinson) v Inland Revenue Commissioners*,[184] the House of Lords had to consider whether the word 'widow' could be read to include 'widower' as a result of section 3 of the Human Rights Act 1998. The court decided that there was no way in which a reasonable reader could understand the word 'widow' to refer to the more general concept of a surviving spouse. The contrary indications in the language of the Act were too strong.[185]

184 [2005] 1 WLR 1718.
185 ibid, [19].

The principal judgment was given by Lord Hoffmann. He said:[186] **7.278**

> I do not believe that section 3 of the 1998 Act was intended to have the effect of requiring the courts to give the language of statutes acontextual meanings. That would be playing games with words. The important change in the process of interpretation which was made by section 3 was to deem the Convention to form a significant part of the background against which all statutes … had to be interpreted. Just as the 'principle of legality' meant that statutes were construed against the background of human rights subsisting at common law …, so now, section 3 requires them to be construed against the background of Convention rights. There is a strong presumption, arising from the fundamental nature of Convention rights, that Parliament did not intend the statute to mean something which would be incompatible with those rights. This of course goes far beyond the old fashioned notion of using background to 'resolve ambiguities' in a text which had notionally been read without raising one's eyes to look beyond it. The Convention, like the rest of the admissible background, forms part of the primary materials for the process of interpretation. But, with the addition of the Convention as background, the question is still one of *interpretation*, i.e. the ascertainment of what, taking into account the presumption created by section 3, Parliament would reasonably be understood to have meant by using the actual language of the statute.

Lord Hoffman continued:[187] **7.279**

> It is therefore sometimes possible, as my noble and learned friend, Lord Nicholls of Birkenhead, pointed out in [*Ghaidan*], to construe a statutory provision as referring to, or qualified by, some general concept implied rather than expressly mentioned in the language used by Parliament. Thus in *Ghaidan*, the words '*as* his or her wife or husband' (my emphasis) were interpreted to refer to a relationship of social and sexual intimacy exemplified by, but not limited to, the heterosexual relationship of husband and wife. The deemed background of the Convention enabled the House to adopt this construction in preference to the more restricted construction adopted before the 1998 Act came into force. It may have come as a surprise to the members of the Parliament which in 1988 enacted the statute construed in the *Ghaidan* case that the relationship to which they were referring could include homosexual relationships. In that sense the construction may have been contrary to the 'intention of Parliament'. But that is not normally what one means by the intention of Parliament. One means the interpretation which the reasonable reader would give to the statute read against its background, including, now, an assumption that it was not intended to be incompatible with Convention rights.

It is this approach to the interpretation of their equivalents of section 3 that has been adopted in both Australia and New Zealand. **7.280**

The New Zealand Bill of Rights Act 1990 contains the following provision in section 6: **7.281**

> Wherever an enactment can be given a meaning that is consistent with the rights and freedoms contained in this Bill of Rights, that meaning shall be preferred to any other meaning.

It was suggested by Lord Steyn in *R v A (No 2)*[188] that the New Zealand provision was 'a slightly weaker model' than the UK Act, but it is hard to see the distinction. The UK Act **7.282**

[186] ibid, [17].
[187] ibid, [18]
[188] [2002] 1 AC 45 at [44].

requires legislation to be read and given effect in a way that is compatible with human rights so far as it is possible to do so. The New Zealand Act requires a meaning to be given to legislation that is consistent with human rights wherever the enactment can be given that meaning. As a matter of interpretation, it is difficult to see the difference.

7.283 This is also true of the Australian provisions. For instance, section 32(1) of the Charter of Human Rights and Responsibilities Act 2006 of Victoria provides that:

> So far as it is possible to do so consistently with their purpose, all statutory provisions must be interpreted in a way that is compatible with human rights.

7.284 It will be seen that the wording of the Victorian provision is even closer to the wording of section 3. But it is suggested that all three statutory provisions are clearly intended to serve the same purpose.

7.285 It is therefore of relevance to understand how the courts in New Zealand and Australia have interpreted their equivalent provisions. And they have both adopted the same approach—one which is consistent with Lord Hoffmann's judgment in *Wilkinson* and opposed to the approach in *Ghaidan*.

7.286 The approach of the New Zealand courts can been seen from the judgment of Cooke J in the New Zealand Court of Appeal in *Ministry of Transport v Noort*.[189] Cooke J said:

> Turning to s 6, it is to be noted that this one of the key features of the New Zealand Bill of Rights Act. It lays down a rule of interpretation comparable in importance to—perhaps of even greater importance than— … the common law presumption which led the House of Lords to hold in *Morris v Beardmore* [1981] AC 446 that a statutory power to require a breath test after an accident did not authorise a constable to demand one from a defendant in his home if the constable was there without the defendant's consent. Section 6 may be seen as to some extent a quid pro quo for the rule of statutory primacy in s 4. The rights and freedoms in part II are not constitutionally entrenched and may be overridden by an ordinary enactment, but in interpreting an enactment a consistent meaning is to be preferred to any other meaning. The preference will come in to play only when the enactment can be given a meaning consistent with the rights and freedoms. This must mean, I think, can reasonably be given such a meaning. A strained interpretation would not be enough.

7.287 The difference in approach of the English courts from those in Australia and New Zealand can be seen clearly in relation to cases concerning the reversal of the onus of proof in criminal cases. The starting point in criminal law is that the prosecution must prove its case beyond reasonable doubt. But it is not uncommon for legislation in particular areas to create a reverse onus of proof in certain circumstances. That erodes one of the fundamental freedoms of citizens, and both the principle of legality and the statutory human rights provisions will therefore come into play.

7.288 The different approaches of the UK courts from those in Australia and New Zealand can be seen by considering four cases:

- *R v Lambert*;[190]
- *R v Phillips*;[191]

[189] [1992] 3 NZLR 260 at 272.
[190] [2002] 2 AC 545.
[191] [1991] 3 NZLR 175.

- *R v Hansen*;[192] and
- *Momcilovic v R*.[193]

In *R v Lambert*,[194] the defendant was charged with possession of a Class A controlled drug with intent to supply contrary to section 5(3) of the Misuse of Drugs Act 1971. Section 5(3) provided: **7.289**

> Subject to section 28 of this Act, it is an offence for a person to have a controlled drug in his possession, whether lawfully or not, with intent to supply it to another . . .

Section 28(2) provided: **7.290**

> Subject to subsection (3) below, in any proceedings for an offence to which this section applies it shall be a defence for the accused to prove that he neither knew of nor suspected nor had reason to suspect the existence of some fact alleged by the prosecution which it is necessary for the prosecution to prove if he is to be convicted of the offence charged.

The defendant claimed that although he had been found in possession of a bag containing a controlled drug, he had neither known nor suspected nor had reason to suspect the nature of the contents of the bag. He appealed against conviction on the ground that he should not have been required to establish his defence on the balance of probabilities because such a requirement conflicted with the presumption of innocence contained in the Human Rights Act. **7.291**

The House of Lords decided that, when applying section 3(1) of the Human Rights Act to the provisions of section 28 of the Misuse of Drugs Act 1971, the expression 'to prove' meant 'to provide sufficient evidence to the contrary'.[195] **7.292**

In the words of Lord Slynn:[196] **7.293**

> Even if the most obvious way to read section 28(2) is that it imposes a legal burden of proof I have no doubt that it is 'possible', without doing violence to the language or to the objective of that section, to read the words as imposing only the evidential burden of proof. Such a reading would in my view be compatible with Convention rights . . .

A similar issue had to be decided by the New Zealand Court of Appeal in *R v Phillips*.[197] A person was convicted under the Misuse of Drugs Act 1975, which provided that 'until the contrary is proved' a person who had 28 g or more of cannabis was deemed to be in possession of the drug for one of the prohibited purposes. He argued that this was inconsistent with a provision of the New Zealand Bill of Rights Act 1990 under which a person was presumed innocent until proved guilty. **7.294**

Section 6 of the Bill of Rights Act 1990 provided: **7.295**

> Wherever an enactment can be given a meaning that is consistent with the rights and freedoms contained in this Bill of Rights, that meaning shall be preferred to any other meaning.

The judgment of the court was given by Cooke P. He said:[198] **7.296**

[192] [2007] 3 NZLR 1.
[193] (2011) 245 CLR 1.
[194] [2002] 2 AC 545.
[195] ibid, [42].
[196] ibid, [17].
[197] [1991] 3 NZLR 175.
[198] ibid, 176–177.

> The suggestion made for the accused is that s 6(6) of the Misuse of Drugs Act is susceptible of that approach. It is said that the expression 'until the contrary is proved' could be taken to mean until some evidential foundation sufficient to create a reasonable doubt appears: that it could be interpreted in such a way as to cast on the defence, not the burden of proving anything in the sense of obtaining a finding of fact, but merely a evidential onus of tendering or pointing to some evidence which, if accepted, might create a reasonable doubt.... [We] are not persuaded that the ordinary and natural meaning of the word 'proof' or 'prove' is capable of extending so far. To suggest that s 6(6) of the Misuse of Drugs Act can be read in the sense contended for is, in our view, a strained and unnatural interpretation which, even with the aid of the New Zealand Bill of Rights Act, this court would not be justified in adopting.

7.297 *Phillips* had been decided before *Lambert* and, in *R v Hansen*,[199] the Supreme Court of New Zealand had to decide which approach to adopt. The defendant had been found in possession of more than 28 g of cannabis and was charged with possession with intent to supply. As in *Phillips*, the question at issue was the meaning of section 6(6) of the Misuse of Drugs Act 1975, under which a person found in possession of more than that amount was deemed to have possession for the purpose of supply or sale 'unless the contrary is proved'. The New Zealand Court of Appeal followed its earlier decision in *Phillips*. On appeal, the Supreme Court of New Zealand reached the same conclusion. The words of section 6(6) were so clear that they simply could not be read in a way that was consistent with the presumption of innocence contained in the Bill of Rights Act. 'Prove' means 'prove'.

7.298 Elias CJ said:[200]

> I am of the view that the presumption of fact in s6(6) ('until the contrary is proved') imposes on the accused a legal burden of proof. There is no other tenable meaning. The provision is not capable of being interpreted to mean that an evidential burden only is transferred, even applying the interpretative direction prescribed by s6 of the Bill of Rights Act.

7.299 Tipping J said that 'The composite "expression' ('until the contrary is proved') has a clear, simple and well-understood legal meaning'.[201] Blanchard J said that the words 'could hardly have been clearer'.[202]

7.300 McGrath J stressed that the question was ultimately one of interpretation. He said:[203]

> Both the heading to s6 of the Bill of Rights and its language indicate that the Court is concerned with an exercise in *interpretation* of the statutory text being considered when it applies the section. This strongly suggests that meanings that can be given are confined to those which are available on the language of the text being interpreted. The section does not qualify the basic principle of interpretation that the text is the primary reference in ascertaining meaning and there is no authority to adopt meanings which go beyond those which the language being interpreted will bear.

7.301 The reference to available meanings is interesting. In relation to contractual interpretation, the necessity to give effect to an available meaning of the relevant words was rejected by Lord

[199] [2007] 3 NZLR 1.
[200] ibid, [5].
[201] ibid, [95].
[202] ibid, [56].
[203] ibid, [237].

Hoffmann in *Investors Compensation Scheme v West Bromwich Building Society*.[204] But that was always a controversial approach, and it was implicitly rejected by the Supreme Court in *Arnold v Britton*.[205] It is suggested that the interpretation of any document confines the interpreter to the available meanings of the words being interpreted, and that this is as true of interpretation under section 3 of the Human Rights Act and of its analogues as it is of any other form of interpretation.

The court considered the approach of the House of Lords in *Lambert*, but rejected it in favour of that in *Phillips*. In *R v A (No 2)*,[206] Lord Steyn had suggested that the New Zealand Act was 'a slightly weaker model' than the English Act. The members of the Supreme Court of New Zealand took a different view. As Elias CJ said:[207] **7.302**

> Despite the considerable authority of these views, I am unable to accept that there is any material difference between the New Zealand and United Kingdom models.

Tipping J described the approach of the UK courts as being more 'adventurous' than those in New Zealand.[208] He saw the reason for this as being 'the more complicated supranational' environment which meant that it was appropriate to 'strike the balance between the judicial and legislative roles in a rather different way'. McGrath J took the same approach. He said: 'In my view the language of s 6 of the New Zealand Bill of Rights is not materially different from the equivalent interpretative instruction in s 3 of the United Kingdom Act . . .'[209] And, like Tipping J, he saw the UK position as being very much influenced by the different constitutional context of the European Union and the approach to interpretation of European legislation. It was therefore not surprising that the UK courts took a different approach from the New Zealand ones. **7.303**

The same issue has also had to be considered in Australia. In *Momcilovic v R*,[210] the High Court of Australia had to consider how to deal with a reverse onus of proof provision in legislation concerning the possession of drugs in the light of a statutory provision in Victoria that required all statutory provisions to be interpreted in a way that is compatible with human rights 'so far as it is possible to do so consistently with their purpose'. **7.304**

The High Court of Australia had to consider whether to follow the approach in *Lambert* or that in *Phillips* and *Hansen*. The defendant argued that the relevant section should be interpreted as imposing only an evidential burden. If the accused could point to some evidence tending to show that he or she was not in possession of the substance, the legal burden would rest on the prosecution of proving possession beyond reasonable doubt. The court unanimously rejected this approach. **7.305**

The court decided that the requirement for the defendant to prove a particular matter meant that he or she must do so on the balance of probabilities. That was what the legislation said, and to adopt a different meaning would require the courts to legislate. **7.306**

Heydon J said:[211] **7.307**

204 [1998] 1 WLR 896 at 914.
205 [2015] AC 1619.
206 [2002] 1 AC 45 at [44].
207 [2007] 3 NZLR 1 at [13].
208 ibid, [156].
209 ibid, [243].
210 (2011) 245 CLR 1.
211 ibid, [454].

> The ordinary meaning of the expression 'satisfies the court to the contrary' in s 5 is 'persuade the court to the contrary on the balance of probabilities'. The recognition, by reason of s 25(1) of a right to be presumed innocent until proved guilty cannot change that meaning. Nor can it support some other available meaning as the correct meaning, for there is no other available meaning. The appellant's submission to the contrary concentrates on what the legislature might have chosen as the desirable meaning for s 5, not on what it actually means. To interpret legislation as having a meaning which is in truth not the actual meaning, but a desired modification of it, is to legislate.

7.308 The members of the court also indicated that the reason for the different approach in the United Kingdom was likely to be because the United Kingdom was, at the time, part of the European Union and therefore subject to a European approach to interpretation.

7.309 The important question raised by these cases is whether the approach of the UK courts should—and will—change now that the United Kingdom is no longer part of the European Union.

7.310 Even when the United Kingdom was a member of the European Union, there was no logic in applying the European approach to the interpretation of section 3. The European approach was relevant to the interpretation of the Convention itself, but there was no necessity to interpret section 3 in the same way. Section 3 was not derived from European legislation or a convention, and should therefore have been interpreted in the way UK statutes are normally interpreted. The problem was that the courts moved from the proposition that the use of section 3 does not require the statutory words to be ambiguous (which is correct) to one that required the courts to give the words a meaning that Parliament could not have intended when passing the legislation concerned (which is not).

7.311 It is sometimes suggested that, on a proper interpretation of section 3, it requires the courts to give effect to Parliament's intention in the Human Rights Act rather than its intention as displayed in the legislation concerned. That might possibly be arguable in relation to legislation passed before the Human Rights Act, but it cannot apply to legislation passed afterwards. Parliament is sovereign. It can change its mind. It can decide that there are good reasons why laws have to be made that do not necessarily comply with the Human Rights Act. The duty of the court is to give effect to the intention of Parliament in the legislation concerned and, if the legislation overrides protections in the Human Rights Act, then the courts have no authority to try to restrict that power.

7.312 It remains to be seen how the courts do interpret section 3 now that the United Kingdom is no longer part of the European Union. It is suggested that the best approach would be to recognise that section 3 is a statutory statement of the common law principle of legality, that it is a principle of interpretation and that it can only be used to give effect to an available meaning of the words that Parliament has used.

7.313 The alternative approach would be to repeal section 3, in which event the principle of legality would hold the field.

7.314 In December 2020, the government established the Independent Human Rights Act Review to examine the wording of the Human Rights Act 1998. The review was chaired by Sir Peter Gross. It reported in October 2021 and the report was presented to Parliament and published in December 2021.[212]

[212] The Independent Human Rights Act Review 2021 (HMSO, December 2021, CP586).

Chapter 5 of the report contains a detailed and useful discussion of the operation of section 3. The panel had been asked to consider whether any change should be made to the framework established by section 3. In particular, it was asked to consider whether section 3 has led the courts to interpret statutes in a manner inconsistent with the intention of Parliament and whether section 3 should be amended or repealed. **7.315**

After a detailed review of the case law, the panel decided that the courts were giving proper effect to section 3 and that it should not be repealed. 'The principles articulated in *Ghaidan* provide clear and sensible guidance to UK courts to apply section 3's interpretative duty.'[213] **7.316**

The report accepted that section 3 did give courts wider powers than they had at common law, and it proposed an amendment to section 3 to make that clear. It would require the court first to interpret the legislation in the normal way and then, if it was not compatible with the Convention rights, the court would use section 3 to try to make it compatible. **7.317**

That is effectively what the courts are already doing, but it is suggested that it is misconceived. Interpretation is a unitary exercise. It requires the interpreter to establish the intention of Parliament from the words it has used. It is not practical to have two different ways of interpreting statutes in the same legal system. **7.318**

The panel also considered that the approach of the courts in *Ghaidan* was to give effect to Parliament's intention rather than acting contrary to it.[214] It is suggested that this may be true of legislation passed before the Human Rights Act came into force. It could be said that Parliament is impliedly amending the earlier legislation. But it cannot be true of subsequent legislation. If Parliament makes its views clear, and they are incompatible with Convention rights, then Parliament has overruled the requirements of the Human Rights Act. Parliament can always change its mind, and the courts must give effect to that intention. **7.319**

The panel considered that section 3 should not be repealed because the UK courts have not misused it.[215] The one change they proposed would set in stone the artificial two-stage approach to interpretation that the courts already adopt. **7.320**

In spite of this endorsement of section 3, the government decided to repeal it as part of a more general reform of human rights law. The Bill of Rights Bill was introduced into Parliament in June 2022. As stated earlier, if it is passed in its form as introduced, it will replace the Human Rights Act 1998 with a Bill of Rights that will not contain any equivalent of section 3. But it is not clear whether the Bill of Rights will ever become law. **7.321**

The problems that section 3 has caused could have been avoided. It was not inevitable that it would be interpreted in the way it has been. The Australian and New Zealand courts both recognised that their equivalents are a statutory recognition of the common law principle that clear words are needed to override a person's fundamental liberties. Instead, the UK courts gave section 3 a broader meaning that cut across the fundamental principle that the purpose of the interpretation of a statute is to establish the objective intention of the legislature. That crossed the boundary between the legislative and judicial functions. Whether or not section 3 is repealed, it is important to restore the proper balance. **7.322**

[213] ibid, para 64.
[214] ibid, paras 59 and 142.
[215] ibid, para 126.

Epilogue

The purpose of the Epilogue is to draw together some of the strands that have been discussed in the various chapters of the book. It is divided into two parts. **Ep.1**

Part I is a case study that illustrates how the various principles of statutory interpretation work together to guide the interpreter to the right conclusion. It also demonstrates how difficult it can be to reach that conclusion and how judgemental the exercise can be. **Ep.2**

When discussing the principles of statutory interpretation, comparisons have been drawn throughout the book with the way in which contracts are interpreted. Part II of the Epilogue draws the discussion together, and explains the similarities and the differences between the interpretation of statutes and of contracts. **Ep.3**

Epilogue Part I

A Case Study

The decision of the Supreme Court in *Hurstwood Properties v Rossendale Borough Council*[1] provides a useful case study for a discussion of how the principles of statutory interpretation are applied in practice in a difficult case. It draws together many of the themes that have been discussed in this book. **Ep.4**

The case was concerned with who was entitled to the possession of land for the purpose of the rating legislation—and thereby liable to pay unoccupied business rates. Business rates are normally levied on the occupier of business property but, where the property is unoccupied, reduced rates are levied on the owner. The legislation defines the owner as being the person entitled to possession of the property; and there is an exemption from liability where that person is in liquidation. **Ep.5**

There is a reluctance on the part of some owners of property to pay rates on unoccupied premises; and schemes were promoted in order to avoid that liability. The promoters of one scheme set up a special purpose company, which was granted a short lease of the property by the original owner. The idea behind the scheme was that the company would then become the person entitled to possession of the property and thereby liable for business rates. Of itself, this would not avoid the liability—it would simply transfer it from the original owner to the company. But the company was established on the basis that it would have no other assets than the lease, and no means to pay business rates. The scheme then worked in one of two ways. **Ep.6**

One method was to put the company into voluntary liquidation in order to take advantage of a statutory provision that exempted a company in liquidation from being liable for unoccupied business rates. The potential flaw with this approach was that a liquidator acting **Ep.7**

[1] [2021] 2 WLR 1125.

Principles of Statutory Interpretation. Richard Calnan, Oxford University Press. © Richard Calnan 2023.
DOI: 10.1093/oso/9780192864673.003.0009

properly would disclaim the lease, thereby re-vesting the liability for unoccupied business rates in the original owner. This problem was avoided—or at least delayed—by using various methods to delay the disclaimer.

Ep.8 The alternative method was to dissolve the company, thereby transferring its assets and liabilities to the Crown by way of *bona vacantia*. Again, the problem would be the Crown then disclaiming the lease—the liability for rates thereby reverting to the original owner. And, again, the scheme relied on the Crown not realising what was happening for long enough to make the scheme worth implementing.

Ep.9 There is no doubt that these schemes involved an abuse of the liquidation procedures in the insolvency legislation or of the dissolution procedures in the companies legislation. And, on any rational basis, they were dishonest. The company was incurring liabilities it could not pay. The original owner could pay, but how could it be liable when the company had a lease and was therefore the person entitled to possession of the property?

Ep.10 One way to avoid the problem would be to decide that the lease was ineffective and therefore that the original owner continued to be the person entitled to possession. That would be the case if the lease were a 'sham', but a document is only a sham if the parties did not intend to create the legal rights and duties contained in the document, and only appeared to do so in order to deceive third parties.[2] The lease to the company was clearly not a sham. The scheme would only work if it did create a valid lease in favour of the company. So the lease was a valid lease.

Ep.11 Rather than treating the lease as a sham, an alternative way of dealing with the problem would be to treat the company as a sham. If one could lift the veil of incorporation, one could treat the company's assets as being assets of the original owner, and thereby make the original owner liable for the rates. But, as the Supreme Court demonstrated in this case, it was not possible to do that. The circumstances in which the veil of incorporation can be lifted are extremely limited, and it was not possible to do so in this case.[3]

Ep.12 Which left one line of argument. Is it possible to conclude that, even though the company was a valid company, and even though the lease to the company was a valid lease, the company was not the person entitled to possession of the land?

Ep.13 Possession is one of those difficult legal concepts which has troubled lawyers for centuries. In spite of the extensive analysis by Pollock and Wright in the leading text *Possession in the Common Law*,[4] the precise nature of possession can sometimes be elusive. A person can possess goods even if it does not have them in its physical possession if it holds a document of title to them[5] or if the person in physical possession has attorned in relation to them.[6]

Ep.14 In relation to land, the person entitled to possession normally means the person who has the immediate legal right to actual physical possession of the property; and this is also the case in the rating legislation.[7] But, in the particular circumstances of this case, the Supreme Court decided that it was the original owner, rather than the company, that was entitled to possession. How did it do this?

[2] *Snook v London and West Riding Investments* [1967] 2 QB 786 at 882.
[3] [2021] 2 WLR 1125 at [63]–[76].
[4] F. Pollock and R. S. Wright, *An Essay on Possession in the Common Law* (Clarendon Press, 1888).
[5] *Sewell v Burdick* (1884–1885) LR 10 App Cas 74.
[6] *Official Assignee of Madras v Mercantile Bank of India* [1935] AC 53 at 58–59.
[7] *Brown v City of London Corporation* [1996] 1 WLR 1070.

The Supreme Court described the key features of the transaction as involving the following elements: **Ep.15**

- The lease was granted solely for the purpose of avoiding liability for business rates.
- The company could do nothing with its rights under the lease, having neither the monetary nor the human resources with which to do so. Those rights were of no value or benefit to the company, which was not intended to carry on business but simply to go into liquidation or dissolution.
- The practical ability to decide whether to continue to leave the property unoccupied remained with the original owner. The lease contained a break clause that enabled the original owner to terminate the lease if it required the property.
- Although the intention was to impose liability for business rates on the company, it was not intended that business rates would actually be paid by the company and, indeed, it had no money with which to do so.
- The schemes constituted a misuse of legal process and involved the directors of the company in breaches of fiduciary duty.

The court then considered what was meant by the entitlement to possession in the context of the rating legislation. It decided that the essential requirement of the entitlement to possession of property is the ability to control the letting of the property.[8] The court also considered why, in the case of unoccupied property, the legislation imposed the liability to pay rates on the person entitled to possession of the property. If it was simply concerned with raising funds, the answer was not obvious. But the background materials showed that the central purpose of unoccupied business rates was to provide an incentive to bring unoccupied property back into use. On that basis, the liability must have been intended to fall on the person who had the ability, in the real world, to achieve that objective.[9] **Ep.16**

In the unusual circumstances of this case, identifying the company as the person entitled to possession would defeat the purpose of the legislation. The company had no real or practical control over whether or not the property was occupied. That control remained with the original owner.[10] **Ep.17**

The Supreme Court therefore said:[11] **Ep.18**

> In our view, Parliament cannot sensibly be taken to have intended that 'the person entitled to possession' of an unoccupied property on whom the liability for rates is imposed should encompass a company which has no real or practical ability to exercise its legal right to possession and on which that legal right has been conferred for no purpose other than the avoidance of liability for rates. Still less can Parliament rationally be taken to have intended that an entitlement created with the aim of acting unlawfully and abusing procedures provided by company and insolvency law should fall within the statutory description.

In the circumstances, the court decided that the company did not become entitled to possession of the property for the purpose of the relevant legislation. That person remained the original owner. **Ep.19**

[8] *Westminster City Council v Haymarket Publishing* [1981] 1 WLR 677 at 680 (Lord Denning MR).
[9] [2021] 2 WLR 1125 at [30].
[10] ibid, [48].
[11] ibid, [49].

Ep.20 The court had this important point to make about the process by which it achieved this result:[12]

> This does not involve ignoring the leases ... Rather it involves their close examination in their context, and a conclusion that they did not transfer to the [companies] the entitlement to possession required by the Act as the badge of ownership. If the [original owners] did not thereby transfer their entitlement to possession it necessarily remained, for the purposes of the Act, with them. The Act requires someone to be identified as the owner. That will be the person who, in any tenurial chain, starting with the freeholder and working downwards, has not disposed of the entitlement to possession of the property in question.

Ep.21 The Supreme Court also emphasised that this conclusion was not founded on the fact that the motive in granting the lease was to avoid paying business rates. The motive was irrelevant. Nor did it think it helpful to use words such as 'artificial' or 'contrived' to describe the leases when it is accepted that they created genuine legal rights. It said:[13]

> Our conclusion is based squarely and solely on a purposive interpretation of the relevant statutory provisions and an analysis of the facts in the light of the provisions so construed.

Ep.22 This is not an easy case. The first instance judge and the Court of Appeal decided that the company was the person entitled to possession of the property because it was the owner of a valid lease of the property. The Supreme Court took a different approach, but it was not a straightforward decision.

Ep.23 The Supreme Court emphasised that its decision was based on a close examination of the statutory words in the light of the purpose of the legislation. The case is as important for what it did not decide as for what it did.

- The fact that the original owner's object was to avoid business rates was not the issue. Its motive was irrelevant.
- The lease could not be ignored. It was a valid lease.
- The company could not be ignored. It was a valid company.

Ep.24 Nevertheless, there are some troubling aspects of the case. The analogy with the *Ramsay* line of cases can only be taken so far. Whether or not a person is entitled to possession of property is essentially a legal question. It is a question of a different kind from whether a person has, or has not, made a profit or a loss in relation to a particular transaction. The Supreme Court considered this point in some detail.[14] But it nevertheless concluded that the words 'entitled to possession' in the relevant section 'are properly construed as being concerned with a real and practical entitlement which carried with it in particular the ability to either occupy the property in question, or to confer a right to its occupation on someone else'.[15] It accepted that a test such as one of 'genuine and real commercial entitlement as owner' is too amorphous a formulation to be acceptable.[16] But it still considered that a proper purposive interpretation had to recognise that entitlement to possession 'is speaking of an entitlement to possession

[12] ibid, [50].
[13] ibid, [51].
[14] ibid, [53]–[61].
[15] ibid, [59].
[16] ibid, [60].

which vests in the person concerned a real and practical ability either to occupy the property or to put someone else into occupation of it'.[17]

The problem with this approach is that it has great potential to create uncertainty. The Supreme Court met this argument by saying that: 'The value of legal certainty does not extend to construing legislation in a way which will guarantee the effectiveness of transactions undertaken solely to avoid the liability which the legislation seeks to impose.'[18] But there are nevertheless grounds for wondering whether a requirement for 'a real and practical ability either to occupy the property or to put someone else into occupation of it' is a great deal clearer than 'a genuine and real commercial entitlement as owner'. **Ep.25**

It would, perhaps, have created less potential for uncertainty if the test had been applied in a negative way, rather than a positive one. In other words, instead of trying to find a formulation that had to be complied with in order to obtain the right to possession, it might have been better to accept that, in most cases—in fact, in practically every case—the right to possession will exist if a person has a legally recognised interest in the property concerned but, in an exceptional case, where it can be established that the person with that interest has been granted that interest without any intention to run a business and without the wherewithal to do so, and has been inserted into the arrangement solely in order to avoid the payment of rates, might create more certainty. The tail should not wag the dog. **Ep.26**

The value of this case as a case study is that it sits on the cusp. It is easy to say that the entitlement to possession is a purely legal matter that is determined by the terms of the documentation, and in particular the lease. It is equally easy to say that no right-thinking person could believe that the proponents of these dishonest schemes should be able to get away with them. What is interesting about the Supreme Court's judgment in this case is that it steers a course between these two extremes and, by close examination of the statutory words in the light of their purpose, the court was able to reach a conclusion that instinctively seems to be the right one. But what is important is to emphasise the extreme nature of the facts of this case, and that this approach can—and should—only be used where the person with the apparent legal right to possession has that right without any expectation or ability to exercise it and is only in that position as part of a dishonest scheme. **Ep.27**

This case can help to illustrate the principles of statutory interpretation. **Ep.28**

Principle 1 describes the guiding principle of statutory interpretation: what did the legislature objectively intend the statute to mean? How would a reasonable person understand the legislature's intention from the words it has used? This was fundamental to the decision of the Supreme Court. It was led to interpret the entitlement to possession in a particular way because it took the view that Parliament could not sensibly be taken to have intended any other outcome.[19] It is dangerous to place too much reliance on what Parliament must have intended if that persuades a court to give insufficient importance to the actual statutory words, but there can be no doubt that interpreters do read the statutory words in the light of what they consider Parliament must reasonably have intended. **Ep.29**

Principle 2 establishes that the words of the statute are the source of the legislature's objective intention. In this case, the Supreme Court made a great point of the fact that it was **Ep.30**

[17] ibid.
[18] ibid, [61].
[19] ibid, [49].

scrupulously conducting a close examination of the statutory words with a view to deciding what they meant in context.

Ep.31 **Principles 3 and 4** require the interpreter to read the statutory words in the context of the statute as a whole and of its relevant background. In this case, the Supreme Court said:[20]

> The particular charging or exempting provision must be construed in the context of the whole statutory scheme within which it is contained. The identification of its purpose may require an even wider review, extending to the history of the statutory provision or scheme and its political or social objective, to the extent that this can reasonably be ascertained from admissible material.

Ep.32 In this case, the court used the words of the minister who promoted the Bill in Parliament to help to establish that the purpose of unoccupied business rates was to encourage owners to bring empty property back into use. This was an integral part of its subsequent reasoning. But it does raise the question whether the wording was sufficiently ambiguous that background materials of this kind ought to have been used. That is, perhaps, one of the more controversial aspects of the decision.

Ep.33 The main battleground in most questions of statutory interpretation is the friction between **Principles 5 and 7**. The words of a statute are nearly always given their ordinary meaning in context, taking account of the purpose of the statute; but, very occasionally, it is clear that the legislature cannot objectively have intended the words it has used to have their ordinary meaning, in which case they are given the meaning which the legislature must objectively have intended.

Ep.34 In this case, the Supreme Court made it clear that it was taking a purposive approach to interpretation. It relied on the *Ramsay* principle, which is discussed in relation to **Principle 5**, to establish that entitlement to possession needed to be given a purposive interpretation. And it used a ministerial statement (**Principle 4**) in order to establish what that purpose was. The Supreme Court based its decision fairly and squarely on a purposive interpretation of the words of the statute. To that extent, it is applying **Principle 5**. But it could equally well have reached the same result under **Principle 7**.

Ep.35 It is possible to argue with the outcome of the case. But, apart from the use of the ministerial statement, it is not possible to argue with the process by which the Supreme Court reached its conclusion. Ultimately, it analysed the particular words used in the statute in the light of the statute as a whole and the relevant background and in the context of the purpose of the legislation. Above everything else, what this case illustrates is the importance of a close analysis of the actual words used in context. But, even when that is done, the outcome can still be controversial. Principles take us so far, but ultimately interpretation is a matter of judgement.

Epilogue Part II

Statutory v Contractual Interpretation

A. The Principles

Ep.36 It would be surprising if the principles of statutory interpretation were materially different from those of contractual interpretation. The basic process of interpretation is common to

[20] ibid, [16].

all texts; and, because statutes and contracts both have legal effect, it should be expected that they will be interpreted in broadly the same way.

The interpretation of any written instrument is ultimately a question of judgement, but that judgement must be exercised in accordance with principle. Interpretation cannot be understood at the level of detailed rules: that would be incompatible with what is essentially a judgemental exercise. But the interpreter of a legal document cannot simply reach a decision untrammelled by legal considerations. In Chapter 6 of *Through the Looking-Glass*, Humpty Dumpty declared that a word means 'just what I choose it to mean—neither more nor less'. That approach is not open to the interpreter of a legal document: it would amount to palm tree justice. The rule of law requires that judgements about the meaning of words are exercised in accordance with principle. And the basic principles of interpretation are applicable to all legal documents. **Ep.37**

The purpose of this part of the Epilogue is to discuss the similarities and differences between the interpretation of statutes and the interpretation of contracts. It draws together the discussion of this question that is contained in the rest of this book.[21] **Ep.38**

Many principles of interpretation apply to all types of writing. Statutes and contracts are both formal legal documents, and it would therefore be expected that they share many of the same principles of interpretation. But they are also fundamentally different types of instrument, and that does have important effects on the way in which they are interpreted. **Ep.39**

The discussion in this Epilogue will be carried out in the context of the principles of interpretation described in the earlier chapters of this book. The seven principles of statutory interpretation will be compared with the ten principles of contractual interpretation contained in the companion volume *Principles of Contractual Interpretation*.[22] **Ep.40**

The principles of contractual and statutory interpretation are both set out below, so that the similarities and differences can been seen: **Ep.41**

Contractual interpretation	Statutory interpretation
Principle 1: The purpose of contractual interpretation is to establish the intention of the parties to the contract. This is done objectively: what would a reasonable person understand their common intention to be from what they have written, said and done?	**Principle 1:** The purpose of interpreting a statute is to establish what the legislature intended the statute to mean. This is done objectively: what would a reasonable person understand the legislature's intention to be from the words it has used in the statute?
Principle 2: Where the contract is in writing, it is the writing which is the primary source of the parties' objective intention.	**Principle 2:** The words of the statute are the source of the legislature's objective intention.
Principle 3: Contracts are read as a whole.	**Principle 3:** The words of the statute are read in the context of the statute as a whole.

21 It is based on a two-part article in *The Journal of Business and Financial Law* (2022) 3 JIBFL 192 and (2022) 5 JIBFL 344.

22 R. Calnan, *Principles of Contractual Interpretation* (Oxford University Press, 2nd edn, 2017).

Contractual interpretation	Statutory interpretation
Principle 4: Contracts are read in the context of their background facts. These are the facts reasonably available to the parties which are relevant to establishing how a reasonable person would understand what the parties intended by the contract when it was entered into.	**Principle 4:** The words of the statute are read in the context of its relevant background. The relevant background consists of publicly available information concerning the law as it was before the statute was passed and the problems that it caused. The object of the relevant background is to provide the context in which the statutory words were used in order to help to establish their purpose. The clearer the statutory words, the more unlikely it is that they can be influenced by the relevant background. The relevant background cannot be used to alter or supplement the statutory words.
Principle 5: Words are nearly always given their ordinary meaning in their context.	**Principle 5:** The words of the statute are nearly always given their ordinary meaning in context, taking account of the purpose of the statute.
Principle 6: If words are ambiguous in their context, they are given the meaning the parties are most likely objectively to have intended.	**Principle 6:** If the words of the statute are reasonably capable of more than one ordinary meaning, they are given the meaning the legislature is most likely objectively to have intended.
Principle 7: Very occasionally, it is clear that the parties cannot objectively have intended words they have used to have their ordinary meaning. If so, they are given the meaning which the parties must objectively have intended. The more unreasonable the result, the more unlikely it is that the parties can have intended it.	**Principle 7:** Very occasionally, it is clear that the legislature cannot objectively have intended the words it has used in the statute to have their ordinary meaning. If so, they are given the meaning that the legislature must objectively have intended. The more unreasonable or unfair the result, the more unlikely it is that the legislature can have intended it. Clear words are therefore needed to override a person's fundamental liberties.
Principle 8: Words are implied into a contract if the parties must objectively have intended them. This will be the case either if they are so obvious that there was no need to express them, or if they are necessary to make the contract work in a business context.	

Contractual interpretation	Statutory interpretation
Principle 9: If a written contract does not record the parties' common intention at the time it was entered into, it will be amended to reflect that intention.	
Principle 10: If the parties to a contract have dealt with each other on the basis of a common understanding about the meaning or effect of the contract, that interpretation will bind them if it would be unjust to go back on it.	

When the principles are seen together, two things stand out. The first is how similar they are. The second is that there are more principles for contracts than for statutes. **Ep.42**

The reason for the latter is that there are some doctrines of contract law which impinge upon the interpretation of contracts but that have no part to play in statutory interpretation. Principles 8 to 10 of the principles of contractual interpretation are not, strictly, principles of interpretation at all. They are concerned with doctrines of the law of contract, but they are so closely entwined with the process of interpretation that it would be misleading not to refer to them. **Ep.43**

More importantly, it will be seen how similar the first seven principles are. They are sometimes expressed in different language in order to cater for the different case law. But their basic thrust is identical. This should come as no surprise. Statutes and contracts are both legal texts, and it would be surprising if the approach to their interpretation were materially different. **Ep.44**

B. Statutes and Contracts: The Differences

Nevertheless, the similarity of the principles can be misleading. Although the principles are broadly the same, their application can be significantly different depending on whether the text concerned is a contract or a statute. **Ep.45**

The reason for this difference of approach is that statutes and contracts are materially different types of legal instrument. **Ep.46**

First, a statute is a unilateral act. It is imposed by the legislature on citizens. It is consensual only in the limited sense that, in a constitutional democracy, we may be taken to have consented to the legislature's power to do this. By contrast, a contract is a voluntary act. **Ep.47**

Secondly, statutes generally apply much more widely than contracts. They tend to be addressed to all citizens, whilst contracts only bind their parties. And statutes are always promulgated by the same body—the legislature of the state concerned. The identity of those who make up the legislature changes over time, but the nature of the body that promulgates the statute is always the same. This is quite different from contracts, which are entered into by all sorts of different persons. **Ep.48**

Thirdly, the purpose of a statute is always broadly the same. They create laws to bind citizens. The nature of the laws varies from statute to statute, but the basic purpose is the same. **Ep.49**

Contracts, on the other hand, are infinitely varied. They are entered into for all sorts of reasons in a multitude of different circumstances.

Ep.50 Fourthly, a statute is a formal instrument. It must be in writing, it is written in a particular form and style and it must be enacted in a particular way. Something is only a statute if it complies with these formal requirements. This is in marked contrast to contracts. They can generally be made informally—orally, or even by conduct. Even if a contract is encapsulated in a document, it does not necessarily follow that all of the terms of the contract are contained in that document. And the drafting style can vary considerably.

Ep.51 For all these reasons, the approach to the interpretation of statutes can differ from contracts. This manifests itself in two ways: one is practical; the other is constitutional.

Ep.52 Taking the practical difference first, contracts are made in all sorts of different circumstances between all sorts of different types of people in order to achieve all sorts of different purposes. Even in a formal written contract, it follows that the meaning of the words used must to some extent be coloured by the context. The identity of the parties, the market in which the parties are operating, the purpose of the contract—these can all influence the way in which the words in the contract will be interpreted. This is less true of a statute. It is a unilateral instrument. It is always issued by the same body. It is normally issued to all citizens. There is much less reason for the background to influence the outcome. It follows that words can be given a more conventional meaning, without as much need to delve into the background.

Ep.53 The other reason for the distinction between statutes and contracts is even more important. We allow the legislature to pass laws that will govern our behaviour. The quid pro quo is that we must know what those laws are so that we can comply with them. Any reasonable person should be able to understand what statutes mean from the words that the legislature has used.

Ep.54 This point cannot be carried too far. A lawyer may well be required in order to establish what the statute really means in practice. But this does not diminish the constitutional importance of our being able to understand what we have signed up to in our social contract.

C. Objective Intention

Ep.55 The guiding principle of the interpretation of any legal text is to establish what was meant by the promulgator of the text. What did they mean when they used the words contained in the text? This is true of most legal systems—civil law as well as common law. But what tends to distinguish the common law systems from those in civil law jurisdictions is the importance that the common law places on objectivity. When interpreting a text, a common law court is rarely concerned with what the promulgator actually meant. What it is normally trying to establish is how a reasonable person would understand what the promulgator meant from what it has written, said and done.

Ep.56 In the case of both contracts and statutes, Principle 1 is therefore Janus-faced. It looks to the intention of the parties or of the legislature, but then confounds that by imposing an objective test. Real intention is irrelevant. All that matters is how a reasonable person would understand that intention from the relevant text. Which begs the question why it is necessary to refer to intention at all.

It is easier to justify the reference to intention in relation to contracts. Contracts are voluntarily entered into, and the whole basis of contractual liability is that it gives effect to what the parties intended. That intention is occasionally judged on a subjective basis but, more often than not, what is relevant is how a reasonable person would understand the parties' intention from what they have written, said and done. It is that which establishes whether a contract has been made, when it comes into existence and what it means. Although, in a written contract, intention is judged from the words used, rather than the parties' real intentions, it is hard to get away from the idea that the interpreter is ultimately giving effect to the objective common intention of the parties. **Ep.57**

It is more difficult to justify the reference to intention when it comes to statutory interpretation. There is no necessity to match the words to particular types of person. Statutes are always issued by the same person—the legislature. They are generally addressed to the same persons—citizens generally. They are required to be written in a particular style and passed in a particular way. Bearing all that in mind, why is intention relevant? Why not just establish the meaning of the words? **Ep.58**

There is no doubt that the actual intentions of the legislature are irrelevant. When we refer to the legislature, we are referring to an idealised body of legislators that is acting reasonably and fairly, rather than to the particular body of people who happen to be the legislators at any particular time. So why not do away with the idea of intention altogether? **Ep.59**

There is much to be said for this view but, ultimately, the reference to intention has been retained—albeit making it clear that it is objectively established. That is partly because the reference to objective intention has a very long history in the case law. But it is mainly because the ultimate aim of the interpreter of any document is to establish what its issuer intended. Words do not exist in a vacuum. They need to be understood by reference to the context in which they were written. Although the legislature is to be judged on what it has done, not on what it intended, the words it has used must have had some purpose, and it is helpful to understand that purpose when reading the words. If legislation is to be interpreted purposively—and there is plenty of authority for that proposition—then the relevant purpose must be that of the legislature, albeit in an idealised form. **Ep.60**

An understanding of the objective intention of the legislature also makes it easier to appreciate why—and therefore when—the courts do occasionally move away from the natural meaning of the statutory words. They do so when they are confident that the natural meaning of the statutory words simply cannot reflect what the legislature must have intended. And it is also easier to understand how courts resolve ambiguities once it is appreciated that they are trying to establish what the legislature must have intended. **Ep.61**

For all these reasons, the concept of the objective intention of the legislature still has a part to play. **Ep.62**

D. The Text

It is axiomatic that the text of any document is the source of its meaning. It is only from its words that one can gauge the intentions of the promulgator. Those words need to be read in the light of the relevant context, but the words that require interpretation can only be found in the text. But establishing the text of a statute is a very different matter from establishing the text of a contract. **Ep.63**

There are very few formalities in the creation of a contract. It rarely has to be made in writing. Even if the terms of a contract are written down in a formal document and signed by the **Ep.64** parties, the document may not contain all of its terms. The terms of the contract are derived from the common intention of the parties, and it may be their objective common intention that other terms are to form part of the contract. That is not very likely if the parties have gone to the trouble of writing down the terms of the contract and signing it, but it is possible. And it is to guard against the concern that a court may have to look at a vast array of documentation in order to decide whether that was the parties' intention that it is common for commercial contracts to contain an entire agreement clause.

Ep.65 None of that is relevant to statutes. A statute must be in writing, made in the appropriate form and approved in the proper way by the legislature concerned. It follows that the terms of the statute are found—and can only be found—in the formal document. Statutes have a built-in entire agreement clause.

Ep.66 In addition, there are two doctrines of the law of contract that have no part to play in relation to statutory interpretation—implied terms and rectification.

Ep.67 Terms can be implied into a contract if they are so obvious that there is no need to express them or if they are necessary to make the contract work in a business context. There is no equivalent doctrine for statutes. But even a brief review of the cases on statutory interpretation illustrates the fact that the courts do add words to statutes when interpreting them. How is this done?

Ep.68 There is little discussion of this problem in the cases, but it is suggested that there is a principled way of distinguishing between the approach to contracts and the approach to statutes. A provision of a document can be varied by interpretation, but a new provision can only be added to a document by the implication of a term. Interpretation is relevant to both contracts and statutes, but terms can only be implied into contracts.

Ep.69 When interpreting an instrument, it is commonplace for courts to interpolate words in order to vary the meaning of an obligation contained in the instrument. Normally, the effect of interpolating the words is to limit the apparent scope of a broad provision—as the Supreme Court did in *Re Sigma Finance*.[23] Occasionally, the effect of doing so is to increase the scope of a provision—as the House of Lords did in *Charter Reinsurance Co v Fagan*.[24] But, in each case, what the court is doing is varying an existing obligation, not creating a new one. This is part of the process of interpretation, and it is as relevant to the interpretation of statutes as it is to the interpretation of contracts.

Ep.70 But it is no part of the process of interpretation to add a new provision to the document being interpreted. That is not interpretation, it is the creation of something for which the instrument does not provide. This cannot be done with a statute; and it can only be done with a contract if the court is able to imply a term in accordance with the strict requirements of the doctrine of implied terms. In *Marks and Spencer v BNP Paribas*,[25] the Supreme Court was only able to require the apportionment of rent in a lease if a term to that effect could be implied; and it could not. The addition of a new obligation could not be effected as a matter of interpretation, but only by the implication of terms.

Ep.71 It follows that the role of the court is more limited in relation to statutes than contracts. By interpretation, it can vary an existing provision of the statute; but it cannot add a new provision. That can only be done by the legislature.

23 [2010] 1 All ER 571.
24 [1997] AC 313.
25 [2016] AC 742.

There is a further way in which statutes differ from contracts. If a party to a contract is unhappy with the ordinary meaning of the words used in the contract, it has a choice. It can claim that, as a matter of interpretation, those words do not mean what they appear to say. Or it can argue that the contract should be rectified in order to give effect to the parties' common intention at the time the contract was entered into. Where there is a dispute of this kind, it is common for both interpretation and rectification to be pleaded, and the court can deal with both in the same hearing—as it did, for instance, in *Chartbrook v Persimmon Homes*.[26] There is no such doctrine for statutes. **Ep.72**

E. The Whole Text

The idea that a text has to be read as a whole is a universal feature of the interpretation of all texts. It was the position in Roman law, and it would seem to be a requirement of all documents in all legal systems. Words take their colour from their surroundings, and a phrase that appears perfectly clear in isolation can mean something quite different when read in context. **Ep.73**

What is interesting is the number of cases which accept this principle but then decide that the words themselves are so clear that the context cannot alter their meaning. This is a particular feature of cases on statutory interpretation, but there is no reason why it is not equally applicable to contracts. **Ep.74**

It is also true of both contracts and statutes that the interpreter must strive to give effect to all the words of the text. In practice, this is a principle honoured more in the breach than the observance, and this is as true of contracts as it is of statutes. The courts recognise that it is a counsel of perfection. Those who draft contracts and statutes share at least one common characteristic. They are not afraid of saying the same thing twice. **Ep.75**

F. The Context

This distinction between statutes and contracts manifests itself in two ways in relation to context. It affects both the extent of available background materials and also the circumstances in which they can be used. **Ep.76**

The first issue concerns the extent of available context. In the contractual sphere, the starting point is that context is always relevant in the interpretation of contracts. The interpreter must be put in the position of having all the background knowledge that would reasonably have been available to the parties in the situation in which they were at the time of the contract (as Lord Hoffmann said in *Investors Compensation Scheme v West Bromwich Building Society*[27]). Certain types of background are excluded (for instance, pre-contractual negotiations and subsequent conduct), but the starting point is that everything is relevant. **Ep.77**

The position is less clear in relation to statutory interpretation. Here, there are certain types of material that are commonly used in the interpretation exercise—for instance, judicial interpretation of the statute and its predecessors, the legislative history of the statute, explanatory notes, public reports on which the statute is based and ministerial statements in Parliament. **Ep.78**

[26] [2009] 1 AC 1101.
[27] [1998] 1 WLR 896 at 912–913.

Ep.79 In spite of this, in some ways the history of the last twenty-five years has seen precisely the opposite approach. The House of Lords has deliberately and substantially reduced the amount of background material available when interpreting contracts[28] and it has deliberately and substantially increased the amount of background material available in the interpretation of statutes.[29] In practice, therefore, the distinction may be quite limited.

Ep.80 The second issue concerns the circumstances in which context is available. There is no doubt that when interpreting a contract, a court is entitled—indeed, bound—to consider relevant background even if the words of the contract themselves are unambiguous on their face.[30] There is some suggestion that the same principle applies to statutory interpretation, but the preponderance of authority—at least for most types of context—is that the court should only look at external materials if the words of the statute, read as a whole, are ambiguous. This is certainly true of legislative history,[31] ministerial statements in *Hansard*[32] and explanatory notes.[33]

Ep.81 In summary, it is suggested that it is—and should be—more difficult to use external materials to interpret a statute than to interpret a contract.

G. Natural Meaning

Ep.82 The principle that words in any document are nearly always given their natural and ordinary meaning in context applies to the interpretation of all types of document. In relation to statutory interpretation, it is normally emphasised that this requires the interpreter to take account of the purpose of the statute. This expression is less frequently used in relation to contractual interpretation but it is no less important in relation to contracts. The most important element of the context of any legal document is the general purpose and object of the instrument concerned. The individual provisions need to be understood in that context.

Ep.83 There is, nevertheless, an important difference in relation to the time at which that meaning is established. Should it be established at the time the document is issued, or at the time the question comes to be determined?

Ep.84 The general position in relation to contracts is that the words of a contract are to be interpreted in the context of the relevant background at the time the contract was entered into.[34] Of course, this is subject to anything the parties may say about the issue in the contract; and contracts frequently do contain specific provisions dealing with potential changes to laws and regulations. But the starting point is to assume that when the parties use particular words and expressions, they intended them to have their natural meanings at the time the contract was entered into.

Ep.85 Statutes are different. They are expected to remain in place for a considerable period of time. Many statutes now in force trace their antecedents back over the centuries. There are therefore a large number of cases in which the courts have had to grapple with this question: should they give the words of an old statute the meaning that they bear now, or should they look to see what those words meant at the time the statute was passed?

28 *Chartbrook v Persimmon Homes* [2009] 1 AC 1101.
29 *Pepper v Hart* [1993] AC 593.
30 *R v National Asylum Support Service* [2002] 1 WLR 2956 at [5] (Lord Steyn).
31 *Mitsui Sumitomo Insurance Co v Mayor's Office for Policing and Crime* [2016] AC 1488.
32 *Pepper v Hart* [1993] AC 593.
33 *R (D) v Secretary of State for Work and Pensions* [2010] 1 WLR 1782 at [45]–[48] (Carnwath LJ).
34 *Lloyds TSB Foundation for Scotland v Lloyds Banking Group* [2013] 1 WLR 366.

There are cases in which the courts do look back to the time the statute was passed,[35] but the more prevalent view, particularly in recent times, is that the words of a statute are 'always speaking' and that the words they contain need to be read in accordance with their meaning at the time the question arises. So, if the meaning of the relevant words has changed since the statute was passed, then it is that new meaning that will be applied.[36] **Ep.86**

The reason for this approach is essentially that it probably represents what the legislature intended. Parliament understands that its legislation may remain in force for a considerable time. It also understands that the meaning of words can change over time, and that it is not normally practicable to require the interpreter of a statute to delve back into the meaning its words had at the time it was passed—or, indeed, the time a predecessor statute was passed. The basic constitutional principle is that citizens should be able to understand the laws that govern them by reading the words of the statutes. As a general rule, it is just not practicable to require anyone reading a statute first to understand when the predecessor of the relevant statute was passed and then to consider whether the words used carried a different meaning at that time. **Ep.87**

In practice, it is often the case that the meaning of the words themselves has not changed, but that the application of those words to the decision of any question will depend on our current understanding, not on what might have been thought in the past.[37] But, either way, we generally need to read statutes by reference to our current understanding of the meaning of the words used. **Ep.88**

The starting assumption for statutes is therefore the opposite of that for contracts. But it is just an assumption, based on what the legislature is likely to have intended. The ultimate question in every case is what the legislature would reasonably have been expected to mean from the words it has used.[38] **Ep.89**

The difference of approach can be illustrated by comparing two cases—one in relation to a contract, the other in relation to a statute. **Ep.90**

In *Lloyds TSB Foundation for Scotland v Lloyds Banking Group*,[39] Lloyds Bank had undertaken in deed to pay to a foundation it had set up for charitable purposes a certain percentage of 'the Pre-Tax Profits (after deduction of Pre-Tax Losses)' for each relevant accounting reference period. 'Pre-Tax Profits' and 'Pre-Tax Losses' were defined to mean: **Ep.91**

> in relation to any Accounting Reference Period ... respectively the 'group profit before taxation' and the 'group loss before taxation' (as the case may be) shown in the Audited Accounts for [the relevant period].

When the deed was entered into, profits could only lawfully be included in a profit and loss account once they had been realised. But the law was subsequently changed and, following an acquisition by Lloyds Bank, its consolidated accounts required it to state a 'gain on acquisition' of over £11bn, although this gain was neither distributable nor taxable. As a result, in the consolidated accounts of the bank, a loss of £10bn was converted into a profit of £1bn. **Ep.92**

35 *The Longford* (1889) 14 PD 34 at 36.
36 *Fitzpatrick v Sterling Housing Association* [2001] 1 AC 27.
37 *Morris v KLM* [2002] 2 AC 628 at [149] (Lord Hobhouse).
38 *R (Quintavalle) v Secretary of State for Health* [2003] 2 AC 687.
39 [2013] 1 WLR 366.

Ep.93 The foundation argued that the 'group profit before taxation' in the audited accounts was, as a result, £1bn, and that was therefore the figure by reference by which the payment should be made. The definition was perfectly clear and must be applied.

Ep.94 Lloyds Bank argued that this was not appropriate. When the deed had been entered into, it was 'unthinkable' that unrealised profits or losses would be taken into account. The change was outside the parties' contemplation at the time of the contract, and therefore the unrealised gain on acquisition should be ignored for the purpose of establishing the amount payable under the deed.

Ep.95 The Supreme Court decided in favour of Lloyds Bank. It was not sufficient simply to read off the figure in the relevant line in the audited accounts. The deed had to be read against the background facts existing at the time—which were that it was unthinkable that unrealised profits of losses would be taken into account. The change was wholly outside the parties' original contemplation, and the question was therefore how the language best operated in fundamentally changed and entirely unforeseen circumstances. The court decided that the answer was evident. It operated best, and quite naturally, by ignoring the unrealised gain on acquisition and treating the loss that existed apart from that as the relevant figure for the purpose of the deed.

Ep.96 In this case, the natural meaning of the words seemed clear. As is so often the case with financial covenants, it seemed that the references in the formula were to particular lines in the relevant accounts. But, because accounting standards had changed after the document had been entered into, the court found it necessary to adjust the text in order to preserve what it considered to have been the intention of the parties at the time the contract was entered into. This is an extreme example of the court reading the contract by reference to circumstances existing at the time it was entered into.

Ep.97 Drafters of contracts are well aware of this and, in consequence, they frequently provide expressly for the way in which changes of circumstance will affect the interpretation of the contract. One specific way in which this is frequently done is in relation to accounting standards. Although the principle is generally that the interpreter must look to the meaning of the contract at the time it was entered into, that is always subject to the terms of the contract itself; and it will frequently require changes in accounting standards to be taken into account.

Ep.98 *The Lloyds Bank* case can be contrasted with *Fitzpatrick v Sterling Housing Association*.[40] The plaintiff had lived with the protected tenant of a flat in a stable and a permanent homosexual relationship between 1976 until the tenant's death in 1994. The plaintiff applied to take over the tenancy, but the defendant (who was the landlord of the flat) refused.

Ep.99 The plaintiff would have been entitled to the tenancy if he were 'a member of the original tenant's family' within paragraph 3(1) of Schedule 1 to the Rent Act 1977.

Ep.100 One of the questions was the meaning of the word 'family'. Should it be interpreted by reference to the meaning of the word in the 1990s (which was when the tenant died) or its meaning in the 1920s (which was when the first antecedent of the Rent Act had been enacted)? It was accepted that, in the 1920s, a homosexual partner would not have been regarded as a member of the tenant's family but, by the 1990s, he would.

[40] [2001] 1 AC 27.

Here the House of Lords did exactly the opposite of what the Supreme Court did in the *Lloyds Bank* case. The majority in the House of Lords decided that the statute had to be read by reference to the facts existing at the time the dispute arose, not by reference to the time the legislation was originally passed. Lord Nicholls accepted that in the 1920s a homosexual partner would not have been regarded as being a member of the tenant's family. But he decided that the underlying legislative purpose was to provide a secure home for those who shared their lives together with the original tenant and that this purpose would be at risk of being stultified if the courts could not have regard to changes in the way people live together and changes in the perception of relationships. The meaning of the word 'family' may not have altered as a matter of language, but what had changed were the precise personal associations to which the concept was then applied. **Ep.101**

The starting point for statutory interpretation is therefore different from that for contractual interpretation. But it is just a starting point. Contracts frequently contain provisions that provide for the updating of certain expressions, and so become 'always speaking' themselves. And it may be clear from the context that a particular reference in a statute is intended to be read in the light of the circumstance at the time the statute was passed. Ultimately, as with all legal texts, the words have to be read in context and in the light of their purpose. **Ep.102**

H. Ambiguity

An interpreter of any text must be prepared to deal with ambiguities. Whether or not the text is ambiguous is always a question of judgement, regardless of the nature of the text concerned. And the resolution of the ambiguity is broadly the same whatever the nature of the text. The first port of call is the rest of the text. In many cases, that will resolve the ambiguity. Failing that, the interpreter will look to the more reasonable of the opposing meanings because that it more likely to be what was intended. This latter point is particularly true of statutes. **Ep.103**

I. Unnatural Meaning

The main problem faced by any practitioner who is trying to second-guess how a court will interpret a provision of a document is whether the court will decide that it cannot give that provision its natural meaning because the promulgator of the document cannot objectively have intended it. In the context of statutory interpretation, the problem is exemplified by *Yemshaw v Hounslow LBC*,[41] where the housing officers, a review panel, the first instance judge and the Court of Appeal all gave the word 'violence' its natural meaning, but the Supreme Court gave it a more extended meaning. In the context of contractual interpretation, it is illustrated by *Investors Compensation Scheme v West Bromwich Building Society*,[42] in which the House of Lords interpreted the words 'any claim (whether sounding in rescission for undue influence or otherwise)' as if they had read 'any claim sounding in rescission (whether for undue influence or otherwise)'. **Ep.104**

In the early years of this millennium, this was a particular problem in relation to contractual interpretation; but, since the Supreme Court gave judgment in *Arnold v Britton*,[43] it now takes a lot to persuade a court that the words of a commercial contract should not be given their natural and ordinary meaning in context. **Ep.105**

41 [2011] 1 WLR 433.
42 [1997] 1 WLR 896.
43 [2015] AC 1619.

Ep.106 It is more of a problem with statutes. The courts are more willing to decide that a statute cannot mean what it appears to say. The reason for this is, again, both practical and constitutional.

Ep.107 We do not necessarily expect contracting parties to act reasonably. It is recognised that parties do not always have equality of bargaining power; and, even if they do, they can make the wrong commercial decision. It is no part of the court's role to rectify a bad bargain. There therefore needs to be a very high level of unreasonableness to persuade a court that the words of a commercial contract do not mean what they say. Adjectives used to describe the nature of the outcome that is to be avoided include that it is 'absurd', 'bizarre', 'irrational', 'utterly fantastic', 'arbitrary', 'aberrant' or 'inconceivable'. Particularly since *Arnold v Britton*,[44] that is a high threshold.

Ep.108 In theory, the same is true of statutory interpretation. In *R (Noone) v Governor of Drake Hall Prison*,[45] the adjectives used by the Supreme Court in a case of statutory interpretation were remarkably similar. The outcome to be avoided was one that was 'absurd', 'irrational', 'indefensible', 'astonishing', 'incapable of contemplation', 'intolerable' or 'anomalous'. But nevertheless the similarity of the way in which the legal principle is expressed does perhaps hide the practical reality—which is that courts are more inclined to give words an unnatural meaning in a statute than in a contract.

Ep.109 There is a good reason for this difference of approach. We may not expect contracting parties to act reasonably, but we certainly do expect Parliament to do so. However much our expectations may be confounded in practice, hope triumphs over experience. The courts expect that what Parliament does will be done in a reasonable and fair way.[46] Of course, Parliament is sovereign. It can pass whatever laws it wants. But the words it has used should be read—if they can—on the assumption that the outcome was intended to be fair and reasonable.

Ep.110 This principle has been applied in a large number of cases in a wide variety of situations. It is as applicable to commercial transactions as it is to other types of case. It is, nevertheless, more compelling in cases involving statutory provisions that appear to impinge on fundamental liberties. It is here that the courts tend to be particularly interventionist. They presume that legislation is not intended to override the fundamental liberties of the citizen unless it does so clearly: general words are insufficient.[47] This principle is sometimes known as the 'principle of legality', although that is an unfortunate choice of words. The sovereignty of Parliament means that anything that it enacts is legal. The principle of legality is not a limit on Parliament's powers. It is a principle of interpretation. If a statute appears to override a fundamental liberty, it will only be taken to do so if it does so clearly.[48]

Ep.111 The distinction between the approach to contracts and the approach to statutes can be illustrated by comparing two cases:

- *Persimmon v Ove Arup*;[49] and
- *Secretary of State for the Home Department v GG*.[50]

44 ibid.
45 [2010] 1 WLR 1743.
46 *Inland Revenue Commissioners v Hinchy* [1960] AC 748 at 676 (Lord Reid).
47 *Raymond v Honey* [1983] 1 AC 1.
48 *R v Secretary of State for the Home Department, ex parte Sims* [2000] 2 AC 115.
49 [2017] EWCA Civ 373.
50 [2010] QB 585.

In *Persimmon v Ove Arup*,[51] Ove Arup were engaged as consulting engineers by Persimmon in relation to the redevelopment of certain old industrial land in South Wales. One of Ove Arup's tasks was to investigate the site for possible contamination and to advise on it. **Ep.112**

The contract contained the following clause: **Ep.113**

> [Ove Arup's] aggregate liability under this Agreement whether in contract, tort (including negligence), for breach of statutory duty or otherwise (other than for death or personal injury caused by [Ove Arup's] negligence) shall be limited to £12,000,000 (twelve million pounds) with the liability for pollution and contamination limited to £5,000,000 (five million pounds) in the aggregate. Liability for any claim in relation to asbestos is excluded.

Persimmon alleged that Ove Arup had been negligent in failing to spot asbestos. Ove Arup denied negligence but argued that, in any event, any liability was excluded by the contract. Persimmon contended that Ove Arup could not rely on the exclusion clause because of the *contra proferentem* rule and the rule in *Canada Steamship v R*.[52] **Ep.114**

The Court of Appeal concluded that Ove Arup was not liable. Exemption clauses were part of the contractual apparatus for distributing risk, and there was no need to approach them with horror or with a mindset determined to cut them down. The words were clear and should be given effect. **Ep.115**

The interpretation of exclusion clauses in contracts was for many years informed by the idea that exclusion clauses were unfair and a way needed to be found to reduce their impact. It was considerations of this kind that led the Privy Council in *Canada Steamship v R*[53] to neuter the effect of a clear exclusion clause. **Ep.116**

The problem with treating exclusion clauses differently from other provisions of the contract is that it fails to appreciate that the purpose of an exclusion clause is to help to establish the extent of the rights and duties of the parties under the contract. It is artificial to treat them any differently from any other clause in the contract. To do so ignores one of the fundamental precepts of the interpretation of any document, which is that it needs to be read as a whole. **Ep.117**

The modern approach to the interpretation of exclusion clauses in contracts is to read them in the same way as any other provision of the contract. The words of Lewison LJ in *Interactive E-solutions v 03b Africa*[54] are instructive: **Ep.118**

> The traditional approach of the courts towards exclusion clauses has been one of hostility. A strict and narrow approach to their interpretation held sway. This began to change with the passing of the Unfair Contract Terms Act 1977. Since then the courts have become more accepting of such clauses, recognising (at least in commercial contracts made between parties of equal bargaining power) that exclusion and limitation clauses are an integral part of pricing and risk allocation ...

This approach can be contrasted with the decision of the Court of Appeal in *Secretary of State for the Home Department v GG*.[55] **Ep.119**

[51] [2017] EWCA Civ 373.
[52] [1952] AC 192.
[53] ibid.
[54] [2018] EWCA Civ 62 at [14].
[55] [2010] QB 585.

Ep.120 The question in this case was whether section 1(3) of the Prevention of Terrorism Act 2005 permitted the Home Secretary to require a person who was the subject of a control order to submit to personal searches.

Ep.121 Section 1(3) provided that:

> The obligations that may be imposed by a control order made against an individual are any obligations that the Secretary of State ... considers necessary for purposes connected with preventing or restricting involvement by that individual in terrorism-related activity.

Ep.122 Section 1(4) then went on to say: 'Those obligations may include, in particular—', and it then set out a series of particular obligations that did not include personal searches.

Ep.123 Did the general words of section 1(3) allow personal searches to be required if the Secretary of State considered them necessary for the relevant purposes? The first instance judge and the Court of Appeal decided that the general words did not authorise the Secretary of State to require personal searches.

Ep.124 As a general matter of the interpretation of written documents, the provisions of section 1(3) were wide enough to include anything that the Secretary of State reasonably regarded as necessary for the relevant purposes. Subsection (4) contained certain specific provisions, but they were clearly not intended to limit the generality of subsection (3). The principle of *eiusdem generis* would not apply here, where the general statement comes first, and then particularly examples are described.

Ep.125 So, in order to reach the conclusion that they did, the court had to decide that the words in subsection (3) did not carry their ordinary meaning. And the basis on which they did this was that freedom from personal search is a fundamental liberty that can only be overridden by an express provision.

Ep.126 The result was that there must be a clear and unambiguous authorisation in a statute to override a fundamental liberty such as the liberty not to be searched. Sedley LJ said:[56]

> It is in my judgment axiomatic that the common law rights of personal security and personal liberty prevent any official search of an individual's clothing or person without explicit statutory authority.

Ep.127 Dyson LJ said:[57]

> [General] words *without more* are insufficient to show that Parliament intended to take away fundamental rights. Something more is required.

Ep.128 A person interpreting any legal text ought to give effect to the natural and ordinary meaning of the words in context unless the effect is so unreasonable that it simply cannot be what was intended. The test is the same for all legal documents, but its application can be different depending on the nature of the text concerned. We do not expect contracting parties always to act reasonably. But we do expect Parliament to do so.

[56] ibid, [12].
[57] ibid, [36].

Index